REA's Test Prep Books Are ... Best!

(a sample of the <u>hundreds of letters</u> REA receives each year)

(more on next page)

(continued from front page)

" I just wanted to thank you for helping me get a great score
on the AP U.S. History exam... Thank you for making great test preps! "
Student, Los Angeles, CA

" I did well because of your wonderful prep books... I just wanted to thank
you for helping me prepare for these tests. "
Student, San Diego, CA

" I used your book to prepare for the test and found that the advice and the
sample tests were highly relevant... Without using any other material, I earned
very high scores and will be going to the graduate school of my choice. "
Student, New Orleans, LA

" What I found in your book was a wealth of information sufficient to shore up
my basic skills in math and verbal... The section on analytical ability was
excellent. The practice tests were challenging and the answer explanations most
helpful. It certainly is the *Best Test Prep for the GRE*! "
Student, Pullman, WA

" I really appreciate the help from your excellent book. Please keep up
the great work. "
Student, Albuquerque, NM

" I am writing to thank you for your test preparation... your book helped me
immeasurably and I have nothing but praise for your *GRE* preparation."
Student, Benton Harbor, MI

(more on back page)

The Best Test Preparation & Review Course

FE/EIT

Fundamentals of Engineering / Engineer-in-Training

PM Exam in Electrical Engineering

Kinh D. Pham, M.S., P.E.
Vice-President, Elcon Associates, Inc.
Portland, OR

Chethan Parameswariah, M.S.
Electrical Engineer
Ruston, LA

Victor Meeldijk
Components Engineering Manager, Dialogic Corp.
Parsippany, NJ

Morel Oprisan, M.Sc., P.Eng.
Electrical Engineer
Neapan, Canada

Edmond Vinarub, S.B.E.E, MSEE
Electrical Engineer, Kimchuk, Inc.
Danbury, CT

And the Staff of REA
Dr. M. Fogiel, Director

Research & Education Association
61 Ethel Road West
Piscataway, New Jersey 08854

The Best Test Preparation and Review Course for the FE/EIT
(Fundamentals of Engineering/Engineer-in-Training)
PM Exam in Electrical Engineering

Printed in the United States of America

Library of Congress Catalog Card Number 99-74248

International Standard Book Number 0-87891-265-7

Research & Education Association
61 Ethel Road West
Piscataway, New Jersey 08854

ABOUT RESEARCH & EDUCATION ASSOCIATION

Research & Education Association (REA) is an organization of educators, scientists, and engineers specializing in various academic fields. Founded in 1959 with the purpose of disseminating the most recently developed scientific information to groups in industry, government, high schools, and universities, REA has since become a successful and highly respected publisher of study aids, test preps, handbooks, and reference works.

REA's Test Preparation series includes study guides for all academic levels in almost all disciplines. Research & Education Association publishes test preps for students who have not yet completed high school, as well as high school students preparing to enter college. For college students seeking advanced degrees, REA publishes test preps for many major graduate school admission examinations in a wide variety of disciplines, including engineering, law, and medicine. Students at every level, in every field, with every ambition can find what they are looking for among REA's publications.

Unlike most test preparation books—which present only a few practice tests that bear little resemblance to the actual exams—REA's series presents tests that accurately depict the official exams in both degree of difficulty and types of questions. REA's practice tests are always based upon the most recently administered exams, and include every type of question that can be expected on the actual exams.

REA's publications and educational materials are highly regarded and continually receive an unprecedented amount of praise from professionals, instructors, librarians, parents, and students. Our authors are as diverse as the fields represented in the books we publish. They are well-known in their respective disciplines and serve on the faculties of prestigious universities throughout the United States.

ACKNOWLEDGMENTS

In addition to our authors, we would like to thank the following:

Dr. Max Fogiel, President, for his overall guidance which has brought this publication to its completion.
Nicole Mimnaugh, New Book Development Manager, for directing the editorial staff throughout each phase of the project.
Kelli A. Wilkins, Assistant Editorial Manager, for coordinating the entire development of the book.
Martin Perzan for typesetting the book. Gary DaGiau, Vincent Biancomano, and James Nobel for their editorial contributions.

CONTENTS

FE/EIT

FE: PM Electrical Engineering Exam

CHAPTER 1

You Can Succeed on the FE: PM Electrical Engineering Exam

CHAPTER 1

YOU CAN SUCCEED ON THE FE: PM ELECTRICAL ENGINEERING EXAM

By reviewing and studying this book, you can succeed on the Fundamentals of Engineering Examination PM Portion in Electrical Engineering. The FE is an eight-hour exam designed to test knowledge of a wide variety of engineering disciplines. The FE was formerly known as the EIT (Engineer-in-Training) exam. The FE Exam format and title have now replaced the EIT completely.

The purpose of REA's *Best Test Preparation and Review Course for the FE: PM Electrical Engineering Exam* is to prepare you sufficiently for the afternoon portion of the Electrical Engineering FE exam by providing 13 review chapters, including sample problems in each review, and two practice tests. The review chapters and practice tests reflect the scope and difficulty level of the actual FE:PM Exam. The reviews provide examples with thorough solutions throughout the text. The practice tests provide simulated FE exams with detailed explanations of answers. While using just the reviews or the practice tests is helpful, an effective study plan should incorporate both a review of concepts and repeated practice with simulated tests under exam conditions.

ABOUT THE TEST

The Fundamentals of Engineering Exam (FE) is one part in the four-step process toward becoming a professional engineer (PE). Graduating from an approved four-year engineering program and passing the FE qualifies you for your certification as an "Engineer-in-Training" or an "Engineer Intern." The final two steps towards licensing as a PE involve completion of four years of additional engineering experience and passing the Principles and Practices of Engineering Examination administered by the National Council of Examiners for Engineering and Surveying (NCEES). Registration as a professional engineer is deemed both highly rewarding and beneficial in the engineering community.

The FE exam is offered in April and October each year. In order to register for the FE, contact your state's Board of Examiners for Professional Engineers and Land Surveyors. To determine the location for the Board in your state, contact the main NCEES office at the following address:

National Council of Examiners for Engineering and Surveying
PO Box 1686
Clemson, SC 29633-1686
(864) 654-6824
Website: http://www.ncees.org

TEST FORMAT

The FE consists of two distinct sections. One section is given in the morning (FE: AM) while the other is administered in the afternoon (FE: PM). This book will prepare you for the FE: PM exam in Electrical Engineering.

The FE: PM is a *supplied reference exam,* and students are not permitted to bring reference material into the test center. Instead, you will be mailed a reference guide when you register for the exam. This guide will provide all the charts, graphs, tables, and formulae you will need. The same book will be given to you in the test center during the test administration.

You will have four hours to complete the exam. The FE: PM consists of 60 questions covering 13 different engineering subjects. The subjects and their corresponding percentages of questions are shown on the next page.

FE: PM ELECTRICAL ENGINEERING SUBJECT DISTRIBUTION

Subject	Percentage of Problems
Analog Electronic Circuits	10
Communication Theory	10
Computer and Numerical Methods	5
Computer Hardware Engineering	5
Computer Software Engineering	5
Control Systems Theory and Analysis	10
Digital Systems	10
Electromagnetic Theory and Applications	10
Instrumentation	5
Network Analysis	10
Power Systems	5
Signal Processing	5
Solid State Electronics and Devices	10

Our review book covers all of these topics. Each subject is explained in detail, with example problems, diagrams, charts, and formulae.

You may want to take a practice exam at various studying stages to measure your strengths and weaknesses. This will help you to determine which topics need more study. Take one test when you finish studying so that you may see how much you have improved. For studying suggestions that will help you to make the best use of your time, see the "Study Schedule" presented after this chapter.

SCORING THE EXAM

Your FE: PM score is based upon the number of correct answers you choose. No points are taken off for incorrect answers. A single score of 0 to 100 is given for the entire (both AM and PM sections) test. Both the AM and PM sections have an equal weight. The grade given is on a pass/

fail basis. The point between passing and failing varies from state to state, although 70 is a general reference point for passing. Thus this general reference point for the FE: PM section alone would be 35.

The pass/fail margin is not a percentage of correct answers, nor a percentage of students who scored lower than you. This number fluctuates from year to year and is reestablished with every test administration. It is based on previous exam administrations and relates your score to those of previous FE examinees. For more specific information on scoring, contact NCEES.

Because this grading system is so variable, there is no real way for you to know exactly what you got on the test. For the purpose of grading the practice tests in this book, however, REA has provided the following formula to calculate your score on the FE: PM practice tests:

$$\left[\frac{\text{No. of questions answered correctly on the FE: PM}}{240}\right] \times 100 = \text{your score}$$

Remember that this formula is meant for the computation of your grade for the practice tests in this book. It does not compute your grade for the actual FE examination.

TEST-TAKING STRATEGIES

How to Beat the Clock

Every second counts, and you will want to use the available test time for each section in the most efficient manner. Here's how:

1. Bring a watch! This will allow you to monitor your time.

2. Become familiar with the test directions. You will save valuable time if you already understand the directions on the day of the test.

3. Pace yourself. Work steadily and quickly. Do not spend too much time on any one question. Remember, you can always return to the problems that gave you the most difficulty. Try to answer the easiest questions first, then return to the ones you missed.

Guessing Strategy

1. When all else fails, guess! The score you achieve depends on the number of correct answers. There is no penalty for wrong answers, so it is a good idea to choose an answer for all of the questions.

2.   If you guess, try to eliminate choices you know to be wrong. This will allow you to make an educated guess.

3.   Begin with the subject areas you know best. This will give you more time and will also build your confidence. If you use this strategy, pay careful attention to your answer sheet; you do not want to mismatch the ovals and answers. It may be a good idea to check the problem number and oval number *each time* you mark down an answer.

4.   Break each problem down into its simplest components. Approach each part one step at a time. Use diagrams and drawings whenever possible, and do not wait until you get a final answer to assign units. If you decide to move onto another problem, this method will allow you to resume your work without too much difficulty.

HOW TO STUDY FOR THE FE: PM EXAM

Two groups of people take the FE examination: college seniors in undergraduate programs and graduate engineers who decide that professional registration is necessary for future growth. Both groups begin their Professional Engineer career with a comprehensive exam covering the entirety of their engineering curriculum. How does one prepare for an exam of such magnitude and importance?

Time is the most important factor when preparing for the FE: PM. Time management is necessary to ensure that each section is reviewed prior to the exam. Once the decision to test has been made, determine how much time you have to study. Divide this time amongst your topics, and make up a schedule which outlines the beginning and ending dates for study of each exam topic and include time for a final practice test followed by a brief review. Set aside extra time for the more difficult subjects, and include a buffer for unexpected events such as college exams or business trips. There is never enough time to prepare, so make the most of the time that you have.

You can determine which subject areas require the most time in several ways. Look at your college grades: those courses with the lowest grades probably need the most study. Those subjects outside your major are generally the least used and most easily forgotten. These will require a good deal of review to bring you up to speed. Some of the subjects may not be familiar at all because you were not required to study them in college. These subjects may be impossible to learn before the examination,

7

although some can be self-taught. The mathematics may be not exceptionally difficult to you and most of the concepts are common sense.

Another way to determine your weakest areas is to take one of the practice tests provided in this book. The included simulated exams will help you assess your strengths and weaknesses. By determining which type of questions you answered incorrectly on the practice tests, you find the areas that need the most work. Be careful not to neglect the other subjects in your review; do not rule out any subject area until you have reviewed it to some degree.

You may also find that a negative attitude is your biggest stumbling block. Many students do not realize the volume of material they have covered in four years of college. Some begin to study and are immediately overwhelmed because they do not have a plan. It is important that you get a good start and that you are positive as you review and study the material.

You will need some way to measure your preparedness, either with problems from books or with a review book that has sample test questions similar to the ones on the FE: PM Electrical Engineering Exam. This book contains sample problems in each section which can be used before, during, or after you review the material to measure your understanding of the subject matter. If you are a wizard in power systems, for example, and are confident in your ability to solve problems, select a few and see what happens. You may want to perform at least a cursory review of the material before jumping into problem solving, since there is always something to learn. If you do well on these initial problems, then momentum has been established. If you do poorly, you might develop a negative attitude. Being positive is essential as you move through the subject areas.

The question that comes to mind at this point is: "How do I review the material?" Before we get into the material itself, let us establish rules which lead to **good study habits**. Time was previously mentioned as the most important issue. When you decide to study you will need blocks of uninterrupted time so that you can get something accomplished. Two hours should be the minimum time block allotted, while four hours should be the maximum. Schedule five-minute breaks into your study period and stay with your schedule. Cramming for the FE can give you poor results, including short-term memory and confusion when synthesis is required.

Next, you need to work in a quiet place, on a flat surface that is not cluttered with other papers or work that needs to be completed before the next day. **Eliminate distractions**—they will rob you of time while you pay attention to them. **Do not eat while you study**; few of us can do two things at once and do them both well. Eating does require a lot of attention and disrupts study. Eating a sensible meal before you study resolves the "eating while you work" problem. We encourage you to have a large glass of water available since water quenches your thirst and fills the void which makes you want to get up and find something to eat. In addition, **you should be well rested when you study**. Late nights and early mornings are good for some, especially if you have a family, but the best results are associated with adequate rest.

Lastly, **study on weekend mornings while most people are still asleep**. This allows for a quiet environment and gives you the remainder of the day to do other things. If you must study at night, we suggest two-hour blocks ending before 11 p.m.

Do not spend time memorizing charts, graphs, and formulae; the FE is a supplied reference exam, and you will be provided a booklet of equations and other essential information during the test. This reference material will be sent to you prior to your examination date. You can use the supplied reference book as a guide while studying, since it will give you an indication of the depth of study you will need to pursue. Furthermore, familiarity with the book will alleviate some test anxiety since you will be given the same book to use during the actual exam.

While you review for the test, use the review book supplied by the NCEES, paper, pencil, and a calculator. Texts can be used, but reliance on them should be avoided. The object of the review is to identify what you know, the positive, and that which requires work, the negative. As you review, move past those equations and concepts that you understand and annotate on the paper those concepts that require more work. Using this method you can review a large quantity of material in a short time and reduce the apparent workload to a manageable amount. Now go back to your time schedule and allocate the remaining time according to the needs of the subject under consideration. Return to the material that requires work and review it or study it until your are satisfied that you can solve problems covering this material. When you have finished the review, you are ready to solve problems.

Solving problems requires practice. To use the problems in this book effectively, you should cover the solution and try to solve the problem on your own. If this is not possible, map out a strategy to answer the problem and then check to see if you have the correct procedure. Remember, that most problems that are not solved correctly were never started correctly. Merely reviewing the solution will not help you to start the problem when you see it again at a later date. Read the problems carefully and in parts. Many people teach that reading the whole problem gives the best overview of what is to come; however, solutions are developed from small clues that are in parts of a sentence. **Read the problem and break it into manageable parts.** Next, **try to avoid numbers until the problem is well formulated.** Too often, numbers are substituted into equations early and become show stoppers. You will need numbers, just use them after the math has been completed. **Be mechanical,** list the knowns, the requirements of the problem, and check off those bits of knowledge you have as they appear. Checking off the intermediate answers and information you know is a positive attitude builder. Continue to solve problems until you are confident or you exceed the time allowed in you schedule for that subject area.

As soon as you complete one subject, move to the next. Retain all of you notes as you complete each section. You will need these for your final overall review right before the exam. After you have completed the entire review, you may want to take a practice test. Taking practice exams will test your understanding of all the engineering subject areas and will help you identify sections that need additional study. With the test and the notes that you retained from the subject reviews, you can determine weak areas requiring some additional work.

You should be ready for the exam if you follow these guidelines:

- Program your time wisely.

- Maintain a positive attitude.

- Develop good study habits.

- Review the material and maximize the learning process.

- Do practice problems and practice tests.

- Review again to finalize your preparation.

GOOD LUCK!

STUDY SCHEDULE

The following is a suggested eight-week study schedule for the Fundamentals of Engineering: PM Exam in Electrical Engineering. You may want to condense or expand the schedule depending on the amount of time remaining before the test. Set aside some time each week, and work straight through the activity without rushing. By following a structured schedule, you will be able to complete an adequate amount of studying, and be more confident and prepared on the day of the exam.

Week 1	Acquaint yourself with this FE: PM Electrical Engineering Test Preparation Book by reading the first chapter: "You Can Succeed on the FE: PM Electrical Engineering" Take Practice Test 1. When you score the test, be sure to look for areas where you missed many questions. Pay special attention to these areas when you read the review chapters.
Week 2	Begin reviewing Chapters 2 and 3. As you read the chapters, try to solve the examples without aid of the solutions. Use the solutions to guide you through any questions you missed.
Week 3	Study and review Chapters 4 and 5. Take notes as you read the chapters; you may even want to write concepts on index cards and thumb through them during the day. As you read the chapters, try to solve the examples without the aid of the solutions.
Week 4	Review any notes you have taken over the last few weeks. Study Chapters 6 and 7. As you read the chapters, try to solve the examples without the aid of the solutions.
Week 5	Study Chapters 8 and 9 while continuing to review your notes. As you read the chapters, try to solve the examples without the aid of the solutions.
Week 6	Study Chapters 10 and 11. As you read the chapters, try to solve the examples without the aid of the solutions to guide you through any questions you missed.

Week 7	Study Chapters 12, 13, and 14. As you read, try to solve the examples without the aid of the solutions. Use the solutions to guide you through any questions you missed.
Week 8	Take Practice Test 2. When you score the text, be sure to look for any improvement in the areas that you missed in Practice Test 1. If you missed any questions in any particular area, go back and review those areas. Be patient and deliberate as you review; with careful study, you can only improve.

FE/EIT

FE: PM Electrical Engineering Exam

CHAPTER 2

Analog Electronic Circuits

CHAPTER 2

ANALOG ELECTRONIC CIRCUITS

OPERATIONAL AMPLIFIER

The equivalent circuit of an operational amplifier is:

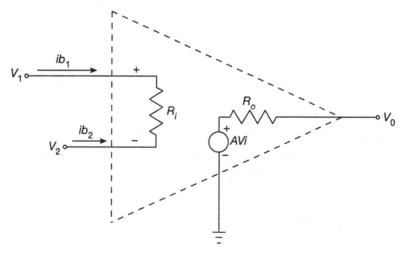

Figure 1

where:

V_1 = voltage at the noninverting input terminal with respect to ground

V_2 = voltage at the inverting input terminal with respect to ground

R_i = input resistance

R_o = output resistance

A = open-loop voltage gain

V_i = differential input voltage ($V_i = V_1 - V_2$)

For an ideal operational amplifier,

$R_i = \infty$, hence $i_{b1} = i_{b2} = 0$

$R_o = 0$

$A = \infty$, hence $V_1 = V_2$

A 741 op-amp has the following typical values:

$R_i = 2 \text{ M}\Omega$

$R_o = 75 \Omega$

$A = 200,000$

The schematic symbol for an op-amp is:

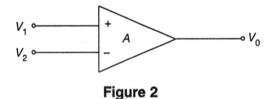

Figure 2

Since the open-loop gain A is very large (200,000), the differential input voltage must be kept very small. For example, a V_i of 1 mV will produce an output voltage of 200 V. Therefore, it is not practical to use op-amp in the open-loop configuration and, therefore, feedback or closed-loop op-amp configuration was introduced.

LINEAR OP-AMP CIRCUITS

In linear op-amp circuits, the output signal is of the same nature as the input signal, i.e., the shape of the input signal is preserved.

Noninverting Amplifier Circuit

Assume that the op-amp is ideal. We have:

$V_2 = V_{\text{in}}$ and $i_2 = 0$

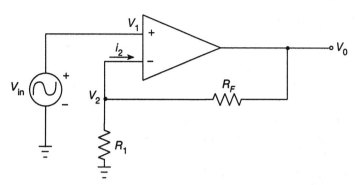

Figure 3

Thus,

$$V_{in} = V_2 = \left[\frac{R_1}{R_1 + R_F}\right] V_o \quad \text{(voltage divider theorem)}$$

$$V_O = \left[\frac{R_1 + R_F}{R_1}\right] V_{in} = \left[1 + \frac{R_F}{R_1}\right] V_{in}$$

The Inverting Amplifier Circuit

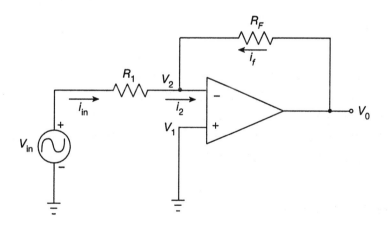

Figure 4

Assume that the op-amp is ideal: $i_2 = 0$ and $V_2 = 0$ (virtual ground)

$$i_{in} = \frac{V_{in}}{R_1} \; ; \qquad i_f = \frac{V_o}{R_f}$$

$$i_{in} = -i_f \quad \Rightarrow \quad \frac{V_{in}}{R_1} = -\frac{V_o}{R_f}$$

Thus,

$$V_0 = -\frac{R_f}{R_1} V_{in}$$

The negative sign indicates a phase inversion between the input and output voltage.

Summing Amplifier

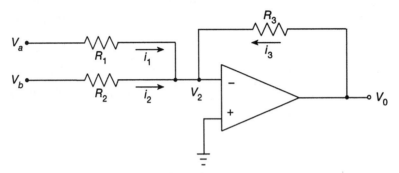

Figure 5

Assume the op-amp is ideal. $V_2 = 0$ (virtual ground), and so we have:

$$i_1 = \frac{V_a}{R_1} \; ; \quad i_2 = \frac{V_b}{R_2} \; ; \quad i_3 = \frac{V_o}{R_3}$$

$$i_1 + i_2 = -i_3 \; (KCL)$$

$$\frac{V_0}{R_3} = -\left(\frac{V_a}{R_1} + \frac{V_b}{R_2}\right)$$

Thus,

$$V_o = -\frac{R_3}{R_1} V_a - \frac{R_3}{R_2} V_b$$

If we select $R_1 = R_2 = R_3$, then:

$$V_o = -V_a - V_b$$

PROBLEM 1:

Determine the load current in the circuit shown.

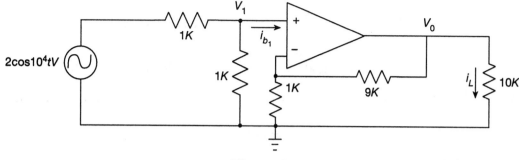

Figure 6

SOLUTION:

Assume that the op-amp is ideal ($i_{b_1} = 0$), we have:

$$V_1 = 2\cos 10^4 t \left[\frac{1K}{1K + 1K} \right] = \cos 10^4 t \text{ (voltage divider theorem)}$$

$$V_o = \left(1 + \frac{9K}{1K} \right) V_1 = 10 \cos 10^4 t V$$

The load current i_L is:

$$\frac{10\cos 10^4 t V}{10K} = 1\cos 10^4 t\, mA$$

PROBLEM 2:

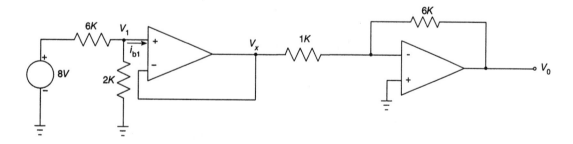

Figure 7

Calculate V_o.

SOLUTION:

Assume that the op-amp is ideal. The current $i_{b_1} = 0$, so we have:

$$V_1 = 8V\left[\frac{2K}{2K+6K}\right] = 2V \text{ (voltage divider)}$$

Since the op-amp is ideal, $V_1 = V_2 = V_x = 2V$. This is called a unity gain voltage follower.

$$V_o = -\frac{6K}{1K}V_x = (-6)(2V) = -12V$$

PROBLEM 3:

Calculate the load current in the circuit below.

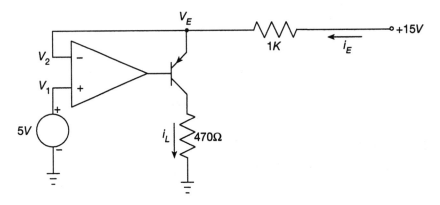

Figure 8

SOLUTION:

Assume that the op-amp is ideal. We have:

$$V_E = V_2 = V_1 = 5V$$

$$i_L \cong i_E = \frac{15V - 5V}{1K} = 10 \text{ mA}$$

This is called a voltage-to-current converter circuit. Note that the load current is independent of the load resistor.

NONLINEAR OP-AMP CIRCUITS

Nonlinear op-amp circuits include the integrator and differentiator.

The Integrating Amplifier

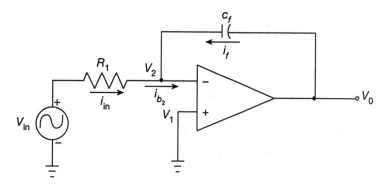

Figure 9

Assuming $V_2 = 0$, we have:

$$i_{in} = \frac{V_{in}}{R_1} \text{ and } i_f = C_f \frac{dV_0}{dt}$$

Assuming $i_{b_2} = 0$, we have:

$$i_{in} + i_f = 0 \text{ (KCL)}$$

$$\frac{V_{in}}{R_1} + C_f \frac{dV_0}{dt} = 0$$

$$\Rightarrow \frac{dV_0}{dt} = -\frac{1}{R_1 C_f} V_{in}$$

Integrating,

$$V_0(t) = -\frac{1}{R_1 C_f} \int_{t_0}^{t} V_{in} dt + V_0(t_0)$$

The Differentiating Amplifier

Assuming that $V_2 = V_1 = 0$, we have:

$$i_{in} = C_1 \frac{dV_{in}}{dt} \text{ and } i_f = \frac{V_0}{R_f}$$

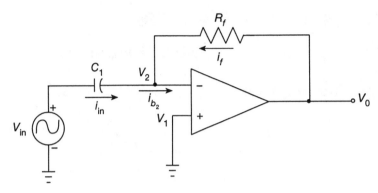

Figure 10

Assuming that $i_{b_2} = 0$, we have:

$$i_{\text{in}} + i_f = 0 \text{ (KCL)}$$

Thus,

$$C_1 \frac{dV_{\text{in}}}{dt} + \frac{V_0}{R_f} = 0$$

Solving for V_0:

$$V_0 = -R_f C_1 \frac{dV_{\text{in}}}{dt}$$

PROBLEM 4:

The input to the integrating amplifier circuit is shown below.

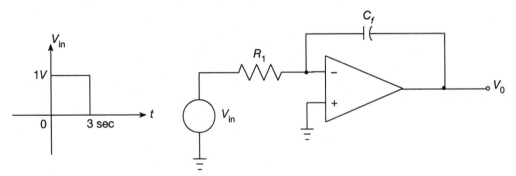

Figure 11

Determine the output voltage and sketch it, assuming that the op-amp is initially nulled and $R_1 C_f = 1$ sec.

SOLUTION:

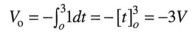

$$V_o = -\int_o^3 1\,dt = -[t]_o^3 = -3V$$

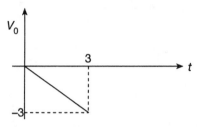

Figure 12

The output waveform is a ramp function with the slope equal to –1 volt/sec.

SMALL-SIGNAL AMPLIFIERS

After a transistor has been biased with a Q point near the middle of the DC load line (see different biasing techniques for bipolar junction transistor circuits discussed in the chapter on solid state devices), a small AC signal can be coupled into the base using a coupling capacitor. This biasing arrangement will produce an amplified output signal with the same shape and frequency as long as the input signal is small and thus swings over only a small portion of the DC load line. We can analyze small-signal transistor amplifier circuits using the superposition theorem to divide the circuit in two separate parts: a DC analysis and an AC analysis.

> **DC analysis:** Reduce the AC source to zero and *open* all capacitors. The circuit remains is called the DC equivalent circuit, which can be used to calculate the DC currents and voltages and the Q point.

> **AC analysis:** Reduce the DC source to zero and *short* all capacitors. The circuit remains is called the AC equivalent circuit, which can be used to calculate the AC currents and voltages. The Ebers-Moll AC model for an NPN transistor is shown in Figure 13.

r_e' is called the AC emitter resistance. r_e' is included in the model due to the change in the emitter voltage and current when the AC signal drives the transistor. The formula for r_e' is:

$$r_e' = \frac{25mV}{I_E}$$

where I_E is the DC emitter current.

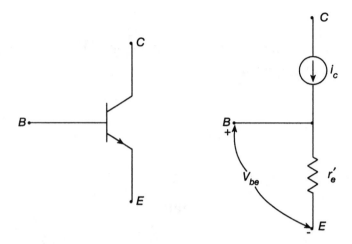

Figure 13

PROBLEM 5:

The figure below shows a common emitter amplifier.

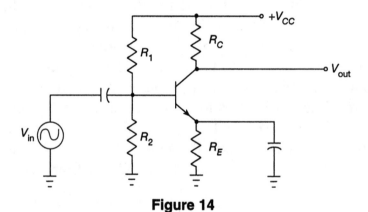

Figure 14

(a) Draw the AC equivalent circuit.

(b) Calculate the voltage gain.

$$A = \frac{V_{out}}{V_{in}}$$

(c) Determine the input impedance.

(d) $R_1 = 10\ K\Omega$, $R_2 = 2\ K\Omega$, $R_C = 2.7\ K\Omega$, $R_E = 1\ K\Omega$, and $V_{CC} = 10V$; the AC input signal is a sinusoidal voltage with a peak value of 1 mV. What is the peak value of the AC output voltage?

SOLUTION:

(a) Reduce V_{CC} to zero and short all the capacitors. We have the following AC equivalent circuit:

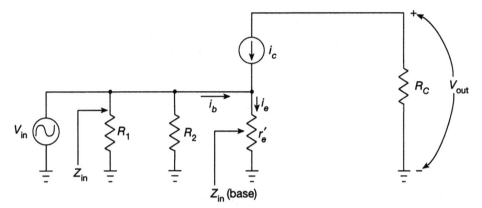

Figure 15

(b) The AC emitter current is:

$$i_e = \frac{V_{in}}{r'_e}$$

Since $i_c \cong i_e$, the output voltage V_{out} is:

$$V_{out} = -i_c R_c = -i_e R_c = -V_{in} \frac{R_c}{r'_e}$$

The voltage gain is therefore equal to:

$$A = \frac{V_{out}}{V_{in}} = -\frac{R_c}{r'_e}$$

The minus sign indicates that there is a phase inversion at the output signal.

(c)
$$Z_{in} \text{ (base)} = \frac{V_{in}}{i_b} = \frac{i_e r'_e}{i_b} \cong \frac{\beta i_b r'_e}{i_b} = \beta r'_e$$

$$\Rightarrow Z_{in} = R_1 // R_2 // \beta r'_e$$

(d)
$$r'_e = \frac{25 \text{ mV}}{I_E}$$

To calculate r'_e, we need to determine the DC emitter current, I_E.

$$V_B = V_{cc}\left[\frac{R_2}{R_1 + R_2}\right] = 10V\left[\frac{2K\Omega}{10K\Omega + 2K\Omega}\right] = 1.67V$$

$$I_E = \frac{V_B - V_{BE}}{R_E} = \frac{1.67V - 0.7V}{1K\Omega} = 0.97 \text{ mA}$$

$$r'_e = \frac{25 \text{ mV}}{0.97 \text{ mA}} = 25.77 \ \Omega$$

The voltage gain is:

$$A = -\frac{2.7K\Omega}{25.77 \ \Omega} = -105$$

The peak AC output voltage is:

$$V_{out} = AV_{in} = (-105)(1 \text{ mV}) = -105 \text{ mV}$$

We can represent this amplifier with the following simplified AC model.

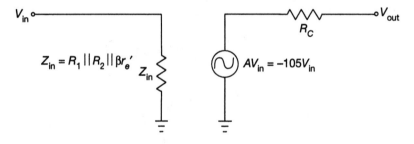

Figure 16

PROBLEM 6:

Figure 17 shows a two-stage amplifier using cascaded CE amplifier circuits. The idea is to use the amplified output from one stage as the input to another stage to obtain a very large overall gain.

The transistors each have $\beta = 160$. Calculate the AC output voltage.

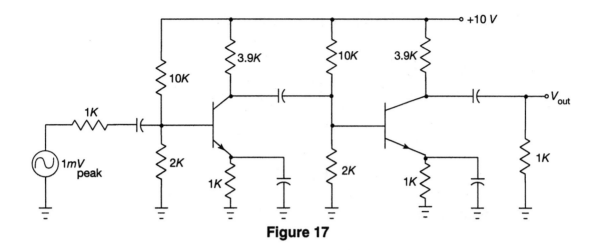

Figure 17

SOLUTION:

Each stage is identical.

$$r_e' = \frac{25 \text{ mV}}{I_E}$$

$$V_B = 10V \frac{2K\Omega}{2K\Omega + 10K\Omega} = 1.67V$$

$$I_E = \frac{V_B - V_{BE}}{R_E} = \frac{1.67V - 0.7V}{1K\Omega} = 0.97 \text{ mA}$$

$$r_e' = \frac{25 \text{ mV}}{0.97 \text{ mA}} = 25.77\Omega$$

The input impedance to each stage is:

$$Z_{\text{in}} = 10K\Omega//2K\Omega//(150)(25.77\Omega) = 1.16K\Omega$$

The output impedance at each stage is:

$$Z_{\text{out}} = 3.9K\Omega$$

Voltage gain for each stage is:

$$-\frac{R_c}{r_e'} = -\frac{3.9K\Omega}{25.77\Omega} = -151$$

The simplified AC model for the two-stage amplifier is:

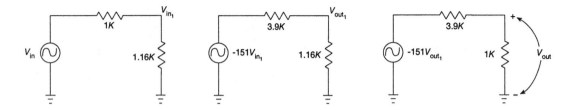

Figure 18

The AC input to the first stage is:

$$V_{in_1} = \left[\frac{1.16K\Omega}{1K\Omega + 1.16K\Omega}\right](1\,mV) = 0.537\,mV$$

$$V_{out_1} = -151V_{in_1}\left[\frac{1.16K\Omega}{3.9K\Omega + 1.16K\Omega}\right] = -18.59\,mV$$

The AC output voltage is:

$$V_{out} = -151V_{out_1}\left[\frac{1K\Omega}{1K\Omega + 3.9K\Omega}\right] = 573\,mV = 0.573V$$

Note that there are two stages of inverted gain. The final output voltage waveform is therefore in phase with the input signal.

FREQUENCY EFFECTS

In the previous section, we analyzed amplifier circuits that operate in the midband frequencies where capacitors have negligible effect. When an amplifier operates outside of the midband, the voltage gain drops off. Consider the following CE amplifier and its AC equivalent circuit.

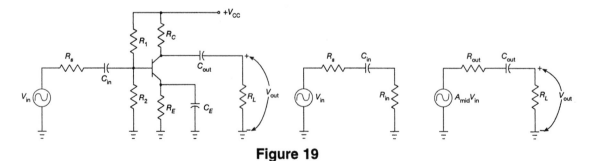

Figure 19

$$R_{in} = R_1//R_2//\beta\, r_e'$$

$$R_{out} = R_c$$

A_{mid} = midband voltage gain

The cutoff frequencies of the input and output of the amplifier circuit are:

$$f_{in} = \frac{1}{2\pi(R_S + R_{in})C_{in}}$$

$$f_{out} = \frac{1}{2\pi(R_{out} + R_L)C_{out}}$$

The higher cutoff frequency is important because it causes the first break in amplifier response. It is called the dominant cutoff frequency. At this frequency, the voltage gain is equal to $0.707A_{mid}$ and the load power is half its maximum.

PROBLEM 7:

For the transistor amplifier in Problem 5, calculate the cutoff frequencies if $\beta = 150$, $C_{in} = 0.47$ µf, $C_{out} = 2.2$ µf and plot the frequency response.

SOLUTION:

We found from Problem 5:

$$r_e' = 25.77\Omega$$

$$A_{mid} = -105$$

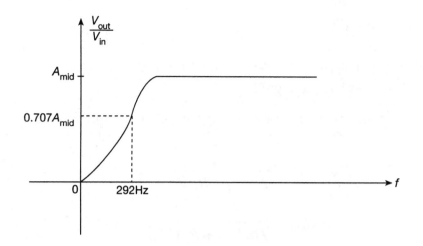

Figure 20

$R_{\text{out}} = R_c = 2.7K\Omega$

$R_{\text{in}} = 10K\Omega//2K\Omega//(150)(25.77\Omega) = 1.16K\Omega$

$$f_{\text{in}} = \frac{1}{2\pi(1.16K\Omega)(0.47\ \mu f)} = 292\ \text{Hz}$$

$$f_{\text{out}} = \frac{1}{2\pi(2.7K\Omega)(2.2\ \mu f)} = 26.8\ \text{Hz}$$

FE/EIT

FE: PM Electrical Engineering Exam

CHAPTER 3

Communication Theory

CHAPTER 3

COMMUNICATION THEORY

In this chapter, we will cover the aspects of both analog and digital communication systems, from modulation to the issues of information rate, equalization, and detection with worked problems and solutions.

MECHANICS OF MODULATION

An information exchange from one point to another or from one person to another or a group is called communication. Communication over long distances is achieved by transmitting an information-bearing signal over the airwaves or through wire media. However, the typical modulating signal, an audio signal, is not generally suited for propagation over long distances. This signal must thus be shifted to a higher frequency by a process called *modulation*.

Modulation

Modulation is the process by which one or more characteristics of a carrier wave are varied according to the message signal (modulating signal). The resultant signal is the modulated signal, which at radio frequencies travels much longer distances than can the modulating (DC – 5KHz audio) signal alone. At the receiving end, the radio wave is demodulated to recover the original audio.

Amplitude and frequency modulation are both so-called continuous wave forms of analog modulation. A sinusoidal signal is used in continuous wave modulation, which is given by the product of the modulating signal and carrier wave:

$$x_c(t) = A_c(t) \times \cos[\omega_c t + \phi(t)] - (1)$$

$$\omega_c = 2\pi f_c,$$

where f_c is the carrier frequency, $A_c(t)$ and $\phi(t)$ are the time-varying amplitude and angle of the carrier.

When the amplitude of the carrier is varied in accordance with the message signal $m(t)$, it is called *amplitude modulation*. If the phase of the carrier is varied, then the result is *angle modulation*, of which there are two types: *phase* and *frequency*. In PM, the carrier's deviation (frequency shift) is directly proportional to the modulation frequency. In FM, the deviation is directly proportional to the modulating signal's amplitude.

Digital communication uses pulse modulation, where the carrier is a periodic train of pulses. The analog modulating signal is converted to digital form, a process called analog-to-digital conversion. There are two general types of analog-to-digital conversion techniques, which result in pulse code modulation and delta modulation.

AMPLITUDE MODULATION

Amplitude modulation is also referred to as linear modulation because the amplitude of the modulated carrier $A(t)$ (i.e., carrier plus sidebands, or envelope) is linearly related to the modulating signal $m(t)$.

In standard amplitude modulation, an audio signal modulates a carrier in the mixer, or multiplier, stage. Let the modulating signal be $KI \cos(\omega_m t)$ and the carrier be $KI \cos(\omega_c t)$. Then using the double angle cosine formula, the modulated output is:

$$e_o = K[\cos(\omega_c + \omega_m) + \cos(\omega_c - \omega_m)]$$

For amplitude modulation, the phase angle $\phi(t)$ is zero, and the amplitude $A_c(t)$ is proportional to message signal $m(t)$.

If we let the proportionality constant be unity, then the modulated signal is given by:

$$x(t) = [A + m(t)] \cos \omega_c t$$

The spectral density of $x(t)$ is given by the modulation theorem as:

$$X(\omega) = \frac{1}{2}M(\omega - \omega_c) + \frac{1}{2}M(\omega + \omega_c) + \pi A[\delta(\omega - \omega_c) + \delta(\omega + \omega_c)]$$

The time and the frequency domain waveforms are as shown below.

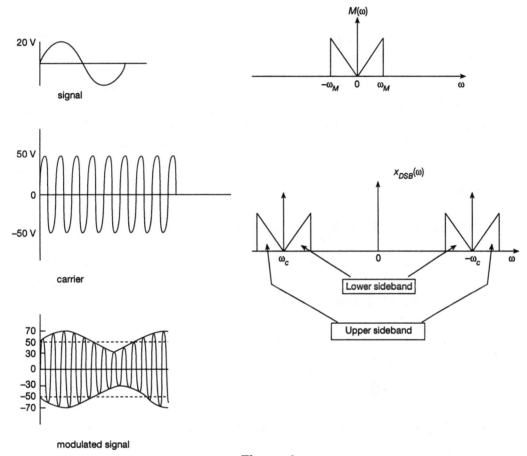

Figure 1

The part of the spectrum that lies above ω_c is called the *upper sideband* and that below it is called the *lower sideband*. The spectral range occupied by the message signal is called the *baseband* and hence it is also referred to as the baseband signal.

The *demodulation* of AM is simple and is most often achieved by envelope detection. If the carrier amplitude, A, is large with respect to the modulating waveform, then the envelope of the modulated signal is proportional to the message signal, $m(t)$. However, if A is not large, then the envelope is not always proportional to $m(t)$ and the original information cannot be fully recovered.

Hence, for successful detection:

$$A \geq |\min\{ m(t)\}|$$

The modulation index μ is given by:

$$\mu = \frac{|\min\{m(t)\}|}{A}$$

and μ is less than or equal to 1. If μ is greater than 1, then the carrier is said to be overmodulated.

PROBLEM 1:

Calculate the communications efficiency of the ordinary AM signal for $\mu = 0.5$.

SOLUTION:

The efficiency of the AM signal is given by:

$$\eta = \frac{P_s}{P_t} \times 100\% = \frac{\frac{1}{4}\mu^2 A^2}{\left(\frac{1}{2} + \frac{1}{4}\mu^2\right)A^2} = \frac{\mu^2}{2 + \mu^2} \times 100\%$$

$$\eta = \frac{0.5^2}{2 + 0.5^2} \times 100\% = 11.1\%$$

This is the percentage power carried by both sidebands. Here we see that most of the power in both sidebands is wasted. The carrier contains no useful information and both sidebands are identical. Thus, one of the sidebands is redundant.

Envelope Detector

A simple envelope detector is shown in Figure 2 on the following page.

During the positive half cycle, the diode is forward biased and the capacitor charges to the peak value of the input signal. Then when the input signal is in the negative half-cycle, the capacitor discharges slowly until the next positive peak turns on the diode. This charges the capacitor to a new peak value, which is the envelope of the signal. The RC values should be chosen such that $1/f_c \ll 1/f_m$.

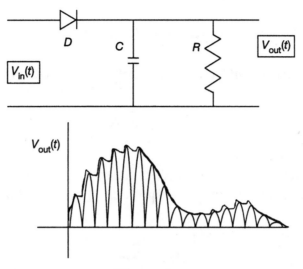

Figure 2

DOUBLE SIDEBAND MODULATION-SUPPRESSED CARRIER

This modulation is the same as the amplitude modulation but the modulated signal's carrier is suppressed before it is transmitted. The DSB-SC is obtained when the carrier $\cos\omega_c t$ is multiplied by the message signal $m(t)$. The modulated signal of DSB-SC is given by:

$$X_{DSB}(t) = m(t) \cos \omega_c t$$

The spectrum of the double sideband (DSB-SC) signal is given by:

$$X(\omega) = \frac{1}{2} M(\omega - \omega_c) + \frac{1}{2} M(\omega + \omega_c)$$

The spectrum of the DSB-SC signal has no carrier in it and hence the modulation is called *double sideband suppressed carrier* modulation.

Demodulation

The information-bearing signal is recovered from the modulated signal by *demodulation*. This can be achieved by multiplying the modulated signal by a local carrier and then passing it through a low-pass filter (LPF) as shown in Figure 3.

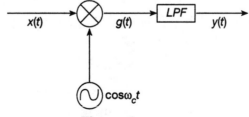

Figure 3

$$g(t) = x(t)\cos\omega_c t = \left[m(t)\cos\omega_c t\right]\cos\omega_c t$$

$$g(t) = \left[m(t)\cos^2\omega_c t\right] = m(t)\left[\frac{1}{2} + \frac{1}{2}\cos 2\omega_c t\right]$$

$$g(t) = \frac{1}{2}m(t) + \frac{1}{2}m(t)\cos 2\omega_c t$$

The low-pass filter is required to separate the double frequency terms from the original spectrum. After passing the $g(t)$ through the low-pass filter, we get:

$$y(t) = \frac{1}{2}m(t)$$

It is important to note that ω_c must be greater than the bandwidth of ω_m for proper signal recovery.

PROBLEM 2:

Show the output when the local carrier has phase (ϕ) or frequency (ω) error.

SOLUTION:

(a) Phase error:

$$g(t) = x(t)\cos\omega_c t = [m(t)\cos\omega_c t]\cos[\omega_c t + \phi]$$

$$g(t) = m(t)\left[\frac{1}{2}\cos\phi + \frac{1}{2}\cos\{2\omega_c t + \phi\}\right]$$

$$g(t) = \frac{1}{2}m(t)\cos\phi + \frac{1}{2}m(t)\cos(2\omega_c t + \phi)$$

The output message signal is equal to:

$$y(t) = \frac{1}{2}m(t)\cos\phi$$

The message signal is a function of the phase error and is zero for:

$$\Phi = \frac{\pi}{2}$$

and is proportional when Φ is constant.

(b) Frequency error:

Similarly, the message signal is multiplied by a low-frequency sine wave and is given by:

$$y(t) = \frac{1}{2} m(t) \cos(\Delta\omega)t$$

The output produced has a beating effect, which is an undesirable distortion. As seen, the receiver must generate a local carrier, which has to be synchronous in phase and frequency with the incoming signal. Thus, this system has some inherent difficulties.

SINGLE SIDEBAND MODULATION

Both the previous types of modulation use a bandwidth equal to twice the bandwidth of the message signal. The message information is complete in either the upper or the lower sideband and so transmission of only one is sufficient. Thus, we have single sideband modulation. There are two major methods of producing SSB signals: *frequency discrimination (filter)* and *phase shift*.

Frequency Discrimination (Filter) Method

The DSB signal is passed through a sideband filter (SBF) to suppress one of the sidebands. This method is called *frequency discrimination* or *filter method*. The filter used must have sharp cutoff response. The process diagrams and frequency spectrum are as shown.

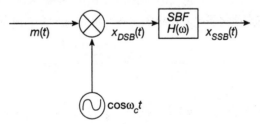

Figure 4(a)

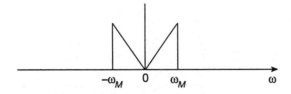

Figure 4(b)

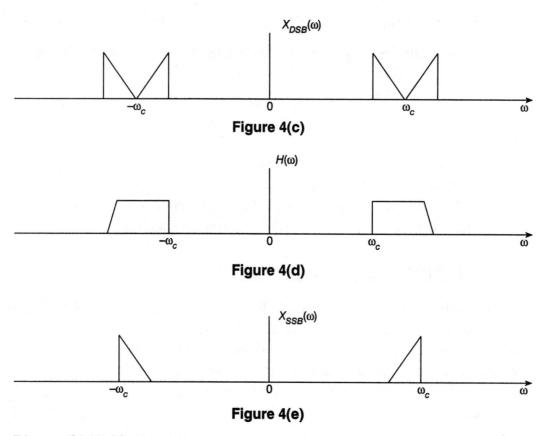

Figure 4(c)

Figure 4(d)

Figure 4(e)

Phase Shift Method

As the name suggests, the carrier and the modulating signals are phase shifted by $\pi/2$, as shown:

$$X_{SSB}(t) = m(t) \cos \omega_c t \pm m(t) \sin \omega_c t$$

where the sum gives the lower sideband signal and the difference gives the upper sideband signal.

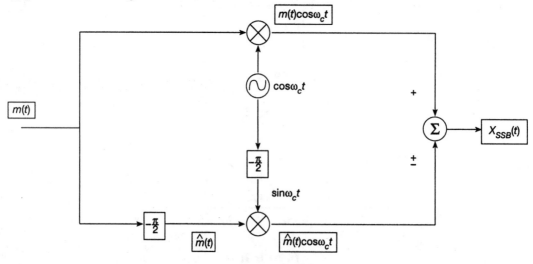

Figure 5

The demodulation of the SSB signal is similar to DSB demodulation.

VESTIGIAL SIDEBAND MODULATION (VSB)

In this system, one sideband is completely transmitted with a trace or vestige of the other. The bandwidth of VSB is about 1.25 times that of SSB. This is used mainly for video signals.

The VSB modulation process is the same as in SSB, except that the filter is a vestigial filter, which has the required sideband shaping characteristics. The VSB modulated frequency domain spectrum is as shown in Figure 6.

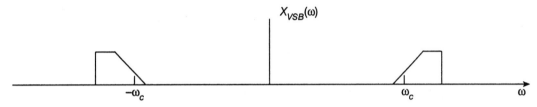

Figure 6

VSB Demodulation

Demodulation is similar to SSB or DSB, using coherent, or synchronous, demodulation. For a distortionless message signal $m(t)$,

$$H(\omega + \omega_c) + H(\omega - \omega_c) = C$$

for $|\omega| \quad \omega_M$ and C is a constant.

QUADRATURE AMPLITUDE MODULATION (QAM)

QAM is a scheme where two different signals can be transmitted or received on the same carrier frequency. Here, the two signals are modulated or demodulated using two carriers at the same frequency but in phase quadrature. It is used in the transmission of color information signals in commercial television.

The modulated output is:

$$X_{QAM}(t) = m_1(t) \cos \omega_c t + m_2(t) \sin \omega_c t$$

The demodulation outputs are given by:

$$X_{QAM}(t)\cos\omega_c t = m_1(t)\cos^2 \omega_c t + m_2 t \sin \omega_c t \cos \omega_c t$$

$$X_{QAM}(t)\cos\omega_c t = \frac{1}{2}m_1(t) + \frac{1}{2}m_1(t)\cos 2\omega_c t + \frac{1}{2}m_2(t)\sin 2\omega_c t$$

$$X_{QAM}(t)\sin\omega_c t = \frac{1}{2}m_2(t) + \frac{1}{2}m_1(t)\sin 2\omega_c t - \frac{1}{2}m_2(t)\cos 2\omega_c t$$

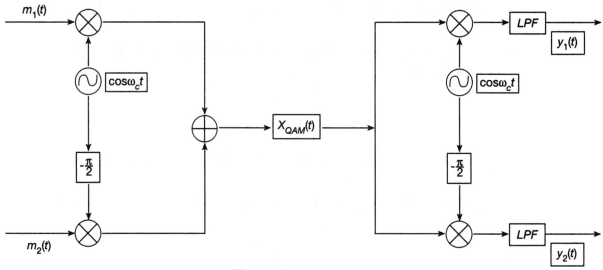

Figure 7

Passing through a LPF filter, we get:

$$y_1(t) = \frac{1}{2} m_1(t)$$

$$y_2(t) = \frac{1}{2} m_2(t)$$

ANGLE MODULATION

Angle modulation is a process by which the phase angle $\phi(t)$ of the sinusoidal carrier wave is changed according to the message signal. Two types of angle modulation are *frequency modulation* and *phase modulation*. The bandwidth of the angle modulated wave is usually greater than twice the message bandwidth. The noise and interference for wideband systems is greatly reduced compared to amplitude modulation systems.

The angle modulated carrier is given by:

$$x_c(t) = A \cos[(\omega_c t + \phi(t)]$$

with A and ω_c the constants, and the phase angle, $\phi(t)$, a function of the message signal.

The instantaneous phase and instantaneous frequency are given by $\theta(t)$ and:

$$\frac{d\theta}{dt}$$

and the maximum radian frequency deviation is given by:

$$\Delta\omega = |\omega_i - \omega_c|$$

FREQUENCY MODULATION

In frequency modulation, the instantaneous frequency deviation is proportional to the message signal:

$$\frac{d\phi(t)}{dt} = k_f m(t)$$

where k_f is the frequency deviation constant, expressed in radians/sec per unit $m(t)$.

The modulated signal is given by:

$$x_{FM}(t) = A \cos[\omega_c t + k_f \int_{-\infty} m(\lambda)d\lambda]$$

The instantaneous frequency ω_i varies linearly with the modulating signal and hence:

$$\omega_i = \omega_c + k_f m(t)$$

Modulation Index

The message signal $m(t) = a_m \cos \omega_m(t)$ gives us a phase angle:

$$\phi(t) = \beta \sin \omega_m(t)$$

where:

$$\beta = \frac{k_f a_m}{\omega_m}$$

β is the modulation index for the sinusoidal FM modulation and is the maximum value of phase deviation.

Therefore,

$$\beta = \frac{\Delta\omega}{\omega_m}$$

where $\Delta\omega$ is the maximum frequency deviation.

PROBLEM 3:

Find the instantaneous frequency of the modulated carrier:

$$20\cos\left(400\pi t + \frac{\pi}{6}\right)$$

SOLUTION:

$$\theta(t) = 400\pi t + \frac{\pi}{6}$$

$$\omega_i = \frac{d\theta}{dt} = 400\pi = 2\pi(200)$$

The instantaneous frequency of the signal is 200 Hz.

PROBLEM 4:

Find the frequency deviation of the modulated signal:

$$x_c(t) = 10 \cos[100\pi t + 10 \cos 50\pi t]$$

SOLUTION:

$$\theta(t) = \omega_c(t) + \phi(t) = 100\pi t + 10 \cos 50\pi t$$

$$\phi(t) = 10 \cos 50\pi t$$

$$\phi'(t) = 10(-50\pi \sin 50\pi t)$$

$$\Delta\omega = |\phi'(t)| = 500\pi \text{ rad/s} = 2\pi(250)$$

The frequency deviation is 250 Hz.

Demodulation

FM demodulation is a process in which the output is proportional to the instantaneous frequency deviation of the input signal, and it is also called frequency discrimination. The modulated wave is given by:

$$x_c(t) = A \cos[\omega_c t + \phi(t)]$$

The output demodulated wave is:

$$y_d(t) = k_d \frac{d\phi(t)}{dt} = k_d k_f m(t)$$

where k_d is the discriminator sensitivity.

The output characteristic is as given below.

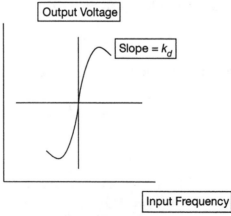

Figure 8

PROBLEM 5:

A modulated signal is given by $x_c(t) = 12 \cos[2\pi 100t + 0.1\sin 100\pi t]$ and if $k_f = 10\pi$, find $m(t)$.

SOLUTION:

Assume $m(t) = a_m \cos 100\pi t$

and from the FM modulated equation:

$$x_{FM}(t) = A\cos\left[\omega_c t + k_f \int_{-\infty} m(\lambda)\, d\lambda\right]$$

$$10\pi \int_{-\infty} m(\lambda)\, d\lambda = 10\pi a_m \int_{-\infty} \cos 100\pi\lambda\, d\lambda$$

$$\frac{a_m}{10}\sin(100)\pi t = 0.1\sin 100\pi t$$

$$a_m = 1.0$$

and
$$m(t) = 10\cos 100\pi t$$

PHASE MODULATION

In phase modulation, the instantaneous frequency given by:

$$\omega_i = \frac{d\theta}{dt}$$

is proportional to the message signal in (t), so that:

$$\phi(t) = k_p m(t)$$

where k_p is the phase deviation constant, expressed in radians per unit $m(t)$. The modulated signal is given by:

$$x_{PM}(t) = A\cos[\omega_c t + k_p m(t)]$$

The instantaneous frequency ω_i varies linearly with the derivative of the modulating signal, and:

$$\omega_i = \omega_c + k_p \frac{dm(t)}{dt}$$

Modulation Index

The message signal $m(t) = a_m \sin \omega_m(t)$ gives us a phase angle:

$$\phi(t) = \beta \sin \omega_m(t)$$

where: $$\beta = k_p a_m$$

β is the modulation index for the sinusoidal phase modulation and is the maximum value of phase deviation. Therefore,

$$\beta = \frac{\Delta \omega}{\omega_m}$$

where $\Delta \omega$ is the maximum frequency deviation.

PROBLEM 6:

In Problem 5, find the maximum phase deviation.

SOLUTION:

$$x_c(t) = 10 \cos[100\pi t + 10 \cos 50\pi t]$$

$$\theta(t) = \omega_c(t) + \phi(t) = 100\pi t + 10 \cos 50\pi t$$

$$\phi(t) = 10 \cos 50\pi t$$

The maximum phase deviation is $|\phi(t)|_{max} = 10$ rad.

PROBLEM 7:

If the PM signal is given by $x_{PM}(t) = 50\cos[100\pi t + 0.1 \sin 100\pi t]$ and the phase deviation constant is 20, find the message signal $m(t)$.

SOLUTION:

$$x_{PM}(t) = A \cos[\omega_c t + k_p m(t)]$$

$$= 50 \cos[100\pi t + 20m(t)]$$

But: $$20m(t) = 0.1 \sin 100\pi t$$

$$m(t) = 0.005 \sin 100\pi t$$

PULSE CODE MODULATION (PCM)

The pulse code modulation process involves sampling, quantizing, and encoding. *Sampling* is a process measuring a signal's amplitude at discrete instants and then representing it by a finite set of levels called *quantizing*. The assignment of a code to the quantized signal is called *encoding*.

Sampling Theorem

If the message signal $m(t)$ is a band limited signal with its highest frequency component less than ω_m, then $m(t)$ can be determined uniquely by its sample values with sampling frequency equal to or greater than $2\omega_m$.

$$m(t) = \sum_{n=-\infty}^{\infty} m(nT_s) \frac{\sin \omega_M (t - nT_s)}{\omega_M (t - nT_s)}$$

where T_s is the sampling period and $f_s = 1/T_s$ is the sampling rate.

The minimum sampling frequency f_s min $= 2\omega_m$.

Ideal Sampling

The signal $m(t)$ sampled at a uniform rate, by a unit impulse train $\delta_T(t)$ yields:

$$m_s(t) = m(t)\delta_{T_s}(t) = \sum_{n=-\infty}^{\infty} m(nT_s)\delta(t - nT_s)$$

where $m_s(t)$ is referred to as the ideal sampled signal.

Natural Sampling

In ideal sampling, the unit impulse function is applied; but in actual practice, a periodic train of rectangular pulse is used. The sampled signal is given by:

$$x_{ns}(t) = m(t)x_p(t)$$

where $x_p(t)$ is the periodic train of rectangular pulses with a period T_s.

We call this process natural sampling, because the top of each pulse maintains the shape of the original analog signal.

Flat Top Sampling

This is the simplest and the most popular sampling method using the sample and hold circuit. The $x_s(t)$ is a pulse amplitude modulated signal with the message signal modulated by a carrier which is the train of rectangular pulses. The modulated signal can be expressed as the convolution of the message signal $m_s(t)$ and the rectangular pulse $p(t)$.

Therefore,

$$x_s(t) = m_s(t) \times p(t)$$

Quantizing

Quantizing is a process in which the infinite levels of the sample signal are translated to a finite number of levels, such as 8, 16, 24, and so on.

Encoding

Assigning of a code to the quantized values is called encoding. The quantized sample is converted to a binary sequence, which is then converted to a sequential string of pulses for transmission. The number of bits in a binary sequence depends on the levels in the quantized sample. The higher the number of bits, the better the resolution and accuracy. The bandwidth of the pulse code modulation is proportional to the number of bits in the binary sequence and the message signal bandwidth f_m and is given by:

$$f_{PCM} = \frac{n}{2} fs \geq nf_m$$

DELTA MODULATION

Delta modulation involves a simpler process to generate a binary sequence than pulse code modulation. It uses a comparator that generates an output, that is the difference of the message signal and the reference signal. The output of the delta modulator is a series of impulses of varying polarity. The block diagram of the delta modulator is as shown in Figure 9.

The output of the delta modulator is given by:

$$x_{DM}(t) = \Delta \sum_{n=-\infty}^{\infty} \text{sgn}\big[e(nTs)\partial(t - nTs)\big]$$

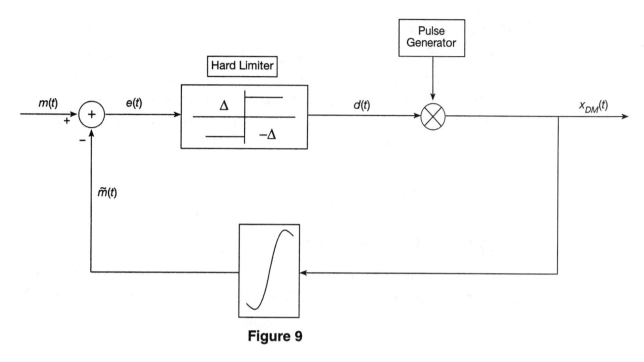

Figure 9

Demodulation

Demodulation of the delta-modulated wave is achieved by integrating the modulated signal and then passing the resulting staircase approximation through a low-pass filter as shown in the following block diagram.

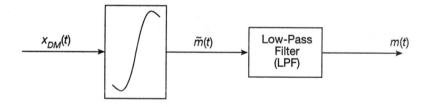

Figure 10

Pulse Shaping

In digital transmission, the carrier is assumed to be a periodic train of rectangular pulses transmitted through a channel, which is linear and distortionless. However, due to the limited bandwidth, the pulses tend to spread and overlap, causing distortion or interference. This is called intersymbol interference. This can be overcome by a process called pulse shaping. The pulse shape shown below produces a zero interference and is given by:

$$h(t) = \frac{1}{Ts} \frac{\sin(\pi t / T_s)}{\pi t / T_s}$$

which is an impulse response of an ideal low-pass filter. This pulse goes through zero at multiples of interval T_s. However, due to the difficulty of realizing an ideal low-pass filter, a raised cosine filter is used in which the frequency response decreases gradually towards zero.

The impulse response of the raised cosine filter is given by:

$$h(t) = \frac{1}{T_s} \frac{\sin Wt}{Wt} \left[\frac{\cos \alpha Wt}{1 - (2\alpha Wt / \pi)^2} \right]$$

where α is the roll-off factor.

DIGITAL CARRIER MODULATION

The process of switching the carrier's amplitude, frequency, or phase between the two values of a binary signal is called shift keying. Hence, we can employ amplitude shift keying, frequency shift keying, and phase shift keying.

Amplitude Shift Keying (ASK)

The modulated signal for one pulse is given by:

$$x_c t = \begin{cases} A \cos \omega_c t & \text{for } 0 < t < T \\ 0 \end{cases}$$

where the modulated signal is on for symbol 1 and off for symbol 0. The waveform is as shown below.

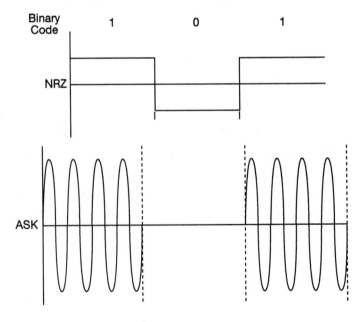

Figure 11

Frequency Shift Keying (FSK)

The modulated signal is given by:

$$x_c t = \begin{cases} A\cos\omega_1 t \\ A\cos\omega_2 t \end{cases}$$

The frequency shift keying is as shown below.

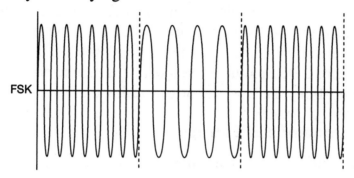

Figure 12

Phase Shift Keying (PSK)

The modulated signal is given by:

$$x_c t = \begin{cases} A\cos\omega_c t \\ A\cos(\omega_c t + \pi) \end{cases}$$

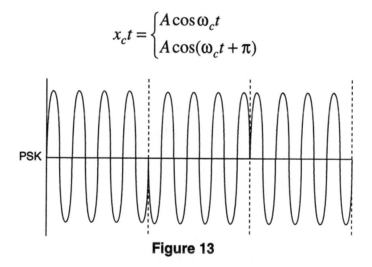

Figure 13

The figure above shows the phase shift keying signal.

INFORMATION THEORY AND CODING

The quantitative measure of the information contained in a message signal is called information theory. It allows us to determine the capacity of the communication system. Coding is the process of improving the efficiency of the system by reducing the redundancy so that the channels can be used with improved reliability.

The information is generated in an information source with or without memory. A memory source is one in which the current symbol depends on the previous symbols. In a memory-less source, the current symbol is independent of the previous symbols. It is characterized by the list of symbols, probability, and the rate of generating these symbols.

Information Content and Entropy

The information content of a symbol x_i, given by $I(x_i)$, is defined by:

$$I(x_i) = -\log_b P(x_i) = \log_b \frac{1}{P(x_i)}$$

In information theory, the logarithmic base $b = 2$ is used, and the corresponding unit of information is "bit" with properties,

$$I(x_i) = 0 \text{ for } P(x_i) = 1$$

$$I(x_i) \quad 0$$

$$I(x_i) > I(x_j) \text{ if } P(x_i) < P(x_j)$$

$$I(x_i x_j) = I(x_i) + I(x_j)$$

if x_1 and x_2 are independent.

The average information of a sequence of symbols is of more importance than the content of a single symbol. The average information content a measure of a so-called entropy is given by:

$$H(X) = -\sum_{i=1}^{m} P(x_i)\log_2 P(x_i) \text{ bits/symbol}$$

PROBLEM 8:

For a binary source with equal probability of its symbols, calculate the source entropy, as given by $H(X)$.

SOLUTION:

$$H(X) = -\sum_{i=1}^{m} P(x_i) \log_2 P(x_i)$$

$$H(X) = -\frac{1}{2} \log_2 \frac{1}{2} - \frac{1}{2} \log_2 \frac{1}{2} = 1 \text{ bit/symbol}$$

Information Rate

Let the rate at which the source X emits symbols be r(symbols/sec). Then the information rate is given by:

$$R = rH(X) \text{ bit/sec}$$

PROBLEM 9:

A black-and-white television consists of 1×10^6 picture elements and 16 different brightness levels with the pictures shown at the rate of 32 per second. Calculate the average information rate if all levels are equiprobable.

SOLUTION:

$$H(X) = \sum_{i=1}^{16} \frac{1}{16} \log_2 \frac{1}{16} = 4 \text{ bit/element}$$

$$r = 1 \times 10^6 \times 32 = 32 \times 10^6 \text{ elements/sec}$$

$$R = rH(X) = 32 \times 10^6 \times 4 = 128 \times 10^6 \text{ bit/sec} = 256 \text{ Mb/sec}$$

Discrete Memory-less Channel

A channel is a medium through which the receiver receives the information. The channel is memory-less when the present output depends only on the present input. If x_i, x_2 ..., x_m are the inputs with probability $P(x_i)$ and the outputs are y_i, y_2, ...,y_n, then the conditional probability of getting an output y_j given input x_l is $P(y_j / x_l)$.

Special Channels

Lossless Channels

The channel described by a matrix with only one nonzero element in each column is called lossless channel. In this channel no information is lost in the channel.

Deterministic Channel

The channel with only one nonzero element in each row is called a deterministic channel. Since each row has only one nonzero element, the value must be unity. It is called deterministic because the output received is clearly known for any input source.

Noiseless Channel

A channel is called noiseless if it is both lossless and deterministic. It has only one element in each row and each column and so this element is unity.

Binary Symmetric Channel

The binary symmetric channel is defined by the channel diagram and its channel matrix. This channel has two inputs and two outputs. The channel is symmetric if the probability of receiving a 1 if a 0 is sent is the same as the probability of receiving a 0 if a 1 is sent.

PROBLEM 10:

From the binary channel shown below determine the channel matrix, the output probabilities, and the joint probabilities $P(x_1, y_2)$ and $P(x_2, y_1)$.

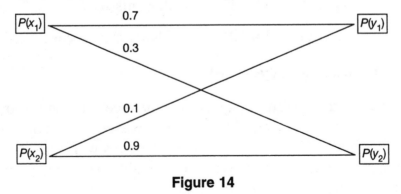

Figure 14

SOLUTION:

The channel matrix is given by:

$$\left[P\!\left(\dfrac{Y}{X}\right) \right] = \begin{bmatrix} P(y_1 / x_1) & P(y_2 / x_1) \\ P(y_1 / x_2) & P(y_2 / x_2) \end{bmatrix} = \begin{bmatrix} 0.7 & 0.3 \\ 0.1 & 0.9 \end{bmatrix}$$

The probability $P(Y)$ is given by:

$$[P(Y)] = [P(X)]\left[P\!\left(\dfrac{Y}{X}\right) \right]$$

$$= [0.5 \quad 0.5] \begin{bmatrix} 0.7 & 0.3 \\ 0.1 & 0.9 \end{bmatrix}$$

$$= [0.40 \quad 0.60] = \left[P(y_1) \; P(y_2) \right]$$

Therefore,
$$P(y_1) = 0.40$$

and
$$P(y_2) = 0.60.$$

The joint probability:

$$[P(X, Y)] = [P(X)]\left[P\!\left(\dfrac{Y}{X}\right) \right]$$

$$= \begin{bmatrix} 0.50 & 0 \\ 0 & 0.50 \end{bmatrix}\begin{bmatrix} 0.7 & 0.3 \\ 0.1 & 0.9 \end{bmatrix}$$

$$= \begin{bmatrix} 0.35 & 0.15 \\ 0.05 & 0.45 \end{bmatrix} = \begin{bmatrix} P(x_1, y_1) & P(x_1, y_2) \\ P(x_2, y_1) & P(x_2, y_2) \end{bmatrix}$$

Therefore,
$$P(x_1, y_2) = 0.15$$

and
$$P(x_2, y_1) = 0.05.$$

SOURCE CODING

Conversion of the output of a discrete memory source (DMS) into a sequence of binary symbols is called *source coding*. The device that performs this conversion is called the *source encoder*.

Code Length and Code Efficiency

The discrete memory-less source generates symbols with their individual probabilities of occurrence $P(x_1)$. The binary code word assigned to the symbol is assumed to have a length of n_1 bits, and the average code word length is given by:

$$L = \sum_{i=1}^{m} P(x_i)n_i$$

where L is the average number of bits per source symbol and the code efficiency is given by:

$$\eta = \frac{L_{min}}{L}$$

PROBLEM 11:

From Problem 10, calculate the average code length, efficiency, and the redundancy.

SOLUTION:

$$L = \sum_{i=1}^{2} P(x_i)n_i = 0.5(1) + 0.5(1) = 1 \text{ bit}$$

$$H(X) = -\sum_{i=1}^{2} P(x_i)\log_2 P(x_i) = -0.5\log_2 0.5 - 0.5\log_2 0.5 = 1 \text{ bit/symbol}$$

The code efficiency is:

$$\eta = \frac{H(X)}{L} = \frac{1}{1} = 100\%$$

The redundancy is:

$$\gamma = 1 - \eta = 1 - 1 = 0 = 0\%$$

Shannon Fano Coding

In this coding scheme, the symbols are placed in a descending order of probability. Then they are partitioned into *equiprobable* sets in step 1 and assigned a 0 (to the top set) and 1 to the bottom set. The assigning of 0's and 1's in this way is continued in successive steps until no further partitioning is possible. The number of symbols in the last step, whether 0 or 1, define n_1, i.e., the code.

PROBLEM 12:

A discrete memory-less source generates four symbols of probabilities $1/2$, $1/4$, $1/8$, and $1/8$, respectively. Write the Shannon Fano code for the same and calculate the average code length and average information content per symbol.

SOLUTION:

x_i	$P(x_i)$	Step 1	Step 2	Step 3	Step 4
x_1	$\frac{1}{2}$	0			0
x_2	$\frac{1}{4}$	1	0		10
x_3	$\frac{1}{8}$	1	1	0	110
x_3	$\frac{1}{8}$	1	1	1	111

Table 1

The average code length is thus:

$$L = \sum_{i=1}^{4} P(x_i)n_i = \frac{1}{2}(1) + \frac{1}{4}(2) + \frac{1}{8}(3) + \frac{1}{8}(3) = 1.75$$

and the average information content per symbol:

$$H(X) = \sum_{i=1}^{4} P(x_i)I(x_i) = \frac{1}{2}(1) + \frac{1}{4}(2) + \frac{1}{8}(3) + \frac{1}{8}(3) = 1.75$$

where

$$I(x_1) = -\log_2 \frac{1}{2} = 1,$$

$$I(x_2) = -\log_2 \frac{1}{4} = 2,$$

and so on . . . .

Huffman Coding

This code is the most efficient. The symbols placed in decreasing order of probabilities are grouped at the two bottom (lower) probabilities and reduced. This is repeated until we have only two probabilities remaining. The last reduction is assigned values of 0 to the top and 1 to the bottom. The 0's and 1's are assigned going back to the reductions formed previously until the first column is reached.

PROBLEM 13:

Construct a Huffman code.

SOLUTION:

x_i	$P(x_i)$	Code						
x_1	$\frac{1}{2}$	0		$\frac{1}{2}$	0		$\frac{1}{2}$	0
x_2	$\frac{1}{4}$	10		$\frac{1}{4}$	10		$\frac{1}{4}$	1
x_3	$\frac{1}{8}$	110		$\frac{1}{4}$	11			
x_4	$\frac{1}{8}$	111						

Table 2

The average code length is:

$$L = \sum_{i=1}^{5} P(x_i)n_i = \frac{1}{2}(1) + \frac{1}{4}(2) + \frac{1}{8}(3) + \frac{1}{8}(3) = 1.75$$

Since the length is the same as that of Shannon Fano coding, the efficiency of both codes is the same in this case.

Block Codes

In block codes, the binary message or data sequence is divided into sequential blocks each k bits long and each block is converted to an $n - b$ block, where, $n > k$. The resultant block is called an (n, k) block code. Thus, in an (n, k) block code, a code word can be represented as:

$c_1, c_2, \ldots c_k$ data bits and

$c_{k+1}, \ldots c_n$ parity-check bits

Error Correcting Codes

These codes can either detect or correct errors, depending on the amount of redundancy contained in the parity-check bits. Codes that can correct errors are known as error correcting codes. Parity-check code is an example of an error correcting code.

PROBLEM 14:

Write a single parity-check code for a (4, 3) format indicating the data, parity-bit, and the final code word. Also, find the probability of an undetected error for two or four bit errors that may occur in the code if the probability of symbol error is 0.1.

SOLUTION:

For a (4, 3) format, $k = 3$, and so, the number of words in the code is $2^3 = 8$.

Data Code	Parity-Bit	Code Word
000	0	0000
001	1	0011
010	1	0101
011	0	0110
100	1	1001
101	0	1010
110	0	1100
111	1	1111

Table 3

The probability of undetected error is:

$$P = \binom{4}{2} p^2 (1-p)^2 + \binom{4}{4} p^4$$
$$= 6p^2 (1-p)^2 + p^4$$
$$= 6(0.1)^2 (0.9)^2 + (0.1)^4 = 0.0487$$

Error Detection; The Hamming Distance

The Hamming distance between the two code vectors is defined as the number of positions in which their elements differ. The Hamming weight of a code vector is defined as the number of 1's in the vector. Thus, the Hamming weight of the vector is the Hamming distance between the vector and 0. The minimum distance is defined as the smallest Hamming distance between any pair of code vectors in the code.

PROBLEM 15:

For the code vectors shown, find the Hamming distances, the Hamming weights, and the minimum distance. Also determine the number of errors the given code can correct.

$$c_1 = [1\ 0\ 0\ 0\ 1]$$

$$c_2 = [0\ 1\ 1\ 1\ 0]$$

$$c_3 = [1\ 1\ 1\ 0\ 1]$$

SOLUTION:

Hamming distances and Hamming weights:

$$d(c_1, c_2) = w(c_1 \oplus c_2) = w[1\ 1\ 1\ 1\ 1] = 5$$

$$d(c_1, c_3) = w(c_1 \oplus c_3) = w[0\ 1\ 1\ 0\ 0] = 2$$

$$d(c_2, c_3) = w(c_2 \oplus c_3) = w[1\ 0\ 0\ 1\ 1] = 3$$

The minimum distance is the smallest Hamming weight of the non-zero vectors in the code.

$$d_{min} = 2$$

$$d_{min} = 2 \geq 2\ t + 1$$

This is satisfied with $t = 0$ and so this code does not correct any error. However, for some codes $t > 0$ and the value of t indicates how many errors the code can correct.

FE/EIT

FE: PM Electrical Engineering Exam

CHAPTER 4

Computer and Numerical Methods

CHAPTER 4

COMPUTER AND NUMERICAL METHODS

COMPUTER METHODS OF CIRCUIT ANALYSIS

Mesh Analysis for a Resistive Circuit with Independent Sources

Consider the following simple two-mesh circuit:

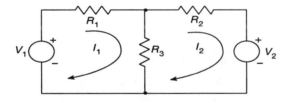

Figure 1

I_1 and I_2 are mesh currents.

Writing Kirchhoff's Voltage Law (KVL) equations for each mesh and rearranging terms, we obtain the following equations:

$$V_1 = (R_1 + R_3) \times I_1 - I_2 \times R_3$$
$$-V_2 = -I_1 \times R_3 + (R_2 + R_3) \times I_2$$

Arranging these equations into the matrix form, we have:

$$\begin{bmatrix} V_1 \\ -V_2 \end{bmatrix} = \begin{bmatrix} R_1 + R_3 & -R_3 \\ -R_3 & R_2 + R_3 \end{bmatrix} \times \begin{bmatrix} I_1 \\ I_2 \end{bmatrix}$$

Observe that:

$R_1 + R_3$:   Sum of resistances in mesh 1.

$R_2 + R_3$:   Sum of resistances in mesh 2.

R_3:   Resistance common to both meshes 1 and 2.

V_1:   Voltage applied around mesh 1.

In general, we have the following procedure for writing mesh equations for a resistive network with independent voltage sources:

$$[V] = [R] \times [I]$$

$$\begin{bmatrix} V_1 \\ V_2 \\ . \\ . \\ . \\ V_n \end{bmatrix} = \begin{bmatrix} R_{11} & R_{12} & \cdots\cdots\cdots & R_{1n} \\ R_{21} & R_{22} & \cdots\cdots\cdots & R_{2n} \\ \multicolumn{4}{c}{\cdots\cdots\cdots\cdots\cdots} \\ \multicolumn{4}{c}{\cdots\cdots\cdots\cdots\cdots} \\ \multicolumn{4}{c}{\cdots\cdots\cdots\cdots\cdots} \\ R_{n1} & R_{n2} & \cdots\cdots\cdots & R_{nn} \end{bmatrix} \times \begin{bmatrix} I_1 \\ I_2 \\ . \\ . \\ . \\ I_n \end{bmatrix}$$

where:

V_i = Summation of all the voltage sources in the ith mesh. Sources constituting a voltage rise are treated as positive while sources constituting a voltage drop are treated as negative.

R_{ij} ($i = j$) = Summation of the values of resistors in the ith mesh.

R_{ij} ($i \neq j$) = Negative sum of the values of resistors that are common to both the ith mesh and j^{th} mesh.

I_i = Unknown mesh currents.

The unknown mesh currents can be found from:

$$[I] = [R]^{-1} \times [V]$$

where $[R]^{-1}$ is the inverse of the resistance matrix $[R]$, and $[R]^{-1}$ can be found by using computers or programmable calculators. Inversion of small matrices such as $[2 \times 2]$ or $[3 \times 3]$ can be done easily by hand.

PROBLEM 1:

Find the current I_X.

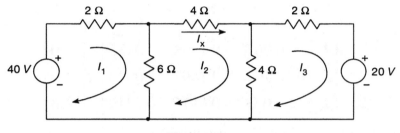

Figure 2

SOLUTION:

The matrix equation $[V] = [R] \times [I]$ can be written by inspection using the above procedure.

$$\begin{bmatrix} 40 \\ 0 \\ -20 \end{bmatrix} = \begin{bmatrix} 8 & -6 & 0 \\ -6 & 14 & -4 \\ 0 & -4 & 6 \end{bmatrix} \times \begin{bmatrix} I_1 \\ I_2 \\ I_3 \end{bmatrix}$$

The current I_X is the same as the mesh current I_2.

$$I_x = I_2 = \frac{\begin{vmatrix} 8 & 40 & 0 \\ -6 & 0 & -4 \\ 0 & -20 & 6 \end{vmatrix}}{\begin{vmatrix} 8 & -6 & 0 \\ -6 & 14 & -4 \\ 0 & -4 & 6 \end{vmatrix}}$$

$$I_x = \frac{8 \begin{vmatrix} 0 & -4 \\ -20 & 6 \end{vmatrix} - 40 \begin{vmatrix} -6 & -4 \\ 0 & 6 \end{vmatrix}}{8 \begin{vmatrix} 14 & -4 \\ -4 & 6 \end{vmatrix} + 6 \begin{vmatrix} -6 & -4 \\ 0 & 6 \end{vmatrix}} = \frac{800}{328} = 2.44$$

Alternately, using a computer or a programmable calculator, $[R]^{-1}$ is found to be equal to:

$$\begin{bmatrix} 0.2073 & 0.1098 & 0.0732 \\ 0.1098 & 0.1463 & 0.0976 \\ 0.0732 & 0.0976 & 0.2317 \end{bmatrix}$$

and

$$\begin{bmatrix} I_1 \\ I_2 \\ I_3 \end{bmatrix} = \begin{bmatrix} 0.2073 & 0.1098 & 0.0732 \\ 0.1098 & 0.1463 & 0.0976 \\ 0.0732 & 0.0976 & 0.2317 \end{bmatrix} \times \begin{bmatrix} 40 \\ 0 \\ -20 \end{bmatrix}$$

$$I_x = I_2 = (0.1098)(40) + (0.0976)(-20) = 2.44 \text{ A}$$

PROBLEM 2:

Write the mesh matrix equation $[V] = [R] \times [I]$ for the following network.

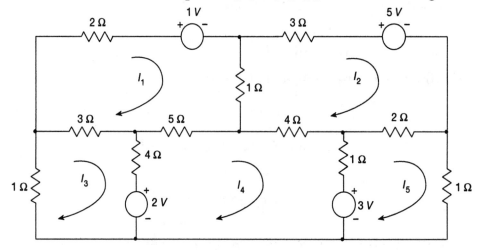

Figure 3

SOLUTION:

The mesh matrix equation $[V] = [R] \times [I]$ becomes:

$$\begin{bmatrix} -1 \\ -5 \\ -2 \\ -1 \\ 3 \end{bmatrix} = \begin{bmatrix} 11 & -1 & -3 & -5 & 0 \\ -1 & 10 & 0 & -4 & -2 \\ -3 & 0 & 8 & -4 & 0 \\ -5 & -4 & -4 & 14 & -1 \\ 0 & -2 & 0 & -1 & 4 \end{bmatrix} \times \begin{bmatrix} I_1 \\ I_2 \\ I_3 \\ I_4 \\ I_5 \end{bmatrix}$$

Using a computer or programmable calculator, we can determine that the mesh currents are:

$$I_1 = -0.9443; \ I_2 = -0.9996; \ I_3 = -1.1099; \ I_4 = -1.0116; \ I_5 = -0.0027$$

Once the mesh currents are known, we can solve for any branch current in the circuit.

Node Analysis for Resistive Circuit with Independent Current Sources

Consider the following simple two-node circuit with conductances and with independent current sources.

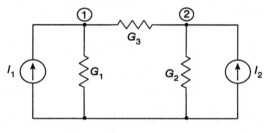

Figure 4

where:

$G = 1/R$ is the conductance in siemens.

Applying Kirchhoff's Current Law (KCL) at nodes 1 and 2 and rearranging terms, we obtain the following equations:

$$I_1 = (G_1 + G_3) \times V_1 - V_2 \times G_3$$

$$I_2 = -V_1 \times G_3 + (G_2 + G_3) \times V_2$$

Arranging these equations in matrix form, we have:

$$\begin{bmatrix} I_1 \\ I_2 \end{bmatrix} = \begin{bmatrix} G_1 + G_3 & -G_3 \\ -G_3 & G_2 + G_3 \end{bmatrix} \times \begin{bmatrix} V_1 \\ V_2 \end{bmatrix}$$

Observe that:

$G_1 + G_3$: Sum of all conductances connected to node 1.

$G_2 + G_3$: Sum of all conductances connected to node 2.

G_3: Conductances connected between nodes 1 and 2.

I_1: Current source connected to node 1.

In general, we have the following procedure for writing node equations for a resistive network with independent current sources:

$$[I] = [G] \times [V]$$

$$
\begin{bmatrix} I_1 \\ I_2 \\ \cdot \\ \cdot \\ \cdot \\ I_n \end{bmatrix}
=
\begin{bmatrix}
G_{11} & G_{12} & \cdots\cdots & G_{1n} \\
G_{21} & G_{22} & \cdots\cdots & G_{2n} \\
& \cdots\cdots\cdots\cdots & & \\
& \cdots\cdots\cdots\cdots & & \\
& \cdots\cdots\cdots\cdots & & \\
G_{n1} & G_{n2} & \cdots\cdots & G_{nn}
\end{bmatrix}
\times
\begin{bmatrix} V_1 \\ V_2 \\ \cdot \\ \cdot \\ \cdot \\ V_n \end{bmatrix}
$$

where:

I_i: The sum of the current sources connected to the ith node. Sources that flow toward the node will be treated as positive while sources that flow away from the node will be treated as negative.

G_{ij} $(i = j)$:   The summation of the values of conductance of all resistors connected to the ith node.

G_{ij} $(i \neq j)$:   The negative of the value of the conductance of any resistor directly connected between the ith node and j^{th} node.

V_i: The unknown node voltage variables.

The unknown node voltages can be found from the following equation:

$$[V] = [G]^{-1} \times [I]$$

where $[G]^{-1}$ is the inverse of the conductance matrix $[G]$, and $[G]^{-1}$ can be found by using computers or programmable calculators.

PROBLEM 3:

Find the node voltages V_1 and V_2 for the circuit shown.

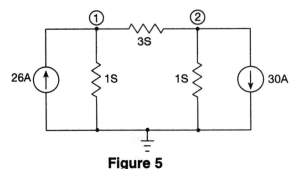

Figure 5

SOLUTION:

The matrix equation $[I] = [G] \times [V]$ can be written by inspection using the procedure:

$$\begin{bmatrix} 26 \\ -30 \end{bmatrix} = \begin{bmatrix} 4 & -3 \\ -3 & 4 \end{bmatrix} \times \begin{bmatrix} V_1 \\ V_2 \end{bmatrix}$$

Solving for V_1 and V_2, we obtain $V_1 = 2V$, and $V_2 = -6V$.

PROBLEM 4:

Set up the nodal matrix equation $[I] = [G] \times [V]$ for the following network.

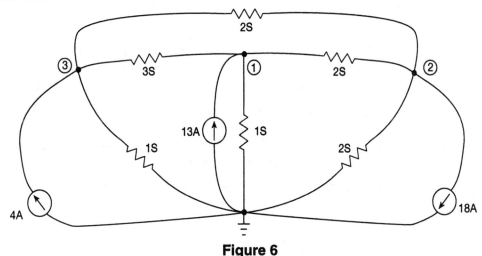

Figure 6

SOLUTION:

The matrix equation $[I] = [G] \times [V]$ is:

$$\begin{bmatrix} 13 \\ -18 \\ 4 \end{bmatrix} = \begin{bmatrix} 6 & -2 & -3 \\ -2 & 6 & -2 \\ -3 & -2 & 6 \end{bmatrix} \times \begin{bmatrix} V_1 \\ V_2 \\ V_3 \end{bmatrix}$$

As an exercise to the reader, verify that the node voltages for V_1, V_2, and V_3 are 2.0, -2.0, and 1.0 respectively by using a programmable calculator.

NUMERICAL DIFFERENTIATION

Successive derivatives at the tabular point x_0 of a function $f(x)$ can be found by using the Gregory-Newton formula:

$$f'(x_0) = \frac{1}{h}\left[\Delta f_0 - \left(\frac{1}{2}\right)\Delta^2 f_0 + \left(\frac{1}{3}\right)\Delta^3 f_0 - \left(\frac{1}{4}\right)\Delta^4 f_0 + \ldots\right]$$

$$f''(x_0) = \frac{1}{h^2}\left[\Delta^2 f_0 - \Delta^3 f_0 + \left(\frac{11}{12}\right)\Delta^4 f_0 + \ldots\right]$$

PROBLEM 5:

Determine the first and second derivatives of $f(x) = \sqrt{x}$ at x = 2.5 from the following table:

x	$\sqrt{x}$	Δ	Δ^2
2.50	1.58114		
2.55	1.59687	0.01573	
2.60	1.61245	0.01558	−0.00015
2.65	1.62788	0.01543	−0.00015

SOLUTION:

We have $x_0 = 2.5$; $h = 0.05$

$$f'(2.5) = \frac{1}{0.05}\left[0.01573 - \left(\frac{1}{2}\right)(-0.00015)\right] = 0.3160$$

$$f''(2.5) = \frac{1}{(0.05)^2}[-0.00015] = -0.06$$

Compare the results with the exact formula:

$$f(x) = \sqrt{x} \Rightarrow f'(x) = \frac{1}{2\sqrt{\chi}} \Rightarrow f''(x) = -\frac{1}{4x\sqrt{x}}$$

$$f'(2.5) = \frac{1}{2\sqrt{2.5}} = 0.31623; \quad f''(2.5) = -\frac{1}{4(2.5)\sqrt{2.5}} = -0.06325$$

NUMERICAL INTEGRATION

For the function $y = f(x)$ defined on the positive interval (a, b), apply n equal subintervals of width Δx where

$$\Delta x = \frac{b-a}{n}.$$

The area bounded by the curve between $x = a$ and $x = b$ is approximately the sum of the trapezoidal areas:

$$A = \int_{a}^{b} f(x)\ dx = \left[\left(\frac{1}{2}\right)f_0 + f_1 + f_2 + \ .... + \left(\frac{1}{2}\right)f_n\right]\Delta x$$

This method is known as the trapezoidal rule of integration.

PROBLEM 6:

Compute $\int_{0}^{1} e^x dx$ by the trapezoidal rule with $h = 0.1$ and check the result using the exact integration formula.

SOLUTION:

x	e^x
0.0	1
0.1	1.1052
0.2	1.2214
0.3	1.3499
0.4	1.4918
0.5	1.6487
0.6	1.8221
0.7	2.0138
0.8	2.2255
0.9	2.4596
1.0	2.7183

$$\int_0^1 e^x dx = [0.5 \ + \ 1.1052 \ + \ 1.2214 \ + \ 1.3499 \ + \ 1.4918 \ + \ 1.6487 \ +$$
$$1.8221 + 2.0138 + 2.2255 + 2.4596 + (0.5)(2.7183)] \times 0.1$$

$$= 1.7197$$

Exact integration formula:

$$\int_0^1 e^x dx = \left[e^x\right]_0^1 = [e-1] = 1.7183.$$

FE/EIT

FE: PM Electrical Engineering Exam

CHAPTER 5

Computer Software Engineering

CHAPTER 5

COMPUTER SOFTWARE ENGINEERING

Today's entry-level engineer is expected to have a working knowledge of computers. In this chapter, we provide an overview of the software topics required for the exam. You will be expected to be familiar with algorithm flow charts, pseudocode, and database management. The material included here is not intended to replace course textbook information, which should be consulted for more detail.

COMPUTER SOFTWARE ENGINEERING

Computer Software Engineering is the process of developing a program that solves a problem. Software consists of source code, the lowest programming level, and executable code, code written in a programming language (that cannot be executed by hardware). The software engineering process, at a minimum, encompasses the following steps:

Software Requirements: A statement of the purpose, or goals and objectives, of the software. The purpose is divided into manageable/ understandable segments.

Specifications: How the requirements are to be satisfied (and in a hardware system design, what parts are implemented in hardware versus software). This is sometimes referred to as the concept formulation phase. During this phase of the program, we examine all advantages and disadvantages and alternative approaches. Some decisions may relate to what parts of the code may be reused from another project, or whether to make the program usable for other future applications.

Design: This phase defines the overall system, from the inputs and outputs required (including GUI, the Graphical User Interface), to the operating system and selection of the programming languages. Here, we decide whether to continue the program or allocate company resources elsewhere.

Programming: This is the portion of the program where actual lines of code are written. CASE (Computer-Aided Software) tools may be used to write/generate the software code.

Test/Debug Phase: Here, we test the software (and the hardware).

Production and Maintenance Phases: Where modifications are made because of changes in the hardware, at the customer's request, or to correct problems that may occur.

THE SOFTWARE ENGINEERING PROJECT

The requirement to develop a piece of software could be the result of an in-house IR&D project or a specific customer order, contract award.

Prior to the start of a software project, upper management, based upon market research, decides if the project is within the business plan of the company, and if it is an area where they can be successful. Management then assesses budgets and manpower, and whether the project is internal or external to the company. Possible competition and time-to-market considerations are also analyzed. If a competitive contract award is involved, the company decides if it is possible to fund the entire project with contract funds or whether internal IR&D money has to be invested.

To facilitate these management decisions, the following metrics must be developed:

- Program milestones (Gantt or Pert charts)

- Manpower hours, broken down by labor grades or categories

- Budgets, estimates of new capital equipment or CASE tools

- Material allocated to the program (new and existing)

- The infrastructure needed to support the project (e.g., LAN and WAN)

- Verification/validation quality assurance tests

Once management has decided to proceed with the project, the company:

1. Forms the Integrated Product (Software Development) Team (IPT) and releases preliminary funding and authorizes the budgeted (labor) hours based upon the preliminary work breakdown structure (WBS).

2. Develops the Hardware Architecture. With the task defined, the team sizes and segments the architecture, then it determines whether single or distributed processing is required (depends upon the application and amount of data involved). At this stage there must be a clear understanding of what is expected from the software. With the objectives properly laid out, tasks can be scheduled and commitments tracked as the project is monitored. Less overtime and rework occurs when this process is followed. The WBS is finalized, which documents all the assumptions made in financing the effort (including cross product commonality savings) as well as the project schedule.

As the project progresses, periodic meetings are held, with defined agendas that generate and track action items and keep records of project decisions. These meetings address project performance and status and problems that are occurring. Problems may result in contingency planning to manage the risks involved. Meeting minutes (software code and product artifacts that define the history of decisions and code development) are maintained in a project library. This facilitates code modification and troubleshooting once the team has been disbanded at the end of the project, or if any team member leaves during the project.

Algorithm Flow Charts

A method to illustrate the logical flow of a computer program (or a process) is to draw it graphically using process (rectangular) boxes and decision (diamond-shaped) boxes. While widely used in the past, these graphs are best applied today for simple programs. Figure 1 illustrates a typical flowchart.

More common today are information, control, or data flow models, as shown in Figure 2.

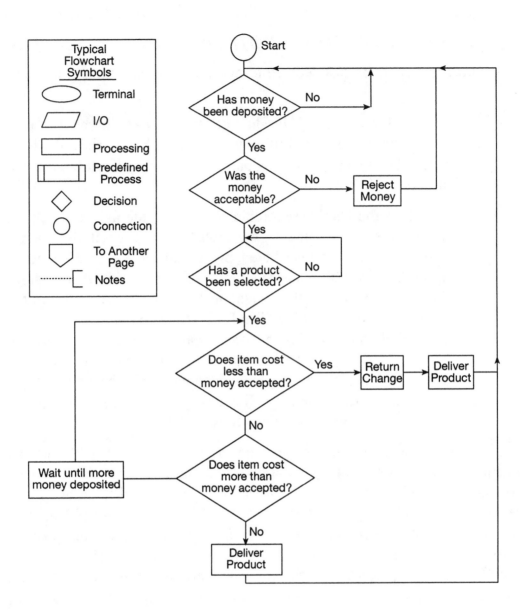

Figure 1. A Basic Flowchart For A Candy Machine.

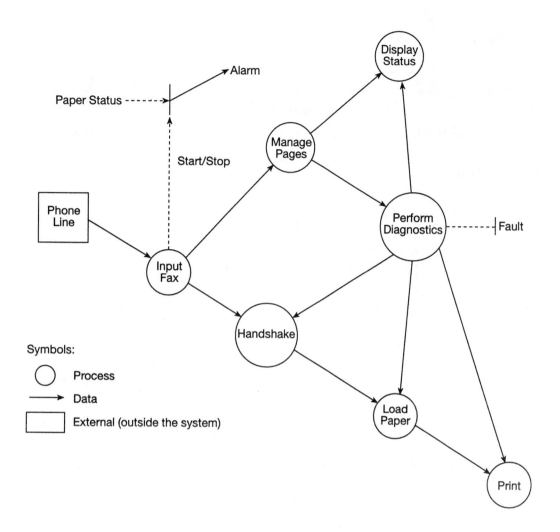

Figure 2. Control of Data Flowchart
(This is a simple flow model of a fax machine.)

PROBLEM 1:

Draw a flowchart illustrating a photocopy machine where a user can input money (assume a dollar bill) and make copies at $0.15 each. The machine should reject unacceptable bills and, when the balance remaining is less than $0.15 return change.

SOLUTION:

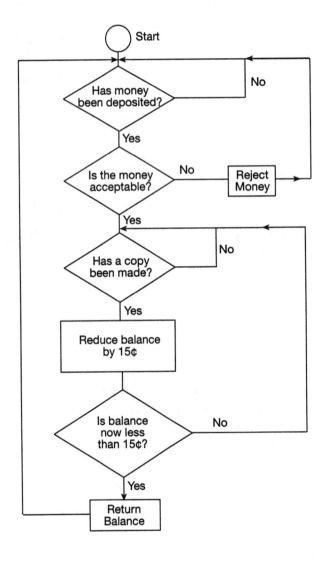

Figure 3. (Problem 1 Solution)

SOFTWARE PROGRAMMING LANGUAGES

Programming languages are selected by their design function (e.g., scientific or business) and their ability to handle concurrent, distributed, or real-time processing. Concurrent programs are sequential programs that execute simultaneously, communicate via shared variables, and call on a centralized operating system to receive a service. A distributed program may execute on different computers that exchange messages via protocols. A real-time program has processor time divided into frames, with tasks divided into segments. Every segment completes in one frame. Alternatively, tasks may be assigned priorities instead of being partitioned (as in the ADA language).

Distributed Programming

In a synchronous communication design, two or more computers communicate with each other via messages that meet a given system protocol. The machines must be at a designated point (rendezvous) in an execution before a message can be transmitted between the sender and receiver units. If one machine reaches the rendezvous point first, it must wait for the other machines to catch up. A system is considered asynchronous if the sender can send messages and continue operating before a reply is received from the receiver.

Concurrent Programming

In concurrent programming, a set of sequential programs run at the same time on a computer. The computer processes communicate via shared variables and can call upon the central operating system for services.

Some properties of concurrent programs are:

Mutual Exclusion Property: When a part of a program needs exclusive access to a computer resource, that part of the program is defined as a critical section. When instructions of two or more critical processes are not interweaved, the program has a "mutual exclusion property."

Freedom from Deadlock State: Deadlock occurs when sequential processes cannot continue because they are making mutually exclusive demands for resources. Concurrent programs detect or prevent this.

Freedom from Starvation State: A "starvation state" results if one process is indefinitely prevented from entering its critical section. Again, concurrent programs detect or prevent this.

Real-Time Programming

Real-time programs must have tasks broken into segments, with the time to execute broken up into frames. A task must execute in a single frame. Tasks may also execute asynchronously, but may be suspended if a higher priority task is ready to execute. Thus, execution of real-time programs is relatively slower as compared to some other types of programming.

Software Programming Languages

Some common software languages you may encounter include:

APL: A Programming language, created in the 1960s by Ken Inverson. Originally with a nonstandard character set, it now uses ISO standard characters and is used on small computers and mainframes. It is a high-level language with simple syntax and few semantic rules, and uses loops (repeated functions) to shorten programs. Its strength is the ability to generate matrixes (row and column data elements).

Assembly Language: Low-level languages that have the same structure and commands as machine languages, but where programmers can use names versus numbers. In the early days of the computer industry, all programs were written in assembly language. Now assembly language is used where speed is critical or where the operation cannot be performed using a higher level language.

C: A high-level general purpose language with a large set of operators that has control flow and data structures. C is written as a series of functions, with the body of the program called the "main function," where the functions call on each other for processing. It is able to operate a computer at a low level (like assembly language) and can be compiled into machine language for most computers. It was developed at AT&T Bell Laboratories and was very popular in the late 1980s. The ANSI X3J11 committee standardized C and so did ISO in 1989.

C++: An extension of C, this high-level programming language was developed by Bjarne Stroustrup of AT&T Bell Laboratories. It adds object-oriented programming features to the structure of the C language. It is widely used for Windows and Macintosh graphical applications.

FORTRAN: (Formula translation) for scientific/engineering applications that require a lot of mathematical computations. John Backus designed it for IBM in the late 1950s. Versions include FORTRAN IV (a USASI standard in 1966) and FORTRAN 77 (ANSI-approved in 1978). There is also an ISO/ANSI version, FORTRAN-90.

Ada: Ada is used for scientific and engineering applications, mainly Department of Defense (DOD). The language is block structured, provides mechanisms for data abstraction and modularization, and supports concurrent processing. The user has control over scheduling and interrupt handling.

BASIC: (Beginners All-purpose Symbolic Instruction Code) Developed in 1964 by Thomas E. Kurtz and John G. Kemeny at Dartmouth University. BASIC is a high-level programming language based upon algebraic notation and developed for solving problems at a computer terminal. (Visual BASIC is for Windows-based programs.)

Cobol: (Common Business Oriented Language) Developed by Grace Hooper of the Pentagon and marketed in 1959. When it was shown at the U.S. Conference on Data System Languages, the language was a prototype with 20 ordinary words (such as inventory, price, and product) that a UNIVAC computer could understand.

Pascal: Developed in 1969 by Niklaus Wirth. Pascal is used to teach programming as a systematic discipline that supports reliable and efficient implementations.

Oracle and *SQL*, or Structured Query Language (originally Sequel or Structured English Query Language designed by IBM in 1975): Languages that control the functions of a relational architecture database management system (DBMS). Oracle Corporation (Redwood, California), a supplier of relational database software was the first to support SQL and introduced SQL commercially in 1979. In 1991 ANSI updated the standard to SAG SQL.

LISP: (List Processor), developed in the early 1960s by John McCarthy of MIT. It is a high-level programming language used for artificial intelligence applications and development tools.

Modula-2: Created by Niklaus Wirth, the author of Pascal, in the late 1970s to address criticisms of his earlier Pascal language, such as the lack of support for separate compilation of modules and multitasking. Modula-2 is generally used in academia and is not often used in general industry applications.

Eiffel: Introduced in 1986, it was created by Bertrand Meyer. It is an advanced programming language that is object oriented and supports a systematic approach to software development. The Eiffel compiler generates C code that can be modified and then recompiled with a C compiler.

Perl: (Practical Extraction Report Language) developed by Larry Wall. An interpretive language originally written to manipulate text and files and perform network tasks. It was designed for processing text with script similar to UNIX.

SGML: (Standard Generalized Markup Language) Developed by ISO in 1986 to manage large documents that are subject to revisions and have to be printed in different formats. SGML is a system that specifies the rules for organizing and tagging elements of a document. These tags are then used to format documents in different ways.

Specialty Software Programming Languages

Special languages such as VHDL (Very High-Density Language) exist for design automation. Languages for the Internet include:

HTML: Hypertext Markup Language, similar to SGML, is an authoring language used to create documents for the World Wide Web. HTML is one way of defining and interpreting tags according to SGML rules.

VRML: Virtual Reality Modeling Language, developed by Silicon Graphics, is useful for 3-D modeling. Files written in VRML have a ".wrl" extension (meaning "world"); a VRML browser or plug-in is needed to view these pages. VRML 2.0 (finalized in August 1996) is officially known as ISO/IEC 14772.

XML: eXtensible Markup Language, a reduced version of SGML designed especially for World Wide Web (WWW) documents. It supports links that can point to multiple documents, as opposed to HTML that can only reference one link. Microsoft Corp. supports it in their Internet Explorer program.

JAVA: A high-level programming language developed by Sun Microsystems that was originally a version of C++ for game and set topbox controller applications. It was renamed JAVA in 1995 and redesigned and simplified for WWW use. This is a cross-platform general-purpose programming language that can operate on any hardware platform (Windows, Macintosh, or UNIX). JAVA applets delivered over the Web execute within a sandbox and cannot directly access hard drives, RAM, or the operating system (A JAVA sandbox is the normally constrained area within JAVA applications that prevents access to the local hard drive or network unless "object signing" privileges are assigned to the application.) Thus, files cannot be modified or deleted. JAVA is therefore considered a secure programming language for the Web. (However, some hackers have developed applets that can directly access system hardware, so absolute security is not guaranteed.) After the software is written, it is run through a compiler to check the source code for syntax errors. Object code is then created for a specific operating system. This object code is run through a linker to construct executable code.

OPERATING SYSTEMS

An operating system manages the application programs that run under its control. Its functions include task control (load, execute, end programs, etc.); file manipulation (open, close, create files); interfacing the computer to hardware peripherals (such as printers, etc.) by storing interrupts in registers then acting on them; and maintenance functions (system data, time, getting tasks). The operating system program consists of the kernel. The kernel services the library, the application programming interface functions, and user documentation. The kernel is an essential set of basic computer services. It includes the interrupt handler, task manager, and the interprocess communication manager. It may also contain the virtual memory manager and the network subsystem manager. Types of operating systems include:

DOS: Disk Operating System, a single-task operating system created by Microsoft Corp. in the early 1980s (was replaced by Windows versions 98, NT, and CE). Prior to DOS, a common operating system was CP/M (Control Program/Microcomputers), developed in 1973 by Gary Kildall, a consultant for Intel Corporation.

Linux: developed by Linus Torvalds, a freeware program (at this time) similar to UNIX. It runs on various hardware platforms (PCs, Macintoshes, and with Intel or Motorola microprocessors).

UNIX: a multitasking operating system developed for research and development of engineering and scientific applications by Bell Labs in 1969. It was one of the first operating systems to be written in C, the high-level programming language. It can be installed on virtually any computer for which a C compiler exists, thus making it very portable. There are two versions of UNIX: (1) by AT&T, known as

System V, and (2) by Berkeley University, BSD4.1, .2, or .3. It is a leading operating system for workstations (now being rivaled by Windows NT).

VMS: (Virtual Memory System), computers used on VAX (Digital Equipment Corp., now owned by Compaq Computer). It is a multiuser, multitasking, and virtual memory operating system. It was introduced in 1979 with the first VAX minicomputer. VMS is now referred to as OpenVMS.

POSIX: (Portable Operating System Interface for UNIX). This is a set of IEEE and ISO standards that define an interface between programs and operating systems. Programs are microkernel, RTOS (real-time operating system), and allow for multiple application-programming interfaces. The IEEE maintains POSIX standards.

ECOS: a real-time operating system (RTOS) by Cygnus Solutions (Sunnyvale, CA) with configurable kernels. It is freeware.

Motif: a GUI (graphical user interface) for UNIX that is a set of user interface guidelines created by the Open Software Foundation. It is used on various hardware platforms and is the standard GUI for UNIX.

OS/2: this operating system was originally developed by IBM and Microsoft Corp. for PCs, but it is sold and managed by IBM, as Microsoft decided to develop Windows instead. Introduced in the late 1980s, it is compatible with Windows and DOS programs (developed by IBM) and competes with the Windows OS.

Microkernel: these operating systems (OS) are used in small hand-held devices that have only small ROM-based storage. They are also used in power management OS where the system may have low power or idle modes.

DATABASE MANAGEMENT SYSTEMS

In the 1960s the term "database" was used by the military relating to data shared by end users of time-sharing computer systems. Today, database management systems (DBMS) have evolved to where there are specialized programs and languages for this application. A DBMS is a method for manipulating data so it can be stored, organized, related, and retrieved in such a manner as to meet the requirements of the user.

Databases tend to be of the following structures:

Hierarchic Data Structure: Records have a root structure with any number of child segments. These child segments may also have child segments associated with them.

Network Data Structure: This structure originated with the association of parts in a bill of materials application. A part can simultaneously be an assembly of other parts and a component of other parts.

Relational Database: Data is represented in a set of tables. Each table has entries of a single type. The rows are the entities in the set and the columns are the attributes that characterize the entity set type. (As with other programming languages, there are now also object-oriented query languages for databases.)

Semantic Data Structure: In this structure the database is developed independently of the application. There are various application-independent models of this type of which the entity relationship is the most common. In this model, data is constructed at two levels—the conceptual level (entities, relationships [i.e., associations between entities], value sets and attributes); and the representation level (where the conceptual level concepts are mapped into tables). Databases may be classified according to their function, such as real-time databases, or structure. In a real-time database the system handles transactions with timing constraints. Real-time transactions must include the CPU processing time and IO time as these constraints. Database structures include the series-parallel database, 2-tree structure, tree structure, and star structure. In addition, query optimization, parallelization strategies, data fragmentation methods, and load balancing properties all contribute to optimizing the database design.

As previously noted, there are various databases and specialized database languages. Common databases used today include Microsoft Access, Oracle, Informix, and Sybase.

SOFTWARE QUALITY ASSURANCE

An essential part of any software development project is proper configuration version control. When various teams, or individuals, are simultaneously working on a project, everyone must be using the same version (or revision) of the software.

Configuration control prevents use of old or unauthorized versions of the code. Generally, in-process tracking is separate from the delivered software. Numbered revisions may be used while the project is developing, and letters after the software is released. When the software is delivered, or incorporated into the hardware, it must be the latest tested and released version per the configuration records. To ensure the quality and reliability of the software, testing is performed. This testing breaks down into three main functions:

- Build verification

- Functionality (regression) tests (makes sure stand-alone functions continue to work with other functions)

- Performance (stress) tests

Testing an operating system includes:

1. verifying that the kernel can receive kernel service requests

2. dispatching requests to the required kernel-service code

3. performing the required operation (application programming interface functions must correctly pass arguments from the application code)

4. exiting properly to the next application level (without loss of context)

5. stress-testing the OS to determine if it can handle heavy interrupt loading and exceptions to normal processing flows

6. checking interoperability of the OS with customer tools

7. verifying if the OS when scaled continues to perform as required

Software problems are reported via bug reporting databases, which may include software troubleshooting test reports sent to the team and appropriate individuals in the organization.

GLOSSARY OF COMPUTER SOFTWARE ENGINEERING TERMS

Applets: JAVA mini-programs, or applications, that can be downloaded from the World Wide Web and executed by a JAVA-capable browser such as Netscape Navigator or Microsoft Internet Explorer.

Bulletin Board Service (BBS): a dial-up service providing technical support information, software, etc.

BPS: bits per second.

Compiler: A high-level language translator that converts the input program to the machine language of a particular computer.

FTP: File Transfer Protocol. This is a protocol used to transfer files over TCP/IP networks, such as the Internet, and was designed to handle (i.e., send) binary files directly without encoding/decoding them. It has functions to log onto the network, list directories, and copy and send files. It can also convert between the ASCII and EBCDIC characters.

GIF: Graphics Interchange Format. A bitmapped graphics file format developed by Compuserve. GIF files are popular for World Wide Web usage, especially scanned images, as GIF supports file compression at various resolutions with 8-bits or 256 colors. There are two versions of these files: (1) GIF Interlaced files gradually become clearer as they download; (2) GIF Transparent files have one color set to transparent so the background shows through. The newer versions of GIF files support animation with sequences of images displayed one after the other.

High-Level Programming Language: In a high-level programming language, each program function defines many machine instructions automatically executed to perform that function. High-level programs are machine dependent, as a compiler converts the source program to the machine language of a particular computer.

HTTP: Hypertext Transfer Protocol. Used by the World Wide Web, it is used to establish a connection to Web servers. It defines how messages are formatted and transmitted. When you select a URL to your Web server, an HTTP command is sent to the Web server, directing it to fetch and transmit the requested Web page to the client Internet browser.

IP Address: a number that identifies a computer on the Internet.

ITU: (International Telecommunication Union). An international organization concerned with telecommunications. It adopts international treaties and develops regulations and standards governing telecommunications.

Shockwave Technology: allows for animations to be played back on the Web in real time, rather than downloaded.

TCP/IP: Transport Control Protocol/Internet Protocol. A network protocol (i.e., rules) that controls communication so computers and networks can work together over the Internet.

Telnet: an Internet protocol that allows the user to log onto a remote computer.

URL: (Uniform Resource Locator) the global address of documents/resources on the World Wide Web.

V.90: A standard for 56 K-bits/s modems approved by the ITU (International Telecommunication Union).

FE/EIT

FE: PM Electrical Engineering Exam

CHAPTER 6

Computer Hardware Engineering

CHAPTER 6

COMPUTER HARDWARE ENGINEERING

Today's entry-level engineer is expected to have a working knowledge of computers. In this chapter, we provide an overview of the hardware topics required for the FE/EIT exam and the material you should be familiar with, most notably in data transmission and storage. The material included herein is not meant to replace course textbook information, which should be consulted for more details, as is appropriate.

COMPUTER HISTORY

In 1833 Charles Babbage of England invented the earliest computing machine (or calculator). He conceived the analytical engine (Difference Engine), which had all the elements of a modern computer, including memory, control, arithmetic unit, and input/output. The memory consisted of counting wheels which were controlled by Jacquard punched cards. Conditional branching, or the ability to modify a calculation based upon intermediate results, was also directed by punched cards. In the late 1880s Herman Hollerith used the method of punched cards to store the results of census questions. He produced machines to punch holes in cards, sort them, and duplicate them.

One of the first electromechanical computers was the Colossus, a World War II code-breaking computer. This machine was the brainchild of Alan Turing and was used to decode the German ENIGMA machine-encrypted messages. It was developed in the 1940s and was located in

Bletchley Park, England. It was kept secret for 30 years. In the United States, the Harvard Mark 1 became operational in 1944. It was a mechanical computer that used wheel positions to store numbers.

In 1946 ENIAC (Electronic Vacuum Tube Computer) was turned on. It was developed by John W. Mauchly and J. Presper Eckert, Jr. at the Moore School of Electrical Engineering at the University of Pennsylvania. ENIAC had 18,000 vacuum tubes, half a million solder joints, and could do 5,000 additions per second. It was built to compute the trajectory of shells to develop firing tables. Before ENIAC, it took four man-years of labor to do the calculations for one table. ENIAC could do it in 20 seconds, 10 seconds less than it took an actual shell to hit a target. Setting 6,000 switches, which activated or deactivated vacuum tubes, and connecting hundreds of cables programmed ENIAC. Eckert and Mauchly left to start the first computer company, which declared bankruptcy five years later because of competition with another emerging computer company, IBM. In 1998 engineers at the University of Pennsylvania created ENIAC on a chip. The chip performs the same tasks as the 30-ton ENIAC computer.

Other developments in the history of computing include the first programmable computer by Allan Turry in 1946, and the first stored program computer, the Manchester Mark 1 (University of Manchester), that used a Williams tube to store the program and executed its first program on June 21, 1948. The first user-friendly computer, the EDSAC, was built by Maurice Wilkes in 1957. Also in 1957, Control Data Corporation was founded and Seymour Cray invented the world's first all transistor computer, the Control Data 1604. Seymour Cray would later become known for his work on supercomputers and the founding of his own company.

The beginning of the semiconductor age of the computer began in 1971 when Intel debuted the first 4-bit microprocessor. Marcian E. (Ted) Hoff, Jr., Frederico Fagin, and Stan Mazor designed it. While history traces the invention of a central processor on a single chip to the then-Intel engineers, in December 1980 Gilbert Hyatt filed for a patent for a processor on a single chip and was granted it, and legal rights to the invention, in 1990. The microprocessor was originally designed by Intel as part of a four-part chip set for use in the 141PF calculator manufactured by the Japanese company Busicom. The parts were the 4001, a 2K ROM; the 4002, a 320-bit RAM; the 4003, a 10-bit serial in parallel outshift register; and the 4004, a 4-bit CPU. It measured one-eighth of an inch wide by one-sixth of an inch long, with 2,300 MOS transistors. It was capable of 60,000 operations per second and had the computing power of the first electronic computer, the ENIAC. The Busicom calculator with printer, which debuted in 1971, eventually sold 100,000 units, but Busicom went bankrupt because of the oil crisis in 1974.

While Intel was the first to market microprocessors, earlier work was done in 1968 by Viatron Inc., a Burlington, Massachusetts company. It announced a data handling system using an 8-bit microprocessor running from a program stored in ROM. The company, however, went bankrupt two years later. During this time, General Electric developed an eight-chip basic logic unit (BLU) that could run different programs in many different terminal designs—essentially what is done with microprocessors.

In March 1972, Intel announced an 8-bit version of the 4004, the 8008, designed by Hal Feeney, Ted Hoff, Frederico Fagin, and Stan Mazor. It was designed as a programmable calculator for Computer Terminals Corporation (CTC, later known as Datapoint) and had 3,300 MOS transistors. It could execute 30,000 operations per second. Two years later Intel introduced the 8080, the first general-purpose microprocessor, with 4,500 transistors executing 200,000 operations per second.

Nineteen seventy-four was a busy year in the computer industry with the introduction of the Motorola 6800, the Texas Instruments (TI) TMS 1000 (designed in March 1971 but then used internally), the RCA 1802, and the National Semiconductor PACE microprocessor. The 6800, a 40-pin DIP packaged device that was the equivalent of about 120 MSI TTL devices, became the first high-volume microprocessor in the industry. A custom derivative of the part was used in 1981 General Motors cars as part of the engine control. The TMS 1000, designed by Gary Boone and Michael Cochran, was the first microcontroller having a microprocessor with built-in RAM, ROM, and I/O. Also that year, Eddie Dingwell at RCA designed the first single-chip CMOS microprocessor, the 1802. The first 16-bit microprocessor, the PACE (Processing and Control Element) from National Semiconductor also debuted. However, it used hole-doped transistors (versus efficient electron-doped transistors) and quickly became obsolete.

A year later, MOS Technology (which later became part of Commodore) debuted the 6502. The 6502 was used in the Apple I and II computers, Atari, Commodore PET, and VIC 20 machines. Also, AMD introduced the 2901, the first bit-slice microprocessor.

In 1977 Zilog introduced the Z80 and the Apple II computer had its debut. A year later Zilog came out with the Z8000, a 16-bit microprocessor. In the summer of 1979, Motorola manufactured the first 68000 microprocessor and Intel debuted the 8088. Today, the main competing microprocessors are the Intel 80x86 devices (with clones by AMD and Cyrix), the Motorola 680x0 line, and the DEC (Digital Equipment Corporation) Alpha (licensed by Samsung and others). This does not include specialized microprocessors, such as those made by Analog Devices and Texas Instruments for signal processing.

The first industry standard PC (the XT) was introduced by IBM in 1981 (it used the Intel 8088 IC). The 286, or AT, followed it. Sales of the 286 peaked about 1989 with over 10 million units sold. The 386 was introduced in October 1985. Its sales peaked in 1992 with about 20 million sold. The 486, introduced in 1989, peaked in 1994 with over 40 million sold. The Pentium (originally known as the P5) was introduced in 1993. Updated variations include the Pentium II and the P7 by AMD. It took four years for 286 computers to be replaced by 386s, but less than three years for Pentiums to replace 486s. Computer turnover now is every 2.5 years compared to 4.5 years early in the 1990s.

THE HARDWARE ENGINEERING PROJECT

The design of circuitry for a computer system may be the result of a specific customer order/contract award or internally generated IR&D.

Prior to the start of any engineering project, upper management decides if the project is within the business plan of the company and if it is an area where they can be successful. Discussions are held regarding the possible competition and the time to market. Budgets and manpower are assessed whether a proposal is required, if the program is being competitively bid, or if the project is internal to the company. When a competitive contract award is involved, the company decides if it is possible to fund the entire project with contract funds, or whether internal IR&D money has to be invested. Once these decisions are made, the process steps in a typical hardware engineering project are:

1. *Statement of the Task to be Performed* (may also be called Statement of Work): This is a description of the project, which includes the hardware function, usage, specific tasks to be performed, and milestones and performance requirements. Details on compliance to third-party requirements are also provided (e.g., Underwriters Laboratory, Canadian Standards Association, CE Marking, FDA CGMP, Military Specifications, etc.). Before a program is formally started, an estimate of the program costs must be developed so that manpower and funds can be allocated. This estimate includes:

- Program milestones (Gantt or Pert charts)

- Manpower hours, broken down by labor grades or categories, and defining new personnel to be hired

- New capital equipment needed or existing material allocated to the program

- Cost of prototype hardware

- Laboratory test costs

- First article tests

- Customer demonstrations

2. *Formation of the Integrated Product Team (IPT)*: Release preliminary funding and authorize the budgeted (labor) hours.

3. *Development of the Hardware Architecture*: With the task defined, the team sizes and segments the architecture.

In early desktop computers (PC XT, 286, 386), functions were placed onto separate circuit cards. The design had a main microprocessor motherboard and the cards that plugged into it included video, modem, memory (in some designs such as the ITT Alcatel), I/O ports, and the disk drive controller. Later designs incorporated more functions onto the microprocessor board (e.g., the I/O ports and video output functions).

The apportionment of the functions includes the following subtasks:

Make or Buy: A particular function, such as a video graphics card, can be designed or purchased. The advantages of designing the card include complete control over the design and functions/features. Production can also be controlled (depending upon material inventories) so card assemblies can be manufactured to meet schedules. The disadvantages include implementing all the design functions including circuit card layouts, obtaining PC cards, necessary procurement staff to buy material, populating (stuffing) the cards, the cost of tooling and labor in building and testing, and extra floor space for raw materials and finished goods. With current EPA controls, permits are also needed for the chemicals used in the manufacture of PC cards (and in conformally coating the cards when necessary for certain customers or applications such as marine environments).

An existing off-the-shelf card can also be purchased. The advantage is that the card comes fully assembled and tested and with a warranty.

The disadvantage is that it may not incorporate all the features needed or may not be available over the total length of the program (unless the contract ensures the item is supplied over the total program time, and that the supplier supports repairs and is responsible for correcting defects that can appear in field use).

Design In-House or Outside: The design can be outsourced to another company, with the risk that the company may not be able to deliver a working product in time (penalty clauses in the contract and/or incentive clauses for early delivery may circumvent this) or may want additional funding to complete the project (unless contractually prohibited from doing so). Advantages include no need to allocate personnel or hire additional personnel and not having to allocate or buy capital equipment and floor space. Some of the design can be implemented in software using IP (intellectual property) cores developed by an outside company. The cores are loaded into programmable devices (e.g., Field Programmable Gate Arrays, or FPGAs).

Make/Buy or Outsource	Advantages	Disadvantages
Make	Control over design and features. Production control over schedules.	Have to design all the functions and features, do layouts, buy the raw cards and materials, have to have staff and facilities to do the assembly. Follow EPA regulations regarding chemicals used in manufacture.
Buy	Fully assembled/tested. Can purchase an extended warranty.	May not have all the features needed. May become obsolete before the end of production schedule.
Outsource Design	Do not need to hire design personnel or procure design equipment (CAD, etc.). No capital equipment or floor space needed.	May not be able to deliver on time or may want additional funds.

Table 1. Summary of Advantages/Disadvantages

COMPUTER ARCHITECTURES, DATA TRANSFER BETWEEN REGISTERS, AND ERROR CORRECTION

Computers were initially grouped by either their processing capability or their physical size. As more processing capability became available in smaller and smaller sizes, the demarcation lines began to blur. Figure 1 shows the structure of a single-processor digital computer system.

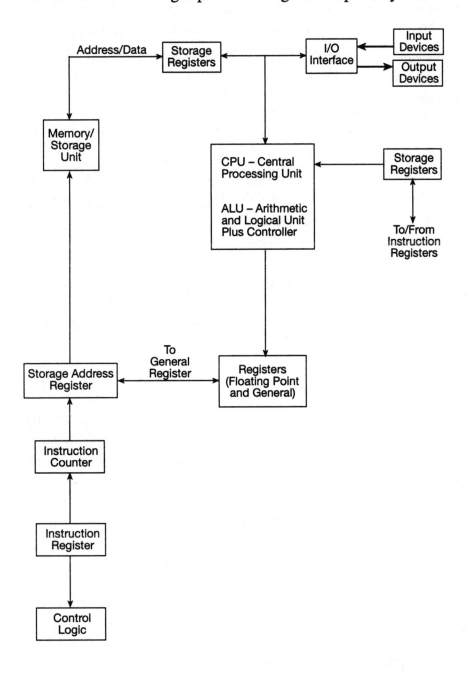

Figure 1. Digital Computer Structure of a Single-Processor System

Computer types may be defined as follows:

Minicomputer: A computer designed for the control of I/O devices, with little computing power.

Microcomputer: The first was the Intel 4004; this may now refer to embedded computers.

Personal Computer: Today the PC has processing power that rivals the workstation or mainframe computers of a few years ago.

Mainframe Computer, or *Maxicomputer*: A general-purpose computer handling tasks that manipulate large amounts of data, such as office payroll.

Supercomputer: Large-scale computer optimized for a particular application, such as mathematical number crunching.

Computer Workstation: A term used to denote a high-end PC connected to a network that is designed for an intensive application (such as 3-D imaging in CAD work). The power of today's PCs rivals that of workstations a few years ago.

COMPUTER PROCESSING METHODS

The way a computer processes data can be grouped into categories that include:

Distributed Processing

A decentralized computer system has processing elements that are interconnected and operates with a distributed control of computer resources. Distributed processing is often described by the way the elements are connected:

- Loop

- Complete interconnection

- Central memory

- Global bus

- Star network

- Loop with central switch

- Bus with central switch

- Regular network

- Irregular network

- Bus window

There are also hybrid forms of these configurations. Processing systems can also be loosely or tightly coupled. In a loosely coupled system, each portion of the system has its own CPU and memory. In a tightly coupled system, each portion has a CPU but shares the same memory. These configurations can be either master-slave (one computer controls another) or client-server (the requesting computer is the client and the requested resource is the server).

Other processing methods include:

Real-Time Processing: Programs run when they are submitted and may have user interaction.

Batch Processing: Programs are grouped into categories that need the same resources (and peripherals) and then processed.

Background/Foreground Processing: Two or more programs run at the same time, with one or more running in the background. This may include real-time programs that run in the foreground, while other programs run in the background.

Teleprocessing: The computer runs from a remote location, such as via a modem.

Concurrent Processing: Two or more programs run concurrently.

Multitasking: Multiple tasks or applications are performed simultaneously.

Time-Sharing: Users take turns using the entire computer memory for short lengths of time (less than a second) under the control of the operating system.

Computer Data Transfer

Data transfer between registers in a digital computer data is by groups of numbers or bits in binary digits. The main computer storage is in bytes, i.e., eight binary bits. Computers read groups of bytes (2, 4, 6, 8) or words from memory in one memory access (the sequence that reads words to or from memory). Addresses in memory run from zero to the largest address. The groups of bits can be a binary word, a signed (the leftmost bit is 1 for a plus sign or 0 for a minus sign) binary number, a floating-point number, a binary-coded decimal number, data characters, or an instruction word. Two's Complement numbers are used for negative numbers and the sign of a decimal number may be indicated by the last four digits, i.e., low-order bits. Some number systems and codes are shown in Table 2.

Common codes used in computers are ASCII (American Standard Code for Information Exchange) and EBCDIC (Extended Binary Coded Decimal Interchange Code. New equipment manufacturers no longer use the BAUDOT code (an internal telegraph code that was also used for teleprinter systems), as it is slower than the other codes.

In arithmetic processors the radix number system is common. For a radix number system with a positive integer radix $r > 2$, there are the binary (2), octal (8), decimal (10), and hexadecimal (16) number systems. Four-bit binary codes that represent decimal digits include the BCD and Gray Codes (where adjacent codes differ by one digit).

Error detection within a computer system will use methods such as:

Residue Code: This is a separable code, where the check bits are separable from the data bits. The residue is over the weighted value

Binary Base-2 (BCD 8421)	Decimal Base-10	Hexa-decimal Base-16	Octal Base-8	BCD Code	Gray Code	Even Parity	Odd Parity
0000	0	0	0	0	0000	0000 0	0000 1
0001	1	1	1	1	0001	0001 1	0001 0
0010	2	2	2	2	0011	0010 1	0010 0
0011	3	3	3	3	0010	0011 0	0011 1
0100	4	4	4	4	0110	0100 1	0100 0
0101	5	5	5	5	0111	0101 0	0101 1
0110	6	6	6	6	0101	0110 0	0110 1
0111	7	7	7	7	0100	0111 1	0111 0
1000	8	8	19	8	1100	1000 1	1000 0
1001	9	9	11	9	1101	1001 0	1001 1
1010	10	A	12	–	1111	1010 0	1010 1
1011	11	B	13	–	1110	1011 1	1011 0
1100	12	C	14	–	1010	1100 0	1100 1
1101	13	D	15	–	1011	1101 1	1101 0
1110	14	E	16	–	1001	1110 1	1110 0
1111	15	F	17	–	1000	1111 0	1111 1

Table 2. Number Systems and Codes

of the radix. The number is divided by the modulus and the result is an integer and a remainder term. The numerator of the remainder is the residue term.

Parity Checking: A separable code where a parity bit is a check bit assigned to a data word. An odd parity check has all bits in the "1" state and the check bit equal to an odd number. Conversely, an even parity check requires that the result equal an even number. Single-bit or odd multiple bit faults in data words, however, will not be detected by this method.

Fixed-Weight Codes: A fixed-weight code will have a fixed number of "1"s in the word. Undetectable errors require that two bits change so that the number of "1"s be equivalent to the correct word.

Error detection external to the computer (or between computers) uses techniques for detecting garbled messages. Two of the simplest and most common techniques are called checksum and CRC. More sophisticated strategies include MNP and CCITT V.42.

A simple error-detection scheme, such as CRC (Cyclic Redundancy Checking), transmits each message accompanied by a numerical value based on the hexadecimal number "1's" in the message. The receiving station checks to make sure the numerical value is the same. If not, there has been an error in the transmission and the signal is retransmitted. In EDAC (Error Detection and Correction), an extra block of data is sent and the receiver returns the block. If they match, the entire data transmission is accepted.

PROBLEM 1:

What is the decimal number 15 in binary base 2?

SOLUTION:

The correct answer is 1111. In binary base 2, each bit is the power of 2. Or, 1111 is 2 to the 3rd power (i.e., 8) + 2 to the 2nd power (i.e., 4) + 2 to the first power (i.e., 2) and 2 to the zero power (i.e., 1).

PROBLEM 2:

Assume you are teleprocessing and want to transfer a 1.44-megabyte file using a 56 K modem line. Approximately how long will this transfer take?

SOLUTION:

The correct answer is 3 minutes and 26 seconds.

A byte is 8 binary bits, so 1.44 megabytes is equivalent to 11.520 megabits in size. The 56 K modem is capable of transferring the file in $11.520 \times 10^6/56 \times 10^3$ s, or 206 seconds, which is 3 minutes 26 seconds.

Computer Buses

There are 15 or so computer bus architectures in existence today. Some are older designs that perhaps should not be used for new projects unless they must interface with older equipment.

Older bus designs include:

XT bus: for the 8088 processor, it ran at 4.77 MHz; throughput was 8 M-bytes/s.

AT bus: The CPU connected to a 16-bit bus, running at 8 MHz, whose throughput was 8 Mbytes/s.

ISA: Industry Standard Architecture requires the CPU or DMA controller to manage all tranfers to and from the bus. During these actions the PC slows to the clock rate on the bus.

EISA: introduced in late 1988 by a group of PC clone manufacturers, this bus has a datapath of 32 bits and data rates as high as 33 M-bytes/s.

ESDI (Enhanced Small Drive Interface): Proposed as an ANSI Standard in 1986, it now is obsolete.

MicroChannel: introduced by IBM, with a 32-bit datapath and 10 MHz clock speed, this bus is able to run independently of the CPU speed. Peak throughput is 20 M-bytes/s.

Other buses include:

EMB: An enhanced master burst extension to version 3.12 of the EISA specification that offer two new modes. The EMB-66 doubles the 32-bit transfer rate to 66 M-bytes/s; the EMB-133 keeps the slower speed transfer rate but widens the datapath to 64 bits.

FC-AL: a serial SCSI interface for fiber, i.e., Fibre Channel-Arbitrated Loop.

EIDE Enhanced IDE (integrated drive electronics) Not a formally established standard.

PCI: A Peripheral Component Interconnect local bus, it is the predominant, universal 32/64-bit general-purpose I/O. The same PCI card can operate in an AT, EISA, or MicroChannel system. An autoconfiguration protocol allows for "plug and play" operation, and no jumpers or switches need to be set to eliminate bus conflicts between the system hardware (such as the CD-ROM and the floppy drive or network card or printer). Variants of the PC/104 specification include Compact PCI, Small PCI, Cardbus PCI, and PC/104-Plus.

AGP: Accelerated Graphics Port. A successor to PCI with a throughput of 532 M-bytes/s for handling 3-D graphics.

SCSI: Small Computer System Interface Popularly known as "scuzzy," it is an industry hardware and software standard for connecting peripheral devices and their controllers to microprocessors. Thus, it is a standard for communications between a host computer and a peripheral. The various types were included in the chapter on computer hard drives.

VL-Bus: VESA (Video Electronics Standards Association) "Local Bus" is a 32-bit high-performance local bus typically used to handle high-bandwidth graphics. The VL-Bus has a "plug and play" concept built around four states: Wait for Key, Sleep, Isolation, and Config (Configuration). When the system is first powered up, all cards start in at the Wait for Key state. At this state, the cards' outputs are disabled while they wait for an initiation key. The sleep state begins after the initiation key is received. The card remains in the sleep state until it is isolated during the isolation procedure, then it receives a unique Card Select Number (CSN) and its resources are read. After all cards in the system are isolated, they are set to the "Config State" and the system configuration takes place.

IEEE 1394 (FireWire): an 800 M-bit/s bus with wide applicability from peripherals to PCs to networks, presently in development.

ATA (AtBus attachment): developed by Quantum Corp. with input from Intel Corp., 66 M-bit/s. Originally known as IDE (Intelligent Drive Electronics) which started development in 1984.

USB (Universal Serial Bus): An up-and-coming standard for basic low-speed peripherals (12 M-bits/s).

There are also standard serial port (RS485 transceivers and RS232 driver/receivers) and the parallel port (RS422), which are used to connect to peripherals.

Card Sizes

The circuit card size is determined by circuit apportionment, make or buy decisions, available space, manufacturing, maintainability, and test-ability considerations. Designing smaller circuit cards has distinct advantages.

Design: EMI/EMC and speed considerations dictate how high-speed functional areas are partitioned. In high-speed circuitry, the propagation delay through interconnections, delays in different IC packages, and trace lengths are critical factors in circuit functionality. When circuits are partitioned between two cards, or located in different areas, the connecting lines may need shielding to prevent coupling of noise onto power and/or signal lines.

Space Considerations: Larger cards may not physically fit into the enclosure.

Manufacturing: Smaller cards may be easier to build, with larger cards requiring stiffeners to prevent warping or flexing (resulting in cracked solder connections or broken parts).

Testability: Larger complex cards are harder to test. Some functions, if split, may need cards to be aligned as a set.

Maintainability: As with testability, cards may have to be replaced as a set (to minimize alignments that may need special setups and equipment).

While circuits can be any size, when developing a custom project, standard-size boards are recommended for compatibility with today's systems. Standard sizes include:

VME (Versa Module Europe): 3U or 6U, grew from Motorola's VERSAbus, defined in 1968 for the 68000, an asynchronous bus. A VMEbus board can be either single or double height. A single-height board (3U) is 100 mm x 160 mm (3.94" x 6.3"); a double-height board (6U) is 233 mm x 160 mm (9.2" x 6.3"). The front edge or face of a typical board is 20 mm wide (.79"). Spacing between backplane slots is 20.32 mm (0.8").

PC/104 cards: physically small cards measuring 91.3 mm x 94.4 mm (3.6" x 3.8").

PCMCIA (Personal Computer Memory Card International Association, a standards association for memory cards): Memory cards are uniformly 2.126" wide and 3.37" (53.9 mm x 85.5 mm) long. They have 68 connector pins. Three types exist (as of late 1992) with the general differences being in the thickness of the card. Type 1, which appeared in 1991, is 3.3 mm (0.13") thick and is primarily used for memory storage and software applications. Type 2 is 5 mm (0.19") thick and is used to add features to portable computers, including network adapters (such as for Ethernet) and modems. Type 3 is 10.5 mm (0.41") thick and can contain hard-disk drives (100 M-bytes).

COMPUTER MEMORY

There are various types of memory used in the architecture of a computer. Some of the types you will encounter include:

BDRAM (Burst DRAM): a DRAM that contains a burst counter.

Burst EDO DRAM: pipeline nibble-mode DRAM.

CAM: Content-Addressable Memory. CAM achieves multiprocessing by examining all memory locations simultaneously instead of sequentially as in RAM operation. CAM arrays include comparators within each memory cell in addition to the SRAM element. Thus, a bit can be compared to the cell's storage element.

CDRAM: Cache DRAM. Included with the DRAM array is a SRAM cache and a synchronous control interface (see 3-D RAM).

DGRAM: Dual Ported Graphics RAM, introduced by Mitsubishi in 1997. It is designed as a frame buffer for graphics accelerators, an interim architecture device between the SGRAM (synchronous graphics RAM) and DRAM (dynamic RAM). The part has two random I/O ports in order to execute two tasks at once. It can also execute smaller triangles, resulting in a higher resolution display.

DMA: Direct Memory Access. Refers to data transferred from memory to memory without using the CPU.

DRAM: Dynamic RAM. A memory device having a temporary memory that must be refreshed with data.

EAROM: Electrically Alterable, Read Only Memory.

E2CMOS: Electrically Erasable CMOS (E2CMOS is a registered trademark of Lattice Semiconductor Corp.).

EDRAM: Enhanced DRAM, introduced by Ramtron International Corporation (Colorado Springs, CO). This device has an on-chip static RAM cache, write-posting register, and additional control lines to allow the SRAM cache and DRAM to operate independently. The cache is integrated into the column decoder of the DRAM and can directly cache one row at a time.

EDO DRAM: Extended-Data-Out DRAM. EDO mode operation allows the data output buffer to remain in a valid state on the rising edge of the DRAM's CAS input. This extends the valid data output time until the buffer is disabled by the falling edge of the CAS clock cycle. Faster system clocks can be used and the data can be written into/out of memory faster. Bandwidth can be as much as 40 percent greater than standard DRAMs.

FCRAM: Fast Cycle RAM. Fujitsu developed this device in 1998, which has a bandwidth of 3.2 G-bytes/s. Rows and columns are addressed simultaneously, cutting random-access cycle time to 20 ns. Activating only a specific array of the core at any one time reduces power dissipation.

Flash Memory: a high-speed nonvolatile random-access memory. It is used in applications where data must be occasionally changed without removing the memory devices from the application, and where costs preclude the use of more expensive EEPROMs (which can be written a byte at a time). The flash parts can be completely erased with one signal and may be preferred over UV-EPROMs that have to be exposed to UV light to be erased and take 15 to 30 minutes for the deprogramming. Flash memory is also preferred over Static RAMs, which have a lower density and need battery backup. It generally has the same footprint as a UV-EPROM of the same capacity. When selecting these devices, one important design parameter is the minimum number of write/erase cycles the device can endure, a measure of device endurance before failure. ("Flash" is a trademark of SEEQ Technology.)

FRAM: Ferroelectric RAM. A nonvolatile memory which in some applications has replaced EPROMs, SRAMs, and EEPROMs (E2PROMs). Developed by Ramtron Corp. (Colorado Springs, CO).

FROM: Field Programmable ROM.

MDRAM: Multibank DRAM, developed by MoSys, Inc. (San Jose, CA). This device is a collection of fully independent memory banks connected to the external interface by a narrow bus.

Memory Card: a credit-card-sized piece of plastic that houses memory chips.

NOVRAM: Non-volatile RAM (also called NVRAM, nvSRAM, or Shadow RAM). Each SRAM cell has an EEPROM element attached to it and in a Store operation, the EEPROM elements are loaded with the contents of the SRAM cells. In a Recall operation, the contents of the EEPROM elements are transferred to the SRAM cells. The memory elements are independent of each other, and independent data can reside in each. Thus, should the SRAM data become corrupted, a Recall operation can restore proper data in the SRAM. (This device also may be known as MOVRAM, for Moving RAM, or nvSRAM, for Shadow RAM, where a nonvolatile portion of the device shadows the volatile part.)

PCMCIA: Personal Computer Memory International Association, a standards association for memory cards. Memory cards are uniformly 2.126" wide and 3.37" long (54 mm x 85.6 mm). They have 68 connector pins. Various types exist.

PEEL: A logic device that is programmable and electrically erasable.

PEROM: Programmable Erasable Read-Only Memory, a term used by Atmel Corporation for their flash CMOS EPROM memories.

Pipeline Nibble-Mode DRAM (also known as Burst EDO DRAM): An EDO DRAM that contains a pipeline stage and a two-bit burst counter. All cycles occur in four-cycle bursts. Bursts longer or shorter than four cycles can be accomplished. This design achieves zero wait state performance at 66 MHz and faster.

RAM: Random Access Memory. A memory that permits access to any of its address locations in any desired sequence, with similar access time for each location. It commonly denotes a read/write memory.

RAMDAC: A graphics chip that usually has three DACs to generate red, green, and blue analog outputs and a small RAM to translate a 4- or 8-bit color specifier into a 24-bit output.

RDRAM: Rambus DRAM, developed by Rambus, Inc. (Mountain View, CA). A DRAM with a byte-wide multiplexed control, address, and data bus. Each RDRAM has its own built-in controller to handle address decoding and page cache management. A memory system can be built with just an RDRAM and a bus controller.

ROM: Read Only Memory. Information in the memory can be accessed but not altered or erased.

SDRAM: Synchronous DRAM. In this DRAM the control lines are operated by a synchronous clock. This device implements on-chip interleaving and burst-mode address generation. Note that not all SDRAMs are compatible; some have two data banks interleaved internally and in operation both RAS and CAS have to be pulsed. In single internal data bank parts, RAS can be held steady while CAS is pulsed. DDR DRAM, developed by Motorola, is a version of this design that doubles the chip bandwidth without increasing the frequency, i.e., in one clock cycle you can read or write two bits of data. (DDR stands for double data rate.)

SGRAM: Synchronous Graphics DRAM It is a synchronous RAM with write-per-bit, block-write, and pixel-masking functions.

SLDRAM: an alternate memory device, introduced by Micron Technology in 1998, to compete against Direct RDRAM and DDR (double data rate) memory ICs.

SRAM: Static RAM. A memory device that continuously retains data except when the power is turned off. It offers high-speed access.

SVRAM: Synchronous VRAM. In this VRAM the control lines are operated by a synchronous clock. This design cannot allocate bandwidth, thus it is not good for multimedia applications (see RDRAM, BDRAM, EDRAM, SDRAM, MDRAM, and SGRAM).

3-D RAM: developed by Mitsubishi Electronics America, Inc. (Sunnyvale, CA) and Sun Microsystems, Inc. It is a RAM specially developed for 3-D graphics on computer workstations and is approximately 10 times faster than VRAMS of comparable cost. It consists of independent DRAM banks, an SRAM pixel buffer, an onboard ALU, serial-access memory video buffers, and a bit bus. It is the next generation of the Mitsubishi Cache Dram (CDRAM).

UVPROM: a PROM that is erased by exposure to ultraviolet light.

UV-EPROM: An electrically programmed ROM that is erased by exposure to ultraviolet light.

VRAM: Video RAM. A DRAM with an additional data port. It cannot allocate bandwidth, thus it is not good for multimedia applications (see RDRAM, BDRAM, EDRAM, SDRAM, MDRAM, and SGRAM).

WRAM: Window RAM. A RAM optimized for use with graphical-user-interface accelerators. It is a RAM that includes a serial port to speed graphical output, but excludes some VRAM features for graphical-user-interface acceleration. WRAMs typically have a frame buffer linked to serial-access memory and data latches, 256-bit wide (or larger) data buses, and a fast page mode function to switch between functions, such as read, write, transfer, and block move. They can also include dual color registers. WRAM was developed by Samsung Semiconductor in 1993. This design cannot allocate bandwidth and thus it is not good for multimedia applications.

Computer Hard Drives

A hard, or fixed, data storage drive consists of an enclosed chamber that contains a head riding on a cushion of air about four microns over a disk platter coated with a magnetic oxide material (a human hair is 80 microns thick). The service life of a hard drive is about five years; failure generally occurs when the bearings wear out.

The types of drives are MFM (Modified Frequency Modulation), older drives usually up to 40 Mb), ESDI (Enhanced Small Drive Interface; proposed as an ANSI Standard in 1986), IDE (Intelligent Drive Electronics; started development in 1984; also known as ATA for AtBus attachment), and SCSI (Small Computer System Interface; has various versions as shown in Table 3).

Other drive types include EIDE (Enhanced IDE; a name, not a formally established standard), USB (Universal Serial bus), and SSA (a serial

Type	Bits	Mega-bits/s	I/O Limits
SCSI-1	8	5	8
Fast	8	10	8
FastWide	16	20	16
Ultra	8	20	4/8 single-ended/differential
WideUltra	16	40	4/16 single-ended/differential
Ultra2	8	40	8
WidUltra2	16	80	16

Table 3. SCSI Versions

SCSI interface). Also under development are P1394 FireWire (IEEE SCSI specification) and FC-AL (a serial SCSI interface for fiber, i.e., Fibre Channel-Arbitrated Loop). Other drive types are Parallel SCSI, Fast SCSI, Fast and Wide SCSI, Fast-20 (SCSI), and Fast-40 (SCSI). (Note: USB specification is at http://www.teleport.com/-USB.) Older computers generally have MFM drives, and PCs have an IDE drive, which is less expensive than an ESDI or SCSI drive.

Hard Drive Capacity Calculations

Different software applications, such as FDISK, CHKDSK, Windows, and BIOS, use different methods and numbering systems to calculate a hard drive storage capacity. Base 10 (decimal) and base 2 (binary) numbering systems are the two most common numeric representations of hard drive capacity. As examples, in CMOS (or DOS FDSK [not the partition on formation] or Windows File Manager) calculate the hard drive size based upon one megabyte equaling 1,048,576 bytes. Disk drive manufacturers define a megabyte as equaling 1,000,000 bytes and CHKDSK calculates size based on this value as well.

The formula to calculate the capacity of a drive is:

$$\text{Cylinders} \times \text{Heads} \times \text{Sectors} \times 512 \text{ (bytes per sector)}$$

This formula calculates the total number of bytes (characters) that can be stored. This is a decimal number. For example, if the drive has 1,024 cylinders, 16 heads, and 63 sectors, the number is 528 megabytes. To convert this number to binary, this value must be divided by the decimal value of a binary MB or GB. Divide by 1,048,576 for binary MB and by 1,073,741,824 for binary GB. Without knowing this conversion factor, you could misinterpret drive sizes from various manufacturers.

PROBLEM 3:

Assume the computer system you are working with has an internal fast wide 10 G-bit SCSI drive. What is the data transfer rate of this drive? How long would it take to transfer all the data from this drive?

SOLUTION:

The SCSI's data transfer rate is 20 M-bit/s. To transfer all the data would take 10 G/20 M, or 500 seconds.

PROBLEM 4:

What is the capacity of a hard drive with 6,800 cylinders, 16 heads, and 63 sectors in decimal? In binary?

SOLUTION:

$6,800 \times 16 \times 63 \times 512 = 3,509,452,800$ bytes, or 3.5 GB using 10^6 or decimal values.

The equivalent in binary MB of this drive is $3,509,452,800 / 1,048,576 = 3,346$ MB.

The equivalent in binary GB is $3,509,452,800 / 1,073,741,824 = 3.268$ GB.

DISPLAYS

If the system requires a display, there are two main choices: the CRT (cathode ray tube) and flat panel displays. In flat panels the designs available include: LCD, Plasma, LED, Vacuum Fluorescent, and Electroluminescent.

The LCD displays can be of various designs including:

AF-LCD-Antiferroelectric Liquid Crystal Display: A black-and-white display that does not exhibit a sticking effect (where the unidirectional row alignment of the ferroelectric crystals causes the display to hold a charge and the previous image remains on the screen momentarily).

AMLCD-Active Matrix Liquid Crystal Displays: Used in aircraft instrumentation with high MTBF of 2,000-5,000 flight hours. The displays are temperature sensitive, with the liquid crystal freezing at low temperatures. Thus, they require heaters (which are often mounted on them).

C-LCD, Cholesteric LCD: These displays, unlike twisted nematic (TN) LCDs, have stable on and off states that maintain an image without any refresh cycle. This display has a very low power demand.

EL-Electroluminescent: a bright display that does not need backlighting. Power consumption is substantially higher than that of LCDs.

FED-Field Emitter Display (LED): This display has much lower power dissipation, wider field of view, lower cost, higher definition, brightness, and contrast, and faster response time than standard LED displays.

PDP-Plasma Display Panel: screen size capability greater than 60 inches, wide viewing angle, nonflickering display, available in opposed discharge and surface discharge designs (reflection type of display). Similar to a CRT in that it uses illuminated phosphors. Has high brightness (180 cd/m^2 typical white peak), high contrast ratio, fast response, wide viewing angle (140^0 or more, twice as wide as an LCD), color capability (260,000 colors, 64 gradations of RGB), unaffected by magnetic fields. Thin ($^1/_{15}$ thickness of a CRT) and lightweight ($^1/_4$ of a CRT).

Phase-Shift Guest-Host LCD: Developed in 1994 by the Sharp Corporation, this reflective LCD display has a bright viewing screen that does not need a backlight. The color LCD display has the liquid crystals in a helical orientation. With applied voltage, the screen is dark and absorbs light. When the voltage rises above a threshold, the helical orientation straightens and the display turns white. This mode acts as a display by controlling the amount of light absorbed. The applied voltage changes the orientation in a material that combines a color pigment of dye (guest) in a liquid crystal material (host).

Plasma LCD: an LCD that uses plasma switches in place of thin film transistors. This design was developed jointly by Tektronix and Sony Corp. In this design millions of thin film transistors are replaced by several hundred lines of plasma switches. It can be produced with low-cost screen printing techniques.

Polysilicon AM LCD: p-Si. These displays are high resolution and compact in size.

RCTN: Reverse Contrast Twisted Nematic, a trademark of Crystaloid. This display has a broader operating range and uses lower drive voltages than a standard dichroic LCD in many applications. It is used in military and commercial applications.

TN AM LCD: Twisted-Nematic Active Matrix LCD. Viewing angles vary based upon the design and range from +/– 40° on the horizontal axis and +10°/–30° or +30°/–0° on the vertical axis (single domain designs), to +/– 38° on the vertical axis and +/– 60° on the horizontal axis (low twist angle).

Passive LCD: These standard LCDs are low cost but have a limited viewing angle.

PD LCDs: The Polmer Dispersed LCD does not require polarizers, and thus avoids the major light losses of TN LCDs. It was developed for LCD projectors.

In 1996 researchers at the University of Washington, Human Interface Technology Lab, and engineers at Micro Vision, Inc., developed the Virtual Retina Display (VRD). This display directs a pinpoint of light in a precise raster pattern to scan an image directly onto the retina of the eye. The one million pixels scanned every 1/60th of a second produce an image that appears continuous and stable to the viewer. More than 300,000 full-color VGA points can be generated.

MECHANICAL DESIGN REQUIREMENTS AND ENVIRONMENTAL FACTORS

Circuit design must take into account end-usage environments. Environments that are detrimental to electronics include:

Humidity: Leakage paths, swelling of materials that absorb moisture, delamination of PWBs and surface-mount ICs (during manufacture entrapped moisture turns to steam).

Salt Fog: (in marine environments), cause metal corrosion and circuit leakage paths. Power switches can become clogged with salt fog residue and permanently short, so equipment cannot be turned off.

Dust: (such as in some manufacturing plants). Controls become intermittent and have a gritty feel. Layers of dust interfere with adequate heat radiation, causing thermal problems.

Uncontrolled Temperatures: High temperatures can cause failure when component junctions exceed their ratings. Low temperatures may cause parts to perform out of specification and timing problems result. Low temperatures can also freeze lubricants and any corresponding rotating components.

Explosive Atmosphere: Contact arcing or metal materials scraping against each other can ignite fuels (aviation, gasoline etc.).

Shock/Vibration: (in vehicles or aircraft). At low shock/vibration levels, socketed components and boards may have intermittent connections. Lower levels that are amplified by resonance conditions can cause components and/or solder joints to crack. Cable insulation can abrade and short circuits can occur.

An electronic enclosure will protect the electronics from the afore-mentioned elements. NEMA (National Electrical Manufacturers Association) has designations that range from NEMA 1 (for indoor use and provides protection against accidental contact with the enclosed equipment, to NEMA 13 (also for indoor use but provides protection against dust, spraying of water, oil, and noncorrosive coolant). Reference: NEMA Standards Publication 250, Enclosures for Electrical Equipment (1000V max.) and IEC Publication 529, Classification of Degrees of Protection by Enclosures. The latter provides a system for specifying the enclosures of electrical equipment on the basis of the degree of protection provided by the enclosure. Many environmental conditions are not tested (e.g., corrosive vapors), therefore exact cross-references from the NEMA to the IEC IP enclosure designations cannot be made.

INTERCONNECTING SYSTEMS

Computers are also externally connected via the following methods:

WAN: Wide Area Network The Public Switched Telephone Network, originally an analog network for voice communication, is now digital with the voice signal sampled at a fixed rate. This network was modernized by ISDN (Integrated Services Digital Network), which has a primary rate service and a faster service for broadband applications. There are also packet-switched networks that allow several data "conversations" to be multiplexed over a single circuit based upon demand, rather than a fixed sampling rate.

LAN: Local Area Network. A data communications network (typically high speed, in the megabit per second range) confined to a localized environment, with distances of several hundred feet to six miles (10 kilometers). All segments of the transmission are located in an office building or campus area, with the user owning the network.

The networks can be categorized into three types: Star, Ring, and Bus. A stretched LAN is a MAN, or Metropolitan Area Network, with communication over a distance of 50 km, and is associated with the IEEE 802.6 MAN Standard. LAN standards include IEEE 802.3 (ISO 8802-3) baseband or broadband LAN with bus topology; IEEE 802.4 (ISO 8802-4) two baseband LANs, broadband LANs utilizing a bus topology and token passing access methods; IEEE 802.5 (ISO 8802-5) ring topology with token passing as the access method. (A token refers to an arbitration method where transmission conflicts are avoided by the use of "tokens" which give permission to a station to send a message. After the message is sent, the token is passed on to the next station.)

Ring Network: In this communications network, the data bus loops on itself and the nodes are embedded in the communications and data pass through each node. The data passes around the ring until the proper node (terminal) is reached. Ring networks use token-passing network accessing methods where node status information (tokens) are appended to the data. IBM's Token Ring Network is a baseband ring network that uses the IEEE 802.5 token-passing method. Data transmission is over twisted pair wires, or fiberoptic media, at 4 or 16 Mbps.

Star Network: all the nodes are connected to a central computer with the advantage that it is easy to add and remove nodes and one malfunctioning node doesn't affect the rest of the network. This scheme, however, has the disadvantages of requiring more cabling than other networks and if the central computer fails, the whole network goes down.

Bus Network: A network (such as Ethernet 10 Base-2 and 10 Base-5) where all the nodes are connected to a single wire (the bus) that has two endpoints.

Ethernet: a network developed by the Xerox Corp. that uses CSMA/CD (Carrier-Sense, Multiple Access with Collision Detection) for access. The IEEE 802.3 standard was derived from the Ethernet standard. Implementations of this LAN are available from most major computer manufacturers, including Intel and Digital Equipment Corporation. Ethernet data transmission is at 10 Mbps, although a single user typically does not have a throughput of more than 1 or 2 Mbps. The transmission is over coaxial cable, with a length from 1640 ft (500 meters) to 4,921 ft (1,500 meters). Using remote repeaters the network length can be extended to 8,202 ft (2.5 km). Each cable segment can have as many as 100 nodes or stations.

FDDI: Fiber Distributed Data Interface, ISO 9314 with a data rate of 100Mbps. An FDDI standard allows for 100 km of wiring (which equates to 200 km of fibers when two fibers are wrapped to form a sausage-shaped ring), with up to 500 nodes. FDDI modes are asynchronous (the normal token-ring mode that dynamically allocates any bandwidth left after the synchronous requirements are met) and synchronous. In synchronous operations, predictable response is required and station management makes sure that the sum of all the allocations (i.e., the time for a maximum length packet and token circulation) does not exceed the target token response time. If the token returns earlier than the target token rotation time, a node can send either synchronous or asynchronous data.

The asynchronous FDDI mode can be either a nonrestricted token mode (the norm, where there is even sharing if bandwidth is between nodes) or restricted (for those times when a pair or group of nodes want to use all the asynchronous bandwidth). There is also an isochronous mode, where transmission is of a steady burst of smaller data units, as opposed to the synchronous mode where large bursts of data are sent.

RELIABILITY

At the earliest stage in design, circuits should be made redundant so if one fails the backup will automatically switch in. In lieu of the procurement of higher reliability parts, devices should be tested and burned in. This burn-in may be static or dynamic (i.e., with power applied just in a high temperature ambient environment or with the temperature cycling from hot to cold, or operating with given signal input).

Critical applications include equipment related to patient care or monitoring and equipment located in remote areas where repairs are not practical (such as in space satellites or in undersea installations).

MAINTAINABILITY

Maintainability concerns need to be addressed in the design stage. Expensive or critical hardware will often have to be replaced in the field by technicians who must be able to repair units quickly and efficiently.

Self-diagnostics built into the equipment, such as the kind found on photocopy machines, can help pinpoint the problem. Diagnostic codes on a display, a sequence of LED lights, or error messages on a bus that can be accessed by a computer can all be used by the servicer. Ease of disassembly and reassembly should also be considered in the design. It is not very advantageous to be able to easily pinpoint a failed part, especially if it is a high failure or wearout item, if half of the machine has to be disassembled to reach that part.

COMPONENT SELECTION CONSIDERATIONS

Component selection is as much an issue related to system reliability as it is to meeting the system's power, voltage, and current requirements. The problem of obsolete parts is also a factor as technology rapidly advances.

The new-product innovation cycle is usually less than three to four years. The life cycle of parts is usually less than five to six years (down from a 10-year availability), with some parts only lasting two years. Any device considered for a new design should be available for a reasonable length of time to support the production of the unit. It is not desirable to complete prototype evaluations and be ready to go into production only to find a critical part is obsolete and a major redesign is necessary.

GLOSSARY OF COMPUTER HARDWARE ENGINEERING TERMS

ASIC: Application Specific Integrated Circuit. A custom IC designed for a specific application. It may be a factory hardwired device or one that has been programmed. ASICs improve performance over general-purpose CPUs as they are made to do a specific job and do not have to act upon stored instructions.

ATM: Asynchronous Transfer Mode. A switching technology that allows simultaneous transmission of video, data, and voice communications at very high speeds (155 M-bits/s to 1 G-bit/s). This compares with Ethernet (10 M-bits/s). It uses short fixed-length packets, or cells.

CSMA/CD: Carrier-Sense, Multiple Access with Collision Detection. A LAN (local area network) access method, standard per IEEE 802.3. In this access method, each node "listens" to the network and if it does not "hear" data, it starts transmitting. If multiple simultaneous transmissions are detected (collisions), the node stops transmitting and waits a random amount of time before transmitting again.

DSP: Digital Signal Processor, a microprocessor that is dedicated to vector and algorithmic processing. These microprocessors have simple memory interfaces and typically execute multiple operations in parallel. Some DSP processors and peripherals (such as multiply and accumulate units [MACs]) are becoming available as standard microprocessors and microcontrollers.

Embedded Processor: a microprocessor in a dedicated (specific) application that is coupled with peripherals and may have on-chip memory.

ESD: Electrostatic Discharge. The instantaneous flow of accumulated charge from a nonconductor to a conductor and/or ultimately to ground. To protect circuit damage, static electricity should be prevented from accumulating and/or gradually bled off to ground.

Fan-out: the number of logic inputs that a digital circuit output can drive.

FIFO: First In, First Out. In electronics, refers to data flow handling of bits in memory.

FIT: Failure In Time. This measurement equals the number of failures in one billion hours.

FLOPS: Floating Point Operations Per Second.

FPCG: Field Programmable Clock Generator. This type of device was introduced by Cypress Semiconductor in 1998.

FPGA: Field Programmable Gate Array. This device is available as a reprogrammable or one-time programmable part. In the reprogrammable design, SRAM bits are used for path transistors to form logic block interconnect switches. In the one-time-programmable device, or antifuse design, a dielectric between two active "wires" is broken when a programming voltage is applied, forming a permanent polysilicon filament connection. The reprogrammable device can be reprogrammed in the system without removing the device. It is, however, slower than the one-time-programmable device because of the programmable elements in the device.

FPSC: Field Programmable System Chip. A term coined by Lucent Technologies in 1998 to identify a hybrid IC that combines field programmable gate array technology with a mask-programmed standard logic on a single device.

FPU: Floating Point Unit. A computer circuit that handles floating point calculations and performs operations, such as graphics processing, faster than standard computer circuits. Microprocessors, such as the Intel 80486 and Pentium units, have built in FPUs. Older generation microprocessors used a separate coprocessor for FPU operations.

GPIB: General Purpose Interface Bus. The IEEE 488 bus, an eight-bit parallel bus, sometimes referred to as a general-purpose instrumentation bus.

Ground: a common reference point for circuit returns (shields or heat sinks), usually considered to mean zero potential with respect to earth.

Ground Bounce: simultaneous switching transients in high-speed circuits. If an octal device simultaneously switches seven outputs into a worse case load of 50 pf and the eighth input is held either low or high, ground bounce would be a transient on the eighth output when the switching occurs. This transient is a result of electrical charge stored in lead inductance that induces a voltage and elevates the internal IC ground to a different level than the system ground. Large ground bounces can cause false logic transitions (because logic thresholds are exceeded) and can cause damage to the input circuit of an IC (when a driver output bounces below ground).

HiPPI: High Performance Parallel Interface. An ANSI standard defining a channel that transfers data between CPUs, and from CPUs to disk arrays, and other peripherals, at a basic rate of 800 M-bits/s.

I/O: Input/Output. refers to any operation, program or device that has to enter data into a computer or to extract data from a computer, such as data transfer between the CPU and a peripheral device.

ISDN: (Integrated Services Digital Network) a high-speed telephone line that carries voice, video, and data communications at speeds up to 128,000 bits/s.

Microcontroller: a single-chip microprocessor that has on-chip memory and peripherals. Some devices can access both external and internal memory.

Microprocessor: a processor on a chip that may or may not include memory and a MMU (Memory Manager Unit). It does have a CPU (Central Processing Unit) with registers, an ALU (Arithmetic Logic Unit), and addressing capability. Some devices have on-chip floating-point units, while others use a support IC.

MIPS: Million Instructions Per Second. Refers to instructions being acted upon by a computer.

MMU: Memory Management Unit. Virtual memory addresses are translated to physical addresses by this IC or circuit.

Parallel Interface: Also known as a Centronics Interface (Centronics Corporation designed the original standard, although today's standard is from the Epson Corporation or a Printer Port.) It is a relatively high bandwidth (as compared to the serial port).

Part Variation Skew: The distribution of propagation delays between the outputs of any two devices. In a distributed clock tree design (which is used to increase device fan out), the part-to-part skew must be minimized to optimize the system clock frequency.

PCI: Peripheral Component Interconnect. A 32-bit processor-independent bus architecture.

PCM: Pulse Code Modulation. A common method of encoding an analog signal into a digital bitstream. It is a digitization technique, but is not a universally standard method.

PCMCIA: Personal Computer Memory Card International Association. A standards association for memory cards.

PEROM: Programmable Erasable Read-Only Memory. A term used by Atmel Corporation for their flash CMOS EPROM memories.

PLA: Programmable Logic Array. A programmable logic IC that contains arrays of programmable AND and OR gates.

PLD: Programmable Logic Device. In this device, arrays of AND and OR gates are connected together by fusible links, which are "blown" to open (or in the case of antifuse technology devices by Actel, fused together), resulting in a gate operation to create complex logic circuits. PLDs can be classified as PROMs (Programmable Read-Only Memories), for small designs, PLAs used for more complex designs, and PLA/GLAs (Programmable Logic Arrays and Generic Logic Arrays), also used for complex designs and generally faster and less expensive than PLAs. Dense parts, used for complicated designs, are referred to as CPLDs, or Complex Programmable Logic Devices. PLDs, unlike gate arrays that are masked in the assembly process to create the required logic circuit, can be programmed in the field. While PLDs may be considered ASICs (Application-Specific ICs), they need not be a programmable device.

Rise Time: For digital circuits, this is the rate at which a signal changes from logic 0 to logic 1 (or from logic 1 to logic 0) and is usually expressed in V/ns. (The opposite of rise time is fall time). For analog circuits, it is the time a pulse takes to rise from 10% to 90% of its final value.

SCSI: Small Computer Interface (pronounced "scuzzy"). This is an industry hardware and software standard for connecting peripheral devices and their controllers to microprocessors (thus it is a standard for communications between a host computer and a peripheral).

SDD: Software Design Description (reference ANSI/IEEE 1016-1987). The standard format for preparing a document that defines the software design of a project.

Server: A networked computer that does tasks for a remote computer(s), or is shared by multiple users. A computer or device on a network that manages network resources (such as a print server that is dedicated to manage printers). The software that manages resources or performs tasks, such as Web Server software.

Three-State (Tri-State) Logic: A logic family that has three output states: high, low, or high impedance. In the high impedance state, the output voltage is unaltered.

UART: Universal Asynchronous Receiver/Transmitter. (USART with a serial I/O).

VL-Bus: VESA (Video Electronics Standards Association) local bus, a 32-bit high-performance local bus typically used to handle high-bandwidth graphics.

von Neumann Architecture: A sequential computer architecture created by John von Neumann based upon the original computer. Containing a CPU, storage area, and secondary fast-access memory, this computer executed instructions sequentially and had common but linked registers.

WDT: Watchdog Timer. A counter that looks for signal activity. If no activity occurs within a certain time, it generates an alarm signal (e.g., a peripheral is not responding because it is offline or has failed).

FE/EIT

FE: PM Electrical Engineering Exam

CHAPTER 7

Control Systems Theory and Analysis

CHAPTER 7

CONTROL SYSTEMS THEORY AND ANALYSIS

TRANSFER FUNCTIONS

Consider the linear time-invariant transfer function model represented by the following block diagram:

$$R(s) \longrightarrow \boxed{H(s)} \longrightarrow C(s)$$

$R(s)$ = Reference input

$C(s)$ = Controlled output

$H(s)$ = Transfer function

The transfer function $H(s)$ can be expressed as the ratio of two polynomials in factored form:

$$H(s) = \frac{C(s)}{R(s)} = \frac{N(s)}{D(s)} = K \frac{\Pi_{m=1}(s - z_m)}{\Pi_{n=1}(s - p_n)}$$

where:

z_m, the roots of the numerator polynomial $N(s)$, are called zeros.

p_n, the roots of the denominator polynomial $D(s)$, are called poles.

$D(s)$ is also called the characteristic polynomial of the system. The order of a system is defined as the degree of its characteristic polynomial.

BLOCK DIAGRAM AND TRANSFER FUNCTION OF SYSTEMS

The canonical form of a feedback control system is shown below:

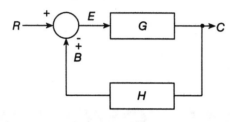

Figure 1

The following definitions refer to this block diagram:

G = direct transfer function

H = feedback transfer function

GH = open-loop transfer function

$\dfrac{C}{R}$ = closed-loop transfer function or control ratio

$\dfrac{E}{R}$ = actuating signal ratio or error ratio

$\dfrac{B}{R}$ = primary feedback ratio

The capital letters R, C, etc., in the block diagram denote Laplace Transform quantities as functions of the complex variable s. We have the following relationships:

$$\frac{C}{R} = \frac{G}{1 \pm GH}$$

$$\frac{E}{R} = \frac{1}{1 \pm GH}$$

$$\frac{B}{R} = \frac{GH}{1 \pm GH}$$

The positive (+) sign in the denominator $1 \pm GH$ refers to a negative feedback system and the negative (–) sign refers to a positive feedback system. The characteristic equation of the system is $1 \pm GH = 0$.

PROBLEM 1:

The block diagram of a negative feedback control system is shown below:

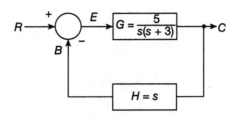

Figure 2

Determine:

 (a) the open-loop transfer function;

 (b) the closed-loop transfer function;

 (c) the error ratio; and

 (d) the primary feedback ratio.

SOLUTION:

(a) The open-loop transfer function is:

$$GH = \frac{5}{s(s+3)} \times s = \frac{5}{s+3}$$

(b) The closed-loop transfer function is:

$$\frac{C}{R} = \frac{G}{1+GH} = \frac{5}{s(s+8)}$$

Note that the positive sign (+) is used in the denominator of the closed-loop transfer function equation for negative feedback.

(c) The error ratio or actuating ratio is:

$$\frac{E}{R} = \frac{1}{1+GH} = \frac{s+3}{s+8}$$

(d) The primary feedback ratio is:

$$\frac{B}{R} = \frac{GH}{1+GH} = \frac{5}{s+8}$$

RESPONSE OF FIRST-ORDER CONTROL SYSTEMS

A simple first-order system in canonical form is represented by the following block diagram:

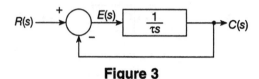

Figure 3

Note that $H(s) = 1$ and this is a unity feedback system; thus, we have:

$$\frac{C}{R} = \frac{1}{1 + \tau s}$$

The block diagram can be further reduced to:

$$R(s) \rightarrow \boxed{\frac{1}{1 + \tau s}} \rightarrow C(s)$$

PROBLEM 2:

A step command, $r(t) = 5u(t)$, is applied to a simple first-order control system whose transfer function is

$$\frac{1}{1 + 3s}.$$

Find the response $c(t)$ for $t > 0$; also identify the transient and steady-state components.

SOLUTION:

$$r(t) = 5u(t)$$

Laplace transformation yields:

$$\text{L}\,[5u(t)] = \frac{5}{s}$$

$$C(s) = \frac{1}{1 + 3s}\frac{5}{s}$$

Convert to the time domain using inverse Laplace transformation:

$$c(t) = 5 - 5.e^{-t/3} \;;\; t \ge 0.$$

The steady-state component is 5, and the transient component is $5\,e^{-t/3}$.

The plot of $c(t)$ is shown below.

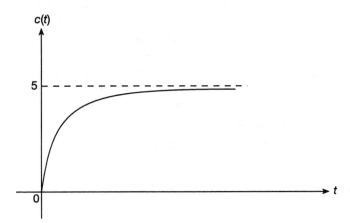

Figure 4

RESPONSE OF SECOND-ORDER SYSTEMS

The transfer function of a simple second-order system can be expressed in parametrix form as:

$$C(s) = \frac{\omega^2_n}{s^2 + 2.\zeta.\omega_n.s + \omega^2_n}$$

where:

ζ = damping ratio

ω_n = natural frequency (rad/sec)

The roots of the characteristic equation, $s^2 + 2.\zeta.\omega_n.s + \omega^2_n = 0$, are

$$s = -\zeta.\omega_n \pm \omega_n\sqrt{\zeta^2 - 1}$$

(a)   If $\zeta > 1$, the roots are real, negative.

(b)   If $\zeta = 1$, the roots are equal to $-\zeta.\omega_n$.

(c)   If $0 < \zeta < 1$, the roots are complex conjugates having negative real parts:

$$s = -\zeta.\omega_n \pm j\omega_n\sqrt{1 - \zeta^2} = -\zeta.\omega_n \pm j\omega_d$$

where $\omega_d = \omega_n\sqrt{1-\zeta^2}$ is called the damped natural frequency.

(d) If $\zeta = 0$, the roots are pure imaginaries (complex conjugate):

$$s = \pm j\zeta.\omega_n$$

(e) If $\zeta < 0$, the roots are complex conjugates having positive real parts.

In cases a, b, and c above, we have roots with negative real parts that correspond to a stable system.

PROBLEM 3:

The following series RLC circuit represents a simple second-order system:

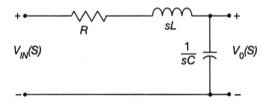

Figure 5

(a) Find the transfer function $\dfrac{V_o(s)}{V_{IN}(s)}$.

(b) Find ζ and ω_n for this circuit.

SOLUTION:

(a) Using voltage divider, we obtain:

$$\frac{V_0(s)}{V_{IN}(s)} = \frac{\dfrac{1}{sC}}{R + sL + \dfrac{1}{sC}} = \frac{1}{s^2LC + sRC + 1}$$

Put this in the parametric form:

$$\frac{V_0(s)}{V_{IN}(s)} = \frac{\dfrac{1}{LC}}{s^2 + \left(\dfrac{R}{L}\right)s + \dfrac{1}{LC}}$$

(b)

$$\omega^2_n = \frac{1}{LC} \Rightarrow \omega_n = \sqrt{\frac{1}{LC}}$$

$$2.\zeta.\omega_n = \frac{R}{L} \Rightarrow \zeta = \left(\frac{R}{2}\right)\sqrt{\frac{C}{L}}$$

STEADY-STATE ERRORS FOR A UNITY FEEDBACK CONTROL SYSTEM

For a unity feedback control system, the steady-state error, $e(\infty)$, is given by the following equation:

$$e(\infty) = \lim_{s \to 0} \left[\frac{sR(s)}{1 + G(s)}\right]$$

(a) For a step input, $r(t) = u(t) \Rightarrow R(s) = \frac{1}{s}$

$$e(\infty) = \lim_{s \to 0} \left[\frac{1}{1 + G(s)}\right] = \frac{1}{1 + \lim_{s \to 0} G(s)}$$

(b) For a ramp input, $r(t) = t.u(t) \Rightarrow R(s) = \frac{1}{s^2}$

$$e(\infty) = \lim_{s \to 0} \left[\frac{1}{s + sG(s)}\right] = \frac{1}{\lim_{s \to 0} sG(s)}$$

(c) For a parabolic input, $r(t) = \left(\frac{1}{2}\right).t^2 \Rightarrow R(s) = \frac{1}{s^3}$

$$e(\infty) = \lim_{s \to 0} \left[\frac{1}{s^2 + s^2 G(s)}\right] = \frac{1}{\lim_{s \to 0} s^2 G(s)}$$

The three limit terms in the denominator of the steady-state error are called the static error constants. Individually, they are:

- The position constant, K_p, where:

$$K_p = \lim_{s \to 0} G(s)$$

- The velocity constant, K_v, where:

$$K_v = \lim_{s \to 0} s\,G(s)$$

- The acceleration constant, K_a, where:

$$K_a = \lim_{s \to 0} s^2 G(s)$$

PROBLEM 4:

Consider the following unity feedback control system:

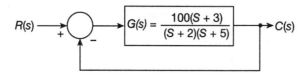

$$R(s) \longrightarrow \bigcirc \longrightarrow G(s) = \frac{100(S+3)}{(S+2)(S+5)} \longrightarrow C(s)$$

Figure 6

Find the steady-state error for the following inputs:

$$u(t),\ t.u(t),\ \text{and}\ \left(\frac{1}{2}\right)t^2.$$

SOLUTION:

(a) For a step input, $r(t) = u(t) \Rightarrow R(s) = \dfrac{1}{s}$

$$e(\infty) = \lim_{s \to 0} \frac{1}{1 + G(s)} = \frac{1}{1 + \lim\limits_{s \to 0} G(s)} = \frac{1}{1+30} = \frac{1}{31}$$

(b) For a ramp input, $r(t) = t.u(t) \Rightarrow R(s) = \dfrac{1}{s^2}$

$$e(\infty) = \lim_{s \to 0} \frac{1}{s + sG(s)} = \frac{1}{\lim\limits_{s \to 0} sG(s)} = \frac{1}{0} = \infty$$

(c)   For a parabolic input, $r(t) = \left(\dfrac{1}{2}\right).t^2 \Rightarrow R(s) = \dfrac{1}{s^3}$

$$e(\infty) = \lim_{s \to 0} \frac{1}{s^2 + s^2 G(s)} = \frac{1}{\lim\limits_{s \to 0} s^2\, G(s)} = \frac{1}{0} = \infty$$

PROBLEM 5:

Consider the following unity feedback system:

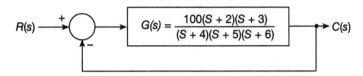

Figure 7

Evaluate the static error constants and determine the steady-state errors for the standard position, velocity, and acceleration inputs.

SOLUTION:

$$K_p = \lim_{s \to 0} G(s) = 5$$

$$K_v = \lim_{s \to 0} s\, G(s) = 0$$

$$K_a = \lim_{s \to 0} s^2 G(s) = 0$$

For a position input:

$$e(\infty) = \frac{1}{1 + K_p} = \frac{1}{1 + 5} = \frac{1}{6}$$

For a velocity input:

$$e(\infty) = \frac{1}{K_v} = \frac{1}{0} = \infty$$

For an acceleration input:

$$e(\infty) = \frac{1}{K_a} = \frac{1}{0} = \infty$$

FE/EIT

FE: PM Electrical Engineering Exam

CHAPTER 8

Digital Systems

CHAPTER 8

DIGITAL SYSTEMS

The study of digital systems covers the fundamental theory of numbers, Boolean algebra, and practical design guidelines and examples for modern logic design.

We will discuss the fundamentals of digital systems and then move on to the basic building blocks—logic gates. With these blocks, we can build more complex and important systems, such as multiplexers, decoders, flip-flops, adders, counters, and shift registers.

NUMBER SYSTEMS

The number system with which we are most familiar is decimal (base 10), but the number system used in digital systems (computers) is binary (base 2). Binary digits 0 and 1 can be represented by low and high voltage, respectively. Digital systems process binary numbers as well as binary-coded numbers of other systems, such as decimal and octal (base 8) numbers. To perform this operation, the system must first convert numbers in other bases to binary form.

Let us consider the three common systems seen most often in digital electronics (decimal, binary, and octal), and study the method of conversion from one to another.

Number System	Base	Example
Decimal	10	875_{10}
Binary	2	$875_{10} = 1101101011_2$
Octal	8	$875_{10} = 1553_8$

Table 1

Conversion of decimal to binary

PROBLEM 1:

Convert 875_{10} to binary.

SOLUTION:

$$
\begin{array}{lll}
2\,\underline{|\,875} & \text{remainder} & \\
2\,\underline{|\,437} & 1 & \\
2\,\underline{|\,218} & 1 & \text{read in reverse order} \\
2\,\underline{|\,109} & 0 & \\
2\,\underline{|\,54} & 1 & \\
2\,\underline{|\,27} & 0 & \\
2\,\underline{|\,13} & 1 & \\
2\,\underline{|\,6} & 1 & \\
2\,\underline{|\,3} & 0 & \\
2\,\underline{|\,1} & 1 & \\
0 & 1 & \\
\end{array}
$$

$875_{10} = 1101101011_2$

Conversion from binary to decimal

PROBLEM 2:

Convert 1101101011_2 to decimal.

SOLUTION:

$$1101101011_2 = 1 \times 2^9 + 1 \times 2^8 + 0 \times 2^7 + 1 \times 2^6 + 1 \times 2^5 + 0 \times 2^4$$
$$+ 1 \times 2^3 + 0 \times 2^2 + 1 \times 2^1 + 1 \times 2^0$$
$$= 512 + 256 + 0 + 64 + 32 + 0 + 8 + 0 + 2 + 1$$
$$= 875_{10}$$

Conversion from binary to octal

PROBLEM 3:

Convert 1101101011_2 to octal.

SOLUTION:

Simply divide the binary number into groups of three bits.

1	101	101	011	
1	5	5	3	$= 1553_8$

Table 2

Conversion of octal to binary

PROBLEM 4:

Convert 247_8 to binary.

SOLUTION:

Convert each octal bit of the number to three-bit binary numbers and then place them next to each other in the same order as shown below.

2	4	7	
010	100	110	$= 010100110_2$

Table 3

Conversion of decimal to octal

PROBLEM 5:

Convert 875_{10} to octal.

SOLUTION:

Convert the decimal number to binary as in Problem 1.

Therefore, $875_{10} = 1101101011_2$

Then convert the binary to octal as in Problem 3.

$1101101011_2 = 1558_8$

BOOLEAN ALGEBRA

Boolean algebra consists of a set, B, that contains at least two elements (e.g., 0 and 1) together with three operations: the AND (Boolean product), the OR (Boolean sum), and the NOT (complement).

For Boolean algebra the following axioms hold:

Idempotent:

$$x \times x = x \qquad\qquad x + x = x$$

Commutative:

$$x \times y = y \times x \qquad\qquad x + y = y + x$$

Associative:

$$x \times (y \times z) = (x \times y) \times z \qquad x + (y + z) = (x + y) + z$$

Absorptive:

$$x \times (x + y) = x \qquad\qquad x + (x \times y) = x$$

Distributive:

$$x \times (y + z) = (x \times y) + (x \times z) \qquad x + (y \times z) = (x + y) \times (x + z)$$

The following definitions also hold:

$$x \times 1 = 1 \times x = x \qquad\qquad x + 0 = 0 + x = x$$

Complement:

$$x \times x' = 0 \qquad\qquad x + x' = 1$$

Canonical Forms of Logic Functions

We define the AND, OR, and NOT operations as follows (two elements A and B are used for this example):

AND (product) operation:

A	B	A × B
0	0	0
0	1	0
1	0	0
1	1	1

Table 4

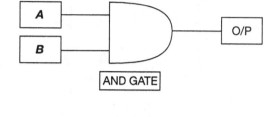

Figure 1

OR (sum) operation:

A	B	A + B
0	0	0
0	1	1
1	0	1
1	1	1

Table 5

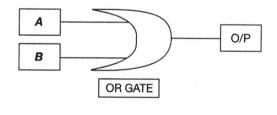

Figure 2

NOT (complement) operation:

NOT (complement)	O/P
A = 0	1
A = 1	0

Table 6

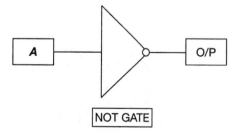

Figure 3

De Morgan's Theorems

1. $\overline{A + B} = \overline{A} \times \overline{B}$

The complement of a sum equals the product of the complements.

A	B	$\overline{A + B}$
0	0	1
0	1	0
1	0	0
1	1	0

Table 7a

A	B	$\overline{A} \times \overline{B}$
0	0	1
0	1	0
1	0	0
1	1	0

Table 7b

The above tables show that for the same values of A and B the last columns are the same.

2. $\overline{A + B} = \overline{A} + \overline{B}$

The complement of a product equals the sum of the complements.

A	B	$\overline{A \times B}$
0	0	1
0	1	1
1	0	1
1	1	0

Table 8a

A	B	$\overline{A} + \overline{B}$
0	0	1
0	1	1
1	0	1
1	1	0

Table 8b

To build a logic circuit associated with any Boolean expression, we can use OR, AND, and NOT gates. Due to the inherent operation of electronics circuitry, the complemented versions of the OR and AND are fundamental gates (NOR and NAND).

As it turns out, NAND gates are all we need to build any logic circuit. The NAND gate is therefore called a universal building block. (NOR gates also are often considered universal blocks.)

Realization of AND, OR, and NOT Gates by a NAND Gate

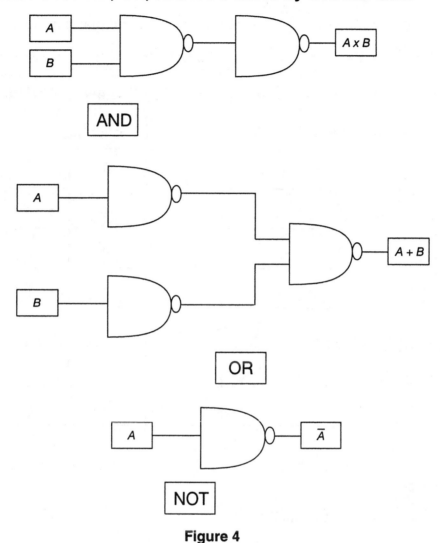

Figure 4

MINTERM AND MAXTERM FORMS

Minterm and maxterm are two common forms of logic equations and the associated arrangement of logic gates.

Minterm Form (Sum of Products)

The sum of products, or minterm, can be written directly by interpreting a 0 under the A or B columns as $\overline{A}$ or $\overline{B}$, respectively. The conditions are written only for rows in which there is a 1 in the output, or F, column. After writing the minterms, the final equation is formed by joining the minterms with the OR (+) symbol. This is the minterm, or sum of products, form.

PROBLEM 6:

Write the minterm equation and draw the logic diagram for the truth table below.

M	A	B	C	F (output)	Minterm
0	0	0	0	0	
1	0	0	1	0	
2	0	1	0	1	$\overline{A} \times B \times \overline{C}$
3	0	1	1	0	
4	1	0	0	1	$A \times \overline{B} \times \overline{C}$
5	1	0	1	0	
6	1	1	0	1	$A \times B \times \overline{C}$
7	1	1	1	0	

Table 9

SOLUTION:

The final minterm equation is:

$$F = (\overline{A} \times B \times \overline{C}) + (A \times \overline{B} \times \overline{C}) + (A \times B \times \overline{C})$$

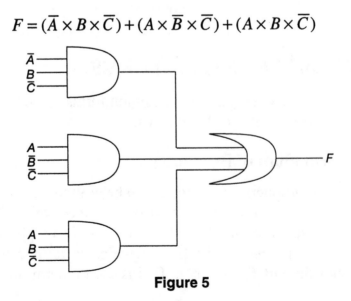

Figure 5

Maxterm Forms (Product of Sums)

The maxterm form is "inverse" to the minterm, in which local variables are joined by the OR (+) function, and the final equation joins the maxterms with the AND (×) function.

PROBLEM 7:

Write the maxterm equation and draw the logic diagram for the truth table below:

M	A	B	C	F (output)	Maxterm
0	0	0	0	0	
1	0	0	1	0	
2	0	1	0	1	$\overline{A} + B + \overline{C}$
3	0	1	1	0	
4	1	0	0	1	$A + \overline{B} + \overline{C}$
5	1	0	1	0	
6	1	1	0	1	$A + B + \overline{C}$
7	1	1	1	0	

Table 10

SOLUTION:

$$F = (\overline{A} + B + \overline{C}) \times (A + \overline{B} + \overline{C}) \times (A + B + \overline{C})$$

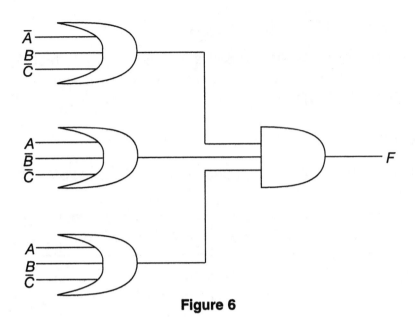

Figure 6

KARNAUGH MAPS

The Karnaugh map is a special truth table designed specifically for simplifying equations. It is constructed such that each square represents one of possible minterms, and any pair of adjacent squares represents a reducible pair of minterms.

The tables below show Karnaugh maps for two, three, and four variables.

Variable	$\overline{A}$	A
$\overline{B}$	$\overline{A}\,\overline{B}$	$A\overline{B}$
B	$\overline{A}B$	AB

Table 11. Two-Variable Karnaugh Map

Variable	$\overline{A}\,\overline{B}$	$\overline{A}B$	AB	$A\overline{B}$
$\overline{C}$	$\overline{A}\,\overline{B}\,\overline{C}$	$\overline{A}B\overline{C}$	$AB\overline{C}$	$A\overline{B}\,\overline{C}$
C	$\overline{A}\,\overline{B}C$	$\overline{A}BC$	ABC	$A\overline{B}C$

Table 12. Three-Variable Karnaugh Map

Variable	$\overline{A}\overline{B}$	$\overline{A}B$	AB	$A\overline{B}$
$\overline{C}\overline{D}$	$\overline{A}\overline{B}\overline{C}\overline{D}$	$\overline{A}B\overline{C}\overline{D}$	$AB\overline{C}\overline{D}$	$A\overline{B}\overline{C}\overline{D}$
$\overline{C}D$	$\overline{A}\overline{B}\overline{C}D$	$\overline{A}B\overline{C}D$	$AB\overline{C}D$	$A\overline{B}\overline{C}D$
CD	$\overline{A}\overline{B}CD$	$\overline{A}BCD$	$ABCD$	$A\overline{B}CD$
$C\overline{D}$	$\overline{A}\overline{B}C\overline{D}$	$\overline{A}BC\overline{D}$	$ABC\overline{D}$	$A\overline{B}C\overline{D}$

Table 13. Four-Variable Karnaugh Map

The size of the map is determined by the number of variables involved and will have as many squares as the number of rows in the standard truth table: 2^n, where n is the number of variables. The squares are filled with 1s for the appropriate minterms and the others left blank. Loops are drawn in the map to reduce the minterms. Each loop must be drawn around the largest group of two, four, eight, and so on. No pairs of terms on the diagonal are reducible.

PROBLEM 8:

Using the example in Problem 6, draw a Karnaugh map and write the simplified equation for the problem. Also draw the logic diagram for the simplified equation.

SOLUTION:

Variable	$\overline{A}\overline{B}$	$\overline{A}B$	AB	$A\overline{B}$
$\overline{C}$		1 _x_	1	1 _y_
C				

Table 14

For loop "x" the term is $B \times C$ and for loop "y" the term is $A \times C$. The final simplified equation is:

$$F = B \times \overline{C} + A \times \overline{C} = (B + A) \times \overline{C}$$

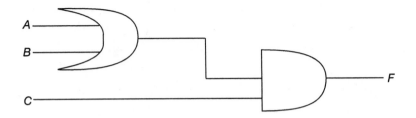

Figure 7. Logic Diagram

The amount of simplification in logic for the same output as in Problem 6 can be clearly seen.

ENCODERS, DECODERS, MULTIPLEXERS, PLAs, AND ROMs

Encoders

Encoders translate from decimal (or some other single input signal) into binary. A decimal to binary encoder consists of four OR gates to convert each key-push signal into its binary equivalent.

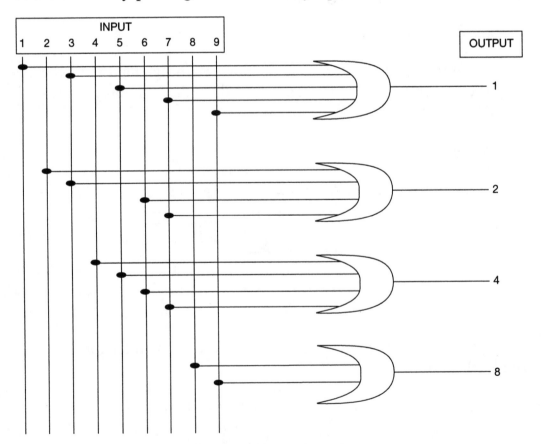

Figure 8. Binary Encoder

PROBLEM 9:

In the previous example, which gates will produce an output for decimal 6?

SOLUTION:

A decimal 6 will produce an output from gates 2 and 4.

Decoders

Decoders essentially reverse the encoding process by converting binary input data or code into a single output signal. Some special applications, such as seven-segment displays, require decoders with multiple outputs.

Two-line to four-line decoder

In this decoder type, the two inputs provide four possible output combinations. In general, n inputs can provide 2^n outputs. The number of AND gates needed is the same as the number of possible output combinations.

Truth Table   **Logic Diagram**

M	A	B
0	0	0
1	0	1
2	1	0
3	1	1

Table 15   **Figure 9**

PROBLEM 10:

For a three-line and four-line input, calculate the number of outputs.

SOLUTION:

For three lines, $n = 3$. Number of outputs $= 2^n = 2^3 = 8$. Therefore, the number of AND gates needed is eight.

For four lines, $n = 4$. Number of outputs $= 2^n = 2^4 = 16$. Therefore, the number of AND gates is 16.

Multiplexers

A *multiplexer/data selector* is the digital equivalent of a multiposition switch. It generally has 2 to 16 data inputs and 1 output. A given data line is selected corresponding to a one to four-bit binary number applied to the device's select inputs. The selected input then becomes available at the output for processing.

PROBLEM 11:

Draw the logic diagram of a four-input multiplexer and its truth table.

SOLUTION:

A four-input multiplexer accepts four input data signals and then, depending on the select inputs, connects one of the four inputs to the output.

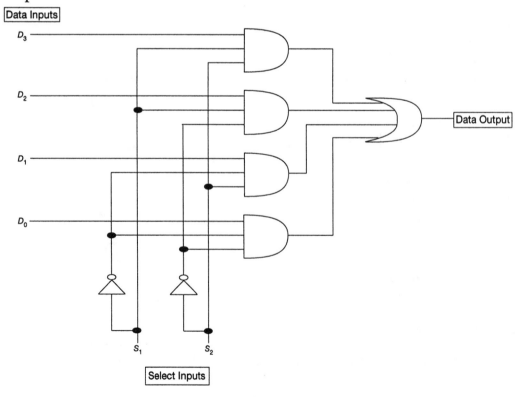

Figure 10

Truth Table

S_1	S_2	Output
0	0	D_0
0	1	D_1
1	0	D_2
1	1	D_3

Table 16

Programmable Logic Arrays

The *programmable logic array* (PLA) is a medium-scale, minterm-type circuit that must be programmed to perform the desired logic functions. The basic device comes with everything connected to generate all the minterms possible for its size. The PLA is programmed by blowing internal fuses to disconnect unwanted circuitry.

The unprogrammed logic array

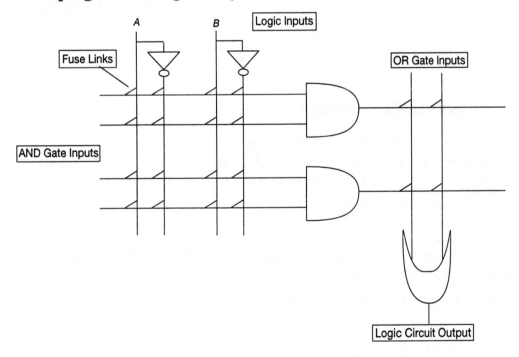

Figure 11

PROBLEM 12:

Draw a programmable logic array that yields an output of

$$F = (\overline{A} \times \overline{B}) + (A \times B)$$

SOLUTION:

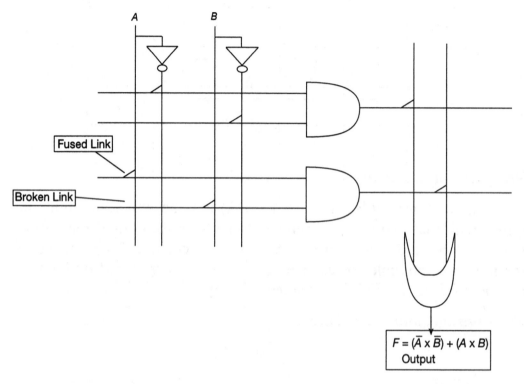

Figure 12

Read-Only Memory (ROM) Logic

The *read-only memory* (ROM) is primarily intended for the part of a computer memory where permanent data are stored. A ROM consists of a number of storage cells arranged in a rectangular grid array, each having a specific address. Each address can activate a corresponding cell which contains a 1 or a 0.

ROM logic is different from gate logic because ROM has no logic inputs as such. In ROM, the logic inputs are the address inputs to the specific cells, and the value stored in the cell is then directed to the output.

PROBLEM 13:

Implement a logic circuit with a ROM for the truth table shown.

	A	B	C	D	F
M_0	0	0	0	0	0
M_1	0	0	0	1	0
M_2	0	0	1	0	0
M_3	0	0	1	1	0
M_4	0	1	0	0	0
M_5	0	1	0	1	0
M_6	0	1	1	0	1
M_7	0	1	1	1	0
M_8	1	0	0	0	0
M_9	1	0	0	1	1
M_{10}	1	0	1	0	0
M_{11}	1	0	1	1	0
M_{12}	1	1	0	0	0
M_{13}	1	1	0	1	0
M_{14}	1	1	1	0	1
M_{15}	1	1	1	1	0

Table 17

SOLUTION:

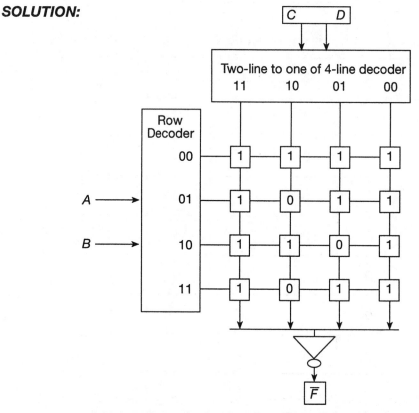

$$F = (\overline{A} \times B \times C \times \overline{D}) + (A \times \overline{B} \times \overline{C} \times D) + (A \times B \times C \times \overline{D})$$

Figure 13

Due to the inverter at the output, the function F is inverted. That is, if $F = 0$, then $\overline{F} = 1$ and vice versa. To understand the operation, consider, for example, the second term $(A \bullet \overline{B} \bullet \overline{C} \bullet D)$. The row decoder puts out a 0 on the row 10 $(A \bullet \overline{B})$. All other row decoder outputs are 1's. The column decoder puts out a 0 on the line 01 $(\overline{C} \bullet D)$. All other column decoder outputs are 1's. The row being selected is at the intersection of the row and the column lines set to 0. When this cell is selected, the value stored in the cell is sent through the output inverter. For the minterm, the value stored in the cell is a 0, and so when the minterm is selected, the output is a 1 after inversion.

ARITHMETIC CIRCUITS

Mathematical operations can be reduced to processes of simple addition. The adder in most computers performs the full range of mathematical operations.

Binary Addition and the Half Adder

The following table defines the binary addition of two binary digits A and B.

A	B	Sum	Carry
0	0	0	0
0	1	1	0
1	0	1	0
1	1	0	1

Table 18

The minterm equations are:

$$\text{Sum} = (\overline{A} \times B) + (A \times \overline{B})$$
$$\text{Carry} = (A \times B)$$

PROBLEM 14:

Draw a logic diagram for the truth table above.

SOLUTION:

Realizing these equations using a logic circuit gives us a half adder.

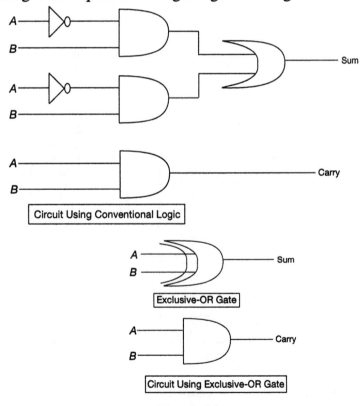

Figure 14

Half Adder Block Diagram

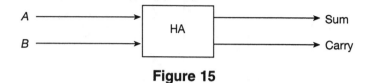

Figure 15

The above is called the half adder because it does not have a provision to add the carry from the preceding addition.

Full Adder

To overcome the limitation of the half adder, the full adder is used. The full adder is composed of two half adders, as shown below.

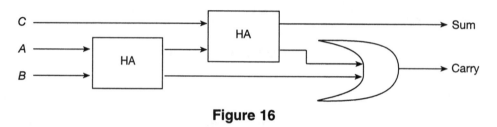

Figure 16

PROBLEM 15:

Write the truth table and the minterm equations for the full adder above.

SOLUTION:

A	B	C	Sum	Carry
0	0	0	0	0
0	0	1	1	0
0	1	0	1	0
0	1	1	0	1
1	0	0	1	0
1	0	1	0	1
1	1	0	0	1
1	1	1	1	1

Table 19

$$\text{Sum} = (\overline{A} \bullet \overline{B} \bullet C) + (\overline{A} \bullet B \bullet \overline{C}) + (A \bullet \overline{B} \bullet \overline{C}) + (A \bullet B \bullet C)$$

$$\text{Carry} = (\overline{A} \bullet B \bullet C) + (A \bullet \overline{B} \bullet C) + (A \bullet B \bullet \overline{C}) + (A \bullet B \bullet C)$$

The Arithmetic Logic Unit (ALU)

The *Arithmetic Logic Unit* is the generally preferred device for most arithmetic circuits. The ALU contains all necessary circuits for performing simple addition and subtraction and logic functions. The functions are selected by programming a set of four select inputs with the appropriate binary combination. The mode control determines if the ALU operates in logic mode or in arithmetic mode.

A CMOS 74HC181 is an ALU device. It has about 75 gates on chips and more devices can be cascaded for longer binary words.

FLIP-FLOPS

A *flip-flop* is a static memory device that consists of two logic gates, with the output of one gate connected to the input of the second gate. The output of the second is then coupled back to the first. Thus, the flip-flop is a device with two stable conditions or states. It can be switched from one state to the other by additional gating. Most flip-flops have a clock control to operate in the synchronous mode.

The R-S Flip-Flop

The R-S flip-flop has two inputs, labeled S and R, and two outputs, Q and $\overline{Q}$. In flip-flops, the two outputs are always complementary, i.e., if Q =1, $\overline{Q} = 0$. The letters S and R often are referred to as set and reset inputs.

PROBLEM 16:

Write the truth table and logic diagram for the R-S flip-flop.

SOLUTION:

The R-S flip-flop using NAND gates and its truth table is as shown.

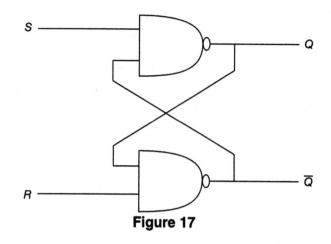

Figure 17

Mode	S	R	Q	$\bar{Q}$	Effect on O/P
Prohibited	0	0	1	1	Do not use
Set	0	1	1	0	Set Q to 1
Reset	1	0	0	1	Reset Q to 0
Hold	1	1	Q	$\bar{Q}$	Previous state

Table 20

The Clocked R-S Flip-Flop

The clocked R-S flip-flop is the same as the R-S flip-flop except it has a clock input. The outputs change only on a clock pulse. This makes the flip-flop operate synchronously.

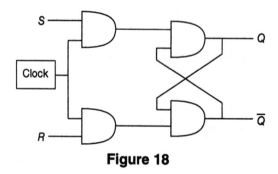

Figure 18

Mode	Clock	S	R	Q	$\overline{Q}$	Effect on O/P
Hold	⎍	0	0	N/C		No change
Reset	⎍	0	1	0	1	Reset Q to 0
Set	⎍	1	0	1	0	Set Q to 1
Prob	⎍	1	1	1	1	Prohibited

Table 21

D Flip-Flop

The *D flip-flop* has only one data input and a clock input. The outputs are labeled Q and $\overline{Q}$. The D flip-flop often is called a delay flip-flop. That is, the data are delayed by one clock pulse from appearing at the output. The D flip-flop is the clocked R-S flip-flop but with only one input that is connected directly to S, and through an inverter to R.

PROBLEM 17:

Draw the logic diagram and write the truth table for a D flip-flop.

SOLUTION:

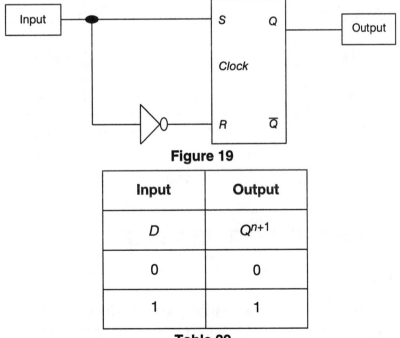

Figure 19

Input	Output
D	Q^{n+1}
0	0
1	1

Table 22

The J-K Flip-Flop

The *J-K flip-flop* is probably the most widely used and popular flip-flop. It is similar to and has all the features of other flip-flops. When both *J* and *K* inputs are 0, the flip-flop is in the hold mode, where the data inputs have no effect on the outputs. When both the inputs are 1, the flip-flop goes into a toggle state, where repeated clock pulses cause the output to turn on and off alternately.

PROBLEM 18:

Draw the logic diagram and write the truth table for a J-K flip-flop.

SOLUTION:

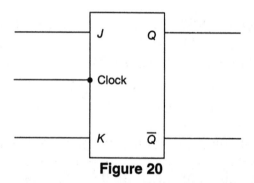

Figure 20

Mode	Clock	J	K	Q	$\overline{Q}$	Effect on O/P
Hold	⎍	0	0	N/C		No change
Reset	⎍	0	1	0	1	Reset Q to 0
Set	⎍	1	0	1	0	Set Q to 1
Toggle	⎍	1	1	Toggle		Changes

Table 23

COUNTERS AND SHIFT REGISTERS

Counters

Counters are used to count pulses, items, and events and are also used to measure frequency by counting cycles referenced to a time period.

Ripple counters are the basic forms of counters implemented with J-K flip-flops. The ripple counter is so named because the output of each flip-flop is connected to the input of the following flip-flop so that the count moves down the line, activating each flip-flop in sequential order.

Four-stage binary ripple counter

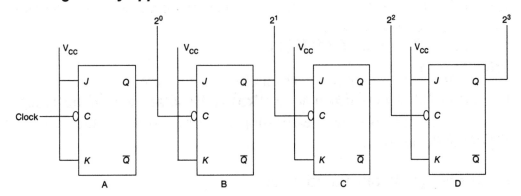

Figure 21

Initially, all flip-flops are reset to 0. The clock input to flip-flop A sets its output to 1 on the negative-going pulse of the clock. Flip-flop B does not change state until its clock input goes to 0, which happens during the second clock pulse when the first output goes to 0. Therefore, the first flip-flop A changes state for every clock pulse but flip-flop B changes for every second pulse. Flip-flop C changes on every fourth pulse and flip-flop D on every sixteenth pulse. On the sixteenth pulse, the outputs are reset to 0. The circuit is called asynchronous because the clock directly controls only the first flip-flop, and the rest are clocked by the output of the preceding flip-flop. The maximum counting frequency is given by:

$$\frac{1}{f_{(max)}} = N (T_p) + T_s$$

where: f = frequency

N = number of flip-flops in the string

T_p = propagation delay of one flip-flop

T_s = strobe time

PROBLEM 19:

Assume a propagation delay of 50 ns per F-F and a decoding time (strobe time) of 50 ns. Calculate the maximum counting frequency for the flip-flop in Figure 21.

SOLUTION:

$$\frac{1}{f} = 4\ (50) + 50 = 250 \text{ ns}$$

$$\frac{f}{(\text{max})} = 4 \text{ MHz}$$

SYNCHRONOUS COUNTERS

Fully *synchronous counters* eliminate the problem of cumulative delay because all data transfers are clocked at the same time. In this type, the propagation delay is only one flip-flop delay regardless of the number of flip-flops in the counter.

A simple synchronous counter

The flip flops are clocked from a common input.

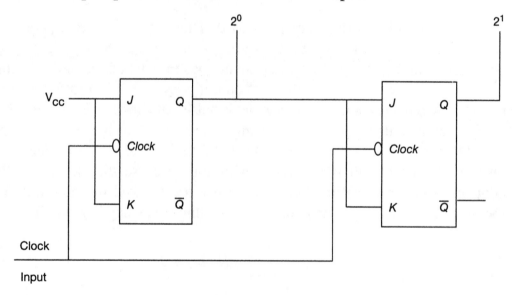

Figure 22

Shift Registers

The *shift register* is a memory system consisting of flip-flops or MOS dynamic memory cells. In the shift registers, data can be transferred from one cell to adjacent cells on command as many times as desired.

Shift registers are synchronous systems using J-K flip-flops or D flip-flops. The Q and $\overline{Q}$ outputs of the preceding stage are connected to the J and K inputs of the next stage. A 1 on the first stage output will be transferred to the second stage. The state on the second will be transferred to the third, and so on. The first stage will remain as before or change states depending on the status of its input lines.

Shift register using J-K flip-flops

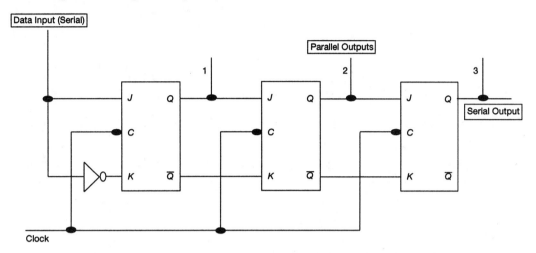

Figure 23. Clock Transfer (Shift) Right

The shift registers are classified as serial-in or parallel-in and serial-out or parallel-out. Any shift register can be used in the serial-in/serial-out mode, but not all have the parallel-in/parallel-out capability.

Parallel-in means that all the data bits can be loaded into the flip-flops at the same time while for serial-in each bit must be loaded into the first flip-flop and shifted over to make room for the next bit until all the bits are loaded. Where parallel-out capability exists, all data bits can be read at the same time while in a serial mode, the data bits are shifted out of the register one at a time. Hence, the shift registers are classified as:

SISO: Serial-in / Serial-out   SIPO: Serial-in / Parallel-out

PISO: Parallel-in / Serial-out   PIPO: Parallel-in / Parallel-out

More advanced shift registers have a useful bidirectional shifting capability and can shift data left or right. This requires that both the parallel inputs and the parallel outputs be available along with some added gates to control the shift direction.

Shift register ring counter

A ring counter can be formed by loading a 1 from the output of an n-stage flip-flop into the circuit's serial and clocking the 1 down the chain. After as many counts as the number of flip-flops, the 1 propagates to the last flip-flop and returns to where it started. The ring counter can produce only four discrete states compared to the binary counter, where 16 discrete states can be achieved. The four states of the ring counter are 1000, 0100, 0010, and 0001, in order. The other states are called the disallowed states. In a ring counter, there are $2^N - N$ disallowed states.

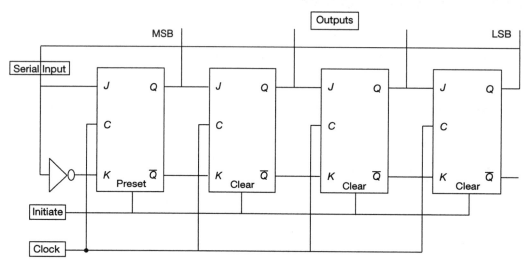

Figure 24. Four Flip-Flop Ring Counter

Truth Table

State	MSB (8)	(4)	(2)	LSB (1)	
1	1	0	0	0	Preloaded
2	0	1	0	0	
3	0	0	1	0	
4	0	0	0	1	

Table 24

The initiate line resets all flip-flops to 0 except the first, which is set to 1. The clock input then shifts the 1. If due to some noise or power shutdown more than one 1 is loaded, then the ring counter enters a disallowed subroutine. The ring counter does not require any decoding gates.

PROBLEM 20:

For the ring counter in Figure 24, how many disallowed states are possible?

SOLUTION:

For the four flip-flop ring counter, there are $2^N - N$ disallowed states.

If the number of flip-flops $N = 4$, then $2^N = 16$, so there are $16 - 4 = 12$ disallowed states.

The Johnson Counter

The counter is virtually the same as the ring counter, except that the complement of the output of the last flip-flop is fed back to the serial input of the shift register. The Johnson counter has $2N$ states and has $2^N - 2N$ disallowed states:

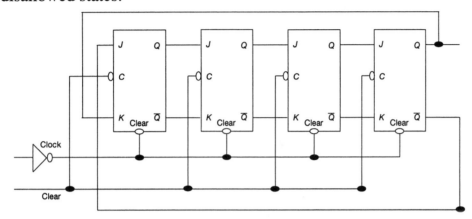

Figure 25

The Johnson counter involves a two-input NAND gate for each decoded output. Each flip-flop drives two gates.

State	Flip-flop A	Flip-flop B	Flip-flop C	Flip-flop D
0	0	0	0	0
1	1	0	0	0
2	1	1	0	0
3	1	1	1	0
4	1	1	1	1
5	0	1	1	1
6	0	0	1	1
7	0	0	0	1

Table 25. Truth Table

Digital Systems

PROBLEM 21:

Draw the decoding circuit for a modulus 4 and modulus 5 Johnson counter.

SOLUTION:

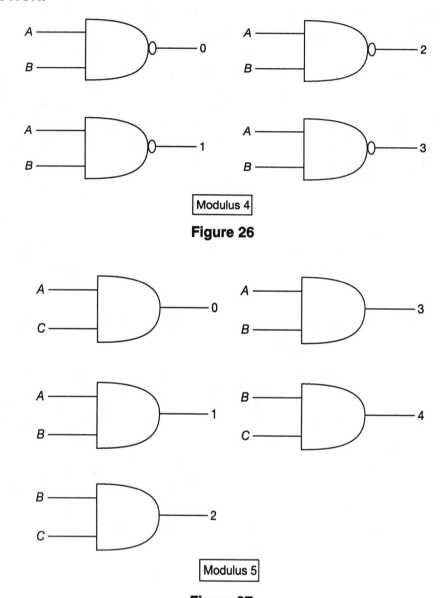

Modulus 4

Figure 26

Modulus 5

Figure 27

SEQUENTIAL CIRCUIT DESIGN, STATE TABLES, AND REDUCTION

A sequential circuit is one whose logic output sequences are functionally dependent on the logic sequences of the input.

A simple electronic sequential circuit is shown in Figure 28. The output F also is fed back to an OR gate. Suppose $R = S = F = 0$. If S goes to 1, node A drops to 0 and F will go to 1 since $R = 0$. Now if S goes back to 0, F remains 1 (as $A = 0$), storing the information that the S input was last a 1.

If now R goes to 1, then F goes to 0. Since $S = 0$, A goes to 1 holding $F = 0$ even after R goes back to 0. The circuit thus stores information that indicates R was last a 1.

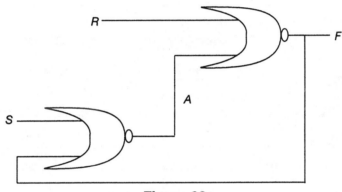

Figure 28

In the general form of sequential circuit, the functional dependence of the outputs (z_1, z_2, ..., z_r) at time t is in general, on the inputs (x_1, x_2, ..., x_p) and the state of the feedback loops (f_1, f_2, ..., f_q). The present values of the system are not only dependent on the present values of the inputs but also on the past history of the input.

To achieve this, the most common memory elements, flip-flops are used in the sequential circuit. Each of these will remember a single binary bit of information. Together, these will constitute what we call the state of the sequential circuit. When the flip-flops change state, the sequential circuit changes state.

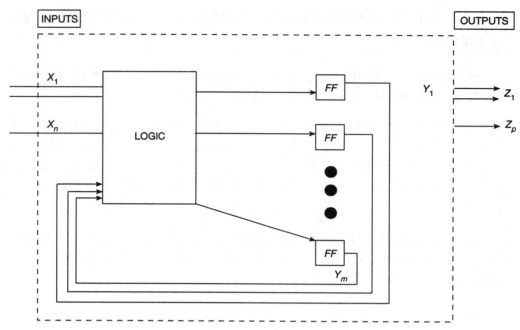

Figure 29. General Sequential Logic Circuit

PROBLEM 22:

Consider a sequential circuit shown in Figure 30 and write the state table.

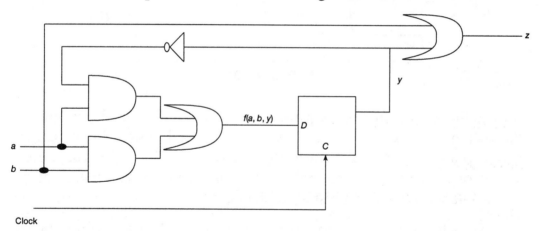

Figure 30

SOLUTION:

To understand the working of this circuit, consider the input to the D flip-flop, which is:

$$f(a,b,y^v) = (ab) + (ay^v)$$

where v is the clock state and y^v is the value of the output y on the vth clock. For the next clock pulse, the value at the D input of the D flip-flop will be the next value of that flip-flop. This leads to:

$$y^{v+1} = f(a, b, y^v) = (ab) + (ay^v)$$

where y^{v+1} is the value of y at the $v + 1$ clock.

This can be represented in a Karnaugh map:

a b	00	01	10	11
y				
0	0	0	1	1
1	0	0	1	0

a b	00	01	10	11
y				
0	0	1	1	0
1	1	1	1	1

Table 26a. State table: y^{v+1}   **Table 26b. State table: Z**

The values represented in the first Karnaugh map are the values of the flip-flop after the next clock pulse. The second Karnaugh map is the output z, which after reduction is given by

$$z = b + y^v$$

In the above maps, a and b are the inputs and y is the present state. The data in the squares give the next state the output assumes for the clock pulse. Hence, these maps are called state tables.

Design of Sequential Networks

PROBLEM 23:

Design a sequential network circuit that generates a "start" signal. The circuit is to have two inputs, "ready" and "go," with a "start" output line, z. A clock input is provided for synchronizing the network. The "start" signal must be generated for one clock period only after the "go" signal has been made high. The "go" signal is generated only after an initial "ready" signal pulse. Once the "start' signal is generated, the next such signal must be generated only after the "ready" signal goes high again. The timing diagram for such a circuit is thus as follows:

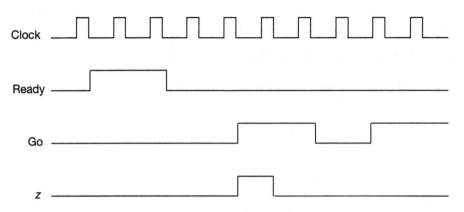

Figure 31. Timing Diagram

SOLUTION:

In this problem, the designer must remember if the "ready" signal has gone to 1 since the last time there was an output signal. If yes, then the "go" signal should generate an output. If not, there should be no output when "go" rises to 1. The timing diagram strongly suggests the need for a flip-flop. Its output "Y" would initially be at 0 until the "ready" signal = 1 and Y would remain at 1 for one clock period after the "go" signal rises to 1.

The state tables from the above description can be written as follows.

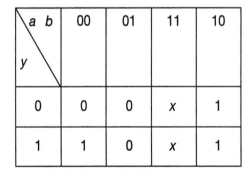

a b \ y	00	01	11	10
0	0	0	x	1
1	1	0	x	1

Table 27a. Y^{v+1}

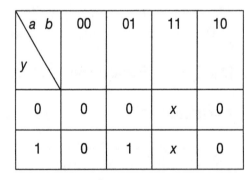

a b \ y	00	01	11	10
0	0	0	x	0
1	0	1	x	0

Table 27b. Z

The x in the state tables are the "don't care" situations. It is assumed that both the "ready" and the "go" signals will not be 1 at the same time.

Writing the minimum sum of products for the output, we have:

$$Z = Y^v \times go$$

Similarly, for the output of the D flip-flop, the logic equation is:

$$D^v = ready + (Y^v \times go)$$

From the two equations, we derive the following circuit:

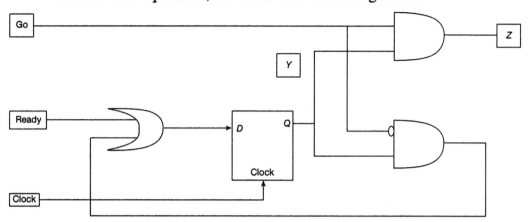

Figure 32

FE/EIT

FE: PM Electrical Engineering Exam

CHAPTER 9

Electromagnetic Theory and Application

CHAPTER 9

ELECTROMAGNETIC THEORY AND APPLICATION

ELECTROSTATICS

Electrostatics describes and analyzes physical phenomena related to the interaction between stationary electric charges or charge distributions in space. Electrostatics divides materials into three large categories: *dielectrics* (insulators), *conductors*, and *semiconductors* and defines two types of electric charges: *positive* and *negative*.

The *law of electric charge conservation* states that the creation of every positive charge $+Q$ results in the creation of a negative charge $-Q$ equal to it in absolute value so that the algebraic sum of all electric charges remains constant.

Coulomb's Law

Coulomb's law states that the interaction force F between two point electric charges Q_1 and Q_2, at a distance r from each other, in a medium of permittivity ε' is:

$$F = \frac{Q_1 \times Q_2}{4\pi\varepsilon' r^2} \tag{1}$$

where F is in newtons (N), Q_1 and Q_2 are in coulombs (C), r is in meters (m), and ε' is in farad/meter (F/m). $\varepsilon' = \varepsilon_0' \, \varepsilon_r$, where ε_r is the relative permittivity of the medium, and ε_0' is the permittivity of free space (vacuum).

$$\varepsilon_0' = \frac{10^7}{(4\pi c^2)} \approx \frac{1}{4\pi \times 9 \times 10^9} \approx 8.8542 \times 10^{-12} \; \frac{F}{m} \tag{2}$$

where $c \approx 2.9979 \times 10^8$ m/s is the speed of light in vacuum. Thus, Coulomb's law can be written as:

$$F = 9 \times 10^9 \frac{Q_1 \times Q_2}{\varepsilon_r \times r^2} \tag{3}$$

Electrostatic Fields

An electrically charged object will apply forces on other electrically charged objects which will cause them to move or rotate. This interaction is the result of the electric field surrounding the electrically charged objects. The electric field surrounding electrically charged conductors is fixed in space and, in a situation of stable equilibrium, is the electrostatic field. The electric field intensity determines the strength of the mechanical force applied to various electrically charged objects in the field. The field intensity, $\vec{E}$, is a vector defined as the ratio between the force and the point charge on which the force acts.

$$\vec{E} = \frac{\vec{F}}{q} \tag{4}$$

When q is equal to one unit of positive charge, $\vec{E} = \vec{F}$, which leads to the definition of electrostatic field intensity as the physical value numerically equal to the force acting on the unit positive charge located at the point of action. Electrostatic Field Intensity is measured in volts/meter (V/m) in the SI system.

Using equation (3):

$$\vec{E} = 9 \times 10^9 \frac{Q}{\varepsilon_r \times r^2} \times \frac{\vec{r}}{r} \tag{5}$$

or, when n point charges are considered Q_i ($i = 1, 2, \ldots, n$), the field intensity is:

$$\vec{E} = \sum_{i=1}^{n} \vec{E}_i \tag{6}$$

where $\vec{E}_i$ is the electric field intensity caused by the charge Q_i. The electric field is said to be uniform if its intensity has the same numeric value, inclination, and direction in all its points. This would be the case for the field between the parallel plates of a capacitor of infinite size.

Since the electrostatic field applies mechanical force on charges in that field, mechanical work results. The ratio between the work A used by the field to move the charge q between points P_1 and P_2 and the charge q is defined as the electrical voltage U between the two points (see Figure 1).

$$\frac{A}{q} = \frac{\int_{P_1}^{P_2} \vec{F}\ d\vec{s}}{q} = \frac{q\int_{P_1}^{P_2} \vec{E}\ d\vec{s}}{q} = \int_{P_1}^{P_2} \vec{E}\ d\vec{s} = U_{1,2}$$

$$A = q \times U_{1,2}$$

$$(7)$$

In the SI system the unit for voltage is the volt (V).

From equations (1), (5), and (7):

$$\frac{A}{q} = \frac{Q}{4\pi\varepsilon'} \times \int_{P_1}^{P_2} \frac{ds \times \cos\alpha}{r^2}$$

$$(8)$$

Since $ds \times \cos\alpha = dr$, as can be seen from Figure 1,

$$\frac{A}{q} = \frac{1}{4\pi\varepsilon'} \times \frac{Q}{r_1} - \frac{1}{4\pi\varepsilon'} \times \frac{Q}{r_2} = V_1 - V_2$$

$$(9)$$

and when $P_2 \rightarrow \infty$ the formula becomes:

$$\frac{A}{q} = \frac{1}{4\pi\varepsilon'} \times \frac{Q}{r_1} = V_1$$

$$(10)$$

V_1 (V_2 respectively) represents the electric potential at P_1 (P_2 respectively) created by the charge Q, and its numerical value is equal to the work needed to move the charge $+1$ from P_1 (P_2) to infinity. The SI unit for electric potential is the volt (V).

From equations (5) and (10), $\vec{E} = -\ \text{grad}\ V$, which means that the intensity of the electrostatic field is equal to, but of opposite sign from, the gradient of the electric potential. Therefore, the curl of $\vec{E}$ is zero ($\nabla \times E = 0$, where $\times$ defines the cross-product), which means that the electrostatic field is irrotational. Surfaces on which the potential V is constant, such as surfaces of charged conductors in electrostatic equilibrium, are called equipotential.

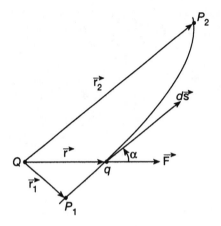

Figure 1

To find the electric field intensity $\vec{E}$ around n electrically charged conductors one must determine the potential $V(x, y, z)$ that satisfies Laplace's equation outside the conductor,

$$\nabla^2 V = 0 \qquad (11)$$

and the boundary conditions: V has given values on the surfaces of given conductors; V becomes 0 at infinity for $\nabla^2 V = 0$ and $V = $ constant on the conductor's surface.

$$\oint_{S_i} \frac{dV}{dn} dS_i = \frac{Q_i}{\varepsilon'} \qquad (12)$$

where Q_i is the total charge of conductor i.

In the case of charged conductors that are in equilibrium, the charges are on the surface while the electric field inside the conductor is zero. Thus, the potential is constant. The electric charge density is defined as:

$$\sigma = \frac{dQ}{dS} \qquad (13)$$

where dQ is the electric charge on the surface element dS. The greater the curvature of the surface, the greater S.

Electric Force Lines/Electric Flux

An electrostatic field is described by the vector $\vec{E}$ (x, y, z) attached to each point of the field. The force lines of the electric field are curves along which their tangent vector $\vec{t}$ (dx, dy, dz), at every point, is along the same line as $\vec{E}$ (E_x, E_y, E_z). The corresponding differential equation is:

$$\frac{dx}{E_x} = \frac{dy}{E_y} = \frac{dz}{E_z}$$

The force lines are open-ended curves, orthogonal on equipotential surfaces. Figure 2 shows the force lines for the field created by a point charge while Figure 3 shows the force lines between the flat plates of a capacitor.

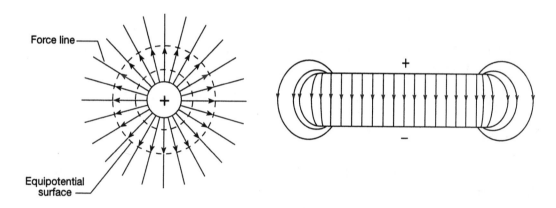

Figure 2   **Figure 3**

The electric flux through the surface S is defined by:

$$\psi = \iint_S \vec{E}\, d\vec{s} \qquad (14)$$

Gauss' theorem states that the electric flux through a closed surface is equal to $\frac{\Sigma Q_i}{\varepsilon'}$, where ΣQ is the sum of charges inside that surface.

$$\oiint_S \vec{E}\, d\vec{s} = \frac{\Sigma Q_i}{\varepsilon'} \qquad (15)$$

or, in its local form:

$$div\ \vec{E} = \frac{\rho}{\varepsilon'} \qquad (16)$$

where ρ is the charge volumic density inside the volume covered by the surface S.

Coulomb's theorem states that in the immediate vicinity of a charged conductor, the electric field intensity is $E = \sigma/\varepsilon'$, while on the conductor's surface $E = \sigma/2\varepsilon'$.

PROBLEM 1:

The glass container of an electroscope is filled with nitrogen at 20°C. The tips of the two poles are at 10 cm distance of each other. Calculate the rejection force between the pole tips if their charge is 0.5 C per pole.

SOLUTION:

From Coulomb's law,

$$F = 9 \times 10^9 \ [(Q_1 \times Q_2)/(\varepsilon_r \times r^2)]. \ Q_1 = Q_2 = 0.5 \ C; \ \varepsilon_r = 1.0006$$

F/m for nitrogen at 20°C (from relative permittivity tables available from technical textbooks);

$$r = 0.1 \ m. \ F = 9 \times 10^9 \times [0.5 \times 0.5 \ )/(1.0006 \times 0.1^2)] \approx 2.25 \times 10^{11} \ N.$$

PROBLEM 2:

Calculate the electric potential of a very small conductor situated at 50 cm from a point charge of 10 C if they are both embedded in the same piece of marble.

SOLUTION:

The electric potential is $V = \dfrac{Q}{4\pi\varepsilon'_r}$. For $Q = 10 \ C$, $r = 0.5 \ m$.

$$\varepsilon' = \varepsilon_0' \times \varepsilon_r = 9^{-1} \times 10^{-9}/4\pi \times 9 = 7.958 \times 10^{-11} \ F/m,$$

where the relative permittivity of marble is between 8 and 10 and an average value of 9 has been selected.

$$V = 10/(4\pi \times 7.958 \times 10^{-11} \times 0.5) = 1.9 \times 10^{10} \ V.$$

PROBLEM 3:

Establish the relation for the electric field intensity for an infinitely large flat surface having a charge density $+ \sigma$ and for the electric field between two infinitely large surfaces with charge density $\pm \sigma$ ($\sigma = dQ/dS$ = const.).

SOLUTION:

Using equation (15) and applying Gauss' theorem to a cylinder with parallel bases, having its height perpendicular to the infinite surface (see figure), we can write:

$$\psi = \frac{Q}{\varepsilon'} = \iint\limits_{S_1} E\,dS + \iint\limits_{S_2} E\,dS + \iint\limits_{S_3} E\,dS = 2ES$$

Thus, the intensity of the electric field of an infinite surface charged with density $+\sigma$ is:

$$E = \frac{Q}{2\varepsilon'S} \quad \text{or} \quad E = \frac{\sigma}{2\varepsilon'}.$$

Similarly, for the infinite size capacitor:

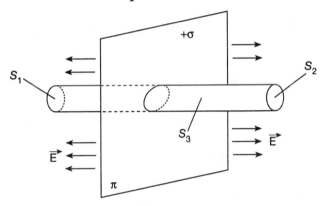

$E = \dfrac{\sigma}{\varepsilon'}$ between plates and $E = 0$ outside the plates.

Figure 4

PROBLEM 4:

Copper is the most used material in electrical applications. Consider an electrically neutral pin made of copper of mass $m = 2.30$ g and determine the charge Q of the pin. For a copper atom: nuclear charge = electron charge = $+4.60 \times 10^{-18}$ C/atom, atomic weight of copper $M_c = 63.54$ g/mole. Avogadro's number (as defined in chemistry and physics textbooks) is $N_A = 6.02 \times 10^{23}$ atoms/mole.

SOLUTION:

In order to determine the charge Q of the pin, the number of copper atoms N_c in the pin must first be calculated.

$$N_A = \frac{N_c \times M_c}{m}$$

Solving for N_c:

$$N_c = \frac{N_A \times m}{M_c} = \frac{6.02 \times 10^{23}[\text{atoms/mole}] \times 2.30[\text{g}]}{63.54[\text{g/mole}]} = 2.18 \times 10^{22} \text{ atoms}$$

Hence, the charge will be:

$$2.18 \times 10^{22} \text{ [atoms]} \times 4.60 \times 10^{-18} \text{ [C/atom]} \approx 1.0 \times 10^5 \text{ C}$$

MAGNETOSTATICS

While electrostatics deals with static charges, magnetostatics deals with stationary currents, i.e., charges moving at constant velocity, and the interaction between these currents.

Magnetic Interaction, Magnetic Field

Coulomb established that magnetic poles of similar polarity reject each other, and poles of opposite polarity attract each other with a force that is a function of the square of the distance between them. That force also depends on the medium in which the magnets are placed. The medium is characterized by the magnetic permeability μ' and is calculated in a similar manner to the way in which the electrostatic force is calculated. Considering two very small loops, C and C', through which currents of densities J and J' respectively flow, the two loops being at distance r from each other, as shown in Figure 5, the force of interaction is:

$$F = -\frac{\mu' J \times J'}{4\pi} \oint_c \oint_{c'} \frac{dl \times dl'}{r^2} \tag{17}$$

$\mu' = \mu_o'\mu_r$, where $\mu_o' = 4\pi \times 10^{-7}$ H/m is the magnetic permeability of vacuum and μ_r is the relative permeability of the medium.

Figure 5

Magnets and conductors carrying electric currents apply mechanical actions on other magnets and currents around them. This is done through the magnetic field surrounding them. The intensity of the magnetic field $\vec{H}$ in a volume V is given by:

$$\vec{H} = \frac{1}{4\pi} \int_V J \frac{d^3 \vec{l}}{r^2} \tag{18}$$

and is measured in A/m or in ampere turns/m.

Magnetic Dipole and Magnetic Moment

Under certain circumstances a small magnet can be considered to be an assembly of two magnetic poles of magnetic quantities $+m$ and $-m$ at a distance l from each other. Such a magnetic dipole, in a magnetic field, would be subjected to forces: $\vec{F} = m\vec{H}$ and $\vec{F}' = -m\ \vec{H}$. The resulting moment is: $M = \vec{l} \times m\vec{H}$ (see Figure 6).

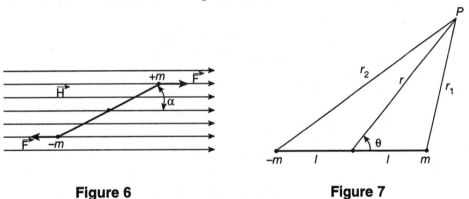

Figure 6　　　　　　　**Figure 7**

The potential of a magnetic dipole (see Figure 7) is:

$$V_H = \left(\frac{m}{r_1} - \frac{m}{r_2} \right) \times \frac{1}{4\pi} \tag{19}$$

The magnetic field components (in polar coordinates) in a plane are:

$$H_r = -\frac{\partial V_H}{\partial r}$$

and

$$H_l = -\frac{1}{r} \frac{\partial V_H}{\partial \theta}.$$

The magnetic field energy in a volume V is:

$$W_m = \iiint_V \frac{\mu' H^2}{2} dV \qquad (20)$$

and the magnetic energy density is:

$$w_m = \frac{\mu' H^2}{2} \qquad (21)$$

PROBLEM 5:

A uniform magnetic field of strength $B = 1.2$ Wb/m^2 (or T) exists within an iron core ($\mu = 1{,}000\mu_0$) as shown in the figure below. If an air gap is cut with the orientation shown, find the magnitude and direction of B_2 in the gap.

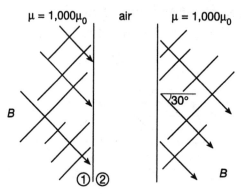

Figure 8

SOLUTION:

Using magnetic boundary conditions,

$B_{n1} = B_{n2}$ (normal components of B are equal)

$H_{t1} = H_{t2}$ (tangential components of H are equal)

$B_{n1} = B_{n2} = B \cos 30° = 1.2\,(0.866) = 1.0\ T$

$H_{t1} = H_{t2}$

$$\frac{B_{t1}}{\mu} = \frac{B_{t2}}{\mu_0}$$

Therefore:

$$B_{t2} = \frac{\mu_0}{1{,}000\mu_0} \times B_{t1} = \frac{1}{1{,}000} B_{t1}$$

$$= \frac{1}{1{,}000}(1.2 \sin 30°) = 0.00006\ T$$

Thus, $B_2 \approx 1.0\ T$ since the tangential component is negligible compared to the normal component.

$$\left(B_2 = \sqrt{B_{n2}^2 + B_{t2}^2}\right)$$

PROBLEM 6:

A thin toroid of permanently magnetized material has a uniform magnetic dipole moment (per unit of volume) of strength M and is oriented concentric to the center of the toroid as shown. Find the direction and magnitude of B and H at point 1 inside the toroid.

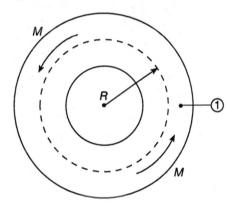

Figure 9

SOLUTION:

Applying Ampere's law:

$$\oint_c \vec{H} \times d\vec{r} = I_{\text{through curve}}$$

$$H2\pi R = I = 0$$

therefore, $H = 0$.

$$\vec{H} = \frac{1}{\mu_0}\vec{B} - \vec{M}$$

therefore,

$$\vec{B} = \mu_0\left(\vec{M} + \vec{H}\right).$$

Since $\qquad \vec{H} = 0, \;\; \vec{B} = \mu_0\vec{M}.$

ELECTROMAGNETISM

There are well defined relationships between the electric and magnetic fields as a consequence of the fact that:

- electric currents are surrounded by magnetic fields;

- the magnetic field intensity of an electric current changes direction as the current changes direction;

- the magnetic field intensity is proportional to the electric current intensity; and

- the magnetic field intensity is a function of the position and shape of the electric circuit.

The magnetic field is described by two vectors: the magnetic field intensity, $\vec{H}$, and the magnetic induction, $\vec{B}$, where $\vec{B} = \mu' H$ and $\mu' = \mu_o' \, \mu_r$ is the absolute permeability, $\mu_o' = 4 \times \pi \times 10^{-7}$ henries per meter (H/m) is the permeability of vacuum, and μ_r is the relative permeability of the medium in which B is calculated. The SI unit for magnetic induction is tesla (T).

The direction of the magnetic field intensity created by an electric current can be determined by the corkscrew rule: the direction of $\vec{H}$ is that in which a corkscrew must be turned so that it would advance in the direction of the current. Magnetic lines of force are closed curves that do not intersect each other.

The *law of magnetic circuit* states that the circulation of $\vec{H}$ is equal to the sum of currents inside the curve C along which the circulation is considered.

$$\oint_C \vec{H}\, dl = \sum_{i=1}^{n} I_k \tag{22}$$

Through generalization, this law led to Maxwell-Ampere's first system of equations.

Laplace's law determines the value of the mechanical force $d\vec{F}$, which acts on the conductor $d\vec{s}$ through which the current I flows, when it is placed in a magnetic field of induction $\vec{B}$:

$$d\vec{F} = I \times d\vec{s} \times \vec{B}. \tag{23}$$

Biot-Savart's law determines the magnetic field intensity around a constant current I that flows through the line element ds at distance r from the point where the field is calculated:

$$d\vec{H} = \frac{I}{4\pi} \times \frac{d\vec{s} \times \vec{r}}{r^3} \tag{24}$$

For a linear conductor of infinite length through which the current I (A) is flowing, the magnetic field at the distance r (m) is

$$H = \frac{I}{2\pi r} \text{(A/m)}.$$

Lorentz's Force is the force acting on a particle of charge q $(q > 0)$ moving at speed v in a magnetic field of induction B.

$$\vec{F} = q \times \vec{v} \times \vec{B} \tag{25}$$

If a current I flows through a circular loop of radius r, the magnetic field and the induction in the center of the loop are:

$$H = \frac{I}{2r} \text{ and } B = \mu' \frac{I}{2r}.$$

For a coil that has a length, l, much larger than its radius, the field in the middle of the coil, on its axis, and far from its ends, will be:

$$H = \frac{NI}{l} \text{ and } B = \mu' \frac{NI}{l}$$

in which N is the coil's number of turns. For a toroid with N_l turns per unit of length, $H = N_l I$ and $B = \mu' N_l I$

Magnetic moment of a closed electric circuit through which current is flowing. The magnetic field of such a circuit is equivalent to that of a thin magnetic sheet having an area identical to that covered by the closed electric circuit. The magnetic moment is $M = \mu' I S$ or, for a multi-turn circuit, $M = \mu' I S N$, in which μ' is the magnetic permeability of the medium in which the circuit is flowing. S is the area covered by the circuit and I the current in the circuit.

Magnetic field around a mobile electrified particle. If a particle q (C) moves at speed v (m/s), which makes the angle α with the direction in which the magnetic field intensity around it is being calculated, then, at distance r (m), the intensity is:

$$H = \frac{q \times v}{4\pi \times r^2} \sin \alpha \qquad (26)$$

Electric Current Interaction

Ampere established experimentally the laws that govern the interaction of two conductors carrying electric currents.

1. Two parallel conductors carrying currents going in opposite directions reject each other.

2. Two parallel conductors carrying currents going in the same direction attract each other.

3. Two conductors crossing each other attract each other when the currents they carry go toward the crossing point and reject each other when the currents flow away from the intersection point.

For two parallel conductors of length l at distance d and carrying the currents I and I' in a medium of relative permeability μ_r (assuming all units are in the SI system), the interaction force is:

$$F = 2 \times 10^{-7} \times \mu_r \times \frac{I \times I'}{d} \times l \qquad (27)$$

Magnetic Flux/Magnetic Circuit

The induction magnetic flux on a surface S is:

$$\Phi = \iint_s \vec{B} \; d\vec{S}$$

$d\vec{S}$ being the directed area element of S. The SI unit for magnetic flux is weber (Wb).

The *magnetic circuit* is the closed tubular circuit that envelopes the force lines of a magnetic field. For a wound toroid where the magnetic induction is $B = \mu' N_1 I$, the magnetic flux in a cross-section is:

$$\Phi = \mu' \frac{N}{l} I \times S = \frac{NI}{\dfrac{l}{\mu' S}} = \frac{F}{R} \qquad (28)$$

in which $F = N \times I$ is the magnetomotive force (mmf) and:

$$R = \frac{1}{\mu' S}$$

is the magnetic circuit reluctance.

Electromagnetic Induction

Electromagnetic induction is the phenomenon by which an electromotive force (emf) is obtained and, therefore, electric currents result through the variation in time of the magnetic flux. Induction emf exists for as long as the flux varies and, if a closed circuit is considered, results in a current. From Faraday's law, emf can be calculated by:

$$e = -\frac{d\Phi}{dt} \qquad (29)$$

The electromagnetic induction is the basis for the operation of electrical machines and many other electrical apparatus. For a conductor of length l moving at speed v across the magnetic force lines, perpendicular on them:

$$e = -B \times l \times v \qquad (30)$$

According to the rule established by Lenz, the direction of the induced current is such that it opposes the variation (either increase or decrease) of the inducing magnetic field.

The energy of the induced current is given by:

$$e\,I\,dt = I\,d\Phi$$

The quantity of electricity (electric charge) induced in an electric circuit of resistance R, when the flux varies from Φ_1 to Φ_2, is:

$$Q = \frac{\Phi_1 - \Phi_2}{R} \qquad (31)$$

Self-induction

Any electric circuit carrying a current creates its own magnetic flux. When the current intensity varies, that flux varies and an emf is created. As the magnetic field intensity is a linear function of I, so is Φ, which can be calculated as:

$$\Phi = L \times I$$

where L is the circuit's inductance or its coefficient of self-inductance. L is measured in henries (H). For a self-induced circuit containing an inductance L, a resistance R, and a voltage source E,

$$e = -L\frac{dI}{dt} \text{ and } I = \frac{E - L\frac{dI}{dt}}{R}. \quad (32)$$

For a very long coil of N turns, each having the area S, if $S_t = N \times S$ and

$$B = \frac{NI}{l}\mu', \Phi = S_t B$$

and

$$L = \frac{N^2}{l}\mu'S$$

For coils with ferromagnetic core, $\mu' = \mu'(I)$. The energy in the magnetic field of a coil is:

$$W = \frac{1}{2}LI^2$$

and the magnetic energy density is:

$$w_m = \frac{\mu'H^2}{2}$$

Mutual Induction

Two electric circuits carrying currents I_1 and I_2, respectively, generate fluxes proportional to these currents. The coefficient M (measured in henries) represents the mutual induction and is used to calculate the emf induced by one circuit into the other.

$$e_1 = -M\frac{dI_2}{dt} \quad (33)$$

If L_1 and L_2 are the inductances of the two circuits, the value:

$$k = \frac{M}{\sqrt{L_1 L_2}}$$

is called the coupling coefficient of the two circuits.

Maxwell's Equations

Maxwell's equations are local forms of the general laws of the electromagnetic field that relate a variable electric field and a variable magnetic field. Maxwell's equations are the analytical expression of this fundamental theory, which states that all electric field variations result in a magnetic field, and magnetic field variations result in an electric field. The equations below apply to macroscopic electrodynamics of stationary media.

Maxwell-Ampere equations are obtained through the generalization of the law of the magnetic circuit by considering a magnetic field around a transfer current. Thus, the displacement current $\vec{j}_d = \vec{D}$ through the dielectric of a capacitor C will be the natural extension of the conduction current, both generating a magnetic field around them according to the same laws.

$$\oint_c \vec{H}\,d\vec{l} = \iint_s \left(\vec{D} + \vec{j}\right)d\vec{S} \tag{34}$$

$$\nabla \times \vec{H} = \vec{j} + \vec{D}$$

where j is the density of the conduction current and S is an area bordered by the closed curve C.

Maxwell-Faraday equations generalize the law of magnetic induction. Thus, Faraday's law applies not only to circuits using conductors, but also to any closed path in a conducting medium, in a dielectric, or in vacuum.

$$\oint \vec{E} \times d\vec{l} = -\frac{\partial \Phi}{\partial t} \tag{35}$$

$$\nabla \times \vec{E} = -\vec{B}$$

To equations (34) and (35) we add the laws of electric flux and magnetic flux (• below defines the dot product):

$$\nabla \bullet \vec{D} = \rho$$
$$\nabla \bullet \vec{B} = 0 \tag{36}$$

and the following relationship equations:

$$\vec{D} = \varepsilon'\vec{E}$$

$$\vec{H} = \frac{1}{\mu'}\vec{B} \tag{37}$$

$$\vec{j} = \sigma\vec{E}$$

In accordance with the theorem of magnetic fields, Maxwell's equations have unique solutions. Maxwell's equations for homogenous and isotropic perfect dielectrics ($\sigma = 0$), without free charges ($\rho = 0$), are:

$$\nabla \times \vec{H} = \varepsilon' \vec{E}$$
$$\nabla \times \vec{E} = -\mu' \vec{H}$$
$$\nabla \bullet \vec{H} = 0 \tag{38}$$
$$\nabla \bullet \vec{E} = 0$$

which lead to the wave equations:

$$\nabla^2 \vec{E} = \frac{1}{v^2} \frac{\partial^2 \vec{E}}{\partial t^2}$$
$$\nabla^2 \vec{H} = \frac{1}{v^2} \frac{\partial^2 \vec{H}}{\partial t^2} \tag{39}$$

where $v^2 = \dfrac{1}{\mu' \varepsilon'}$.

The equations of the magnetic field in a homogenous, isotropic, and conducting medium (where e', m', and σ are constant) are:

$$\nabla^2 \vec{E} = \frac{1}{v^2} \frac{\partial^2 \vec{E}}{\partial t^2} + \sigma \mu' \frac{\partial \vec{E}}{\partial t}$$
$$\nabla^2 \vec{H} = \frac{1}{v^2} \frac{\partial^2 \vec{H}}{\partial t^2} + \sigma \mu' \frac{\partial \vec{H}}{\partial t} \tag{40}$$

in a sinusoidal regime, $\vec{E} = \vec{E}_0\, e^{j\omega t}, \vec{H} = \vec{H}_0\, e^{j\omega t}$ resulting in:

$$\nabla^2 \vec{E} = \frac{1}{v_c^2} \frac{\partial^2 \vec{E}}{\partial t^2}$$
$$\nabla^2 \vec{H} = \frac{1}{v_c^2} \frac{\partial^2 \vec{H}}{\partial t^2} \tag{41}$$

where $v_c^2 = \dfrac{1}{\mu' \varepsilon_c}$ and $\varepsilon_c = \varepsilon' + \dfrac{\sigma}{j\omega}$ is the complex dielectric constant.

Equations (39) and (40), which are partial derivative equations of second degree in hyperbolic form, describe the propagation of the electromagnetic field. Their solutions describe the electromagnetic wave.

If V and $\vec{A}$ are the scalar and respectively vectorial potentials,

$$\vec{E} = -grad \quad V - \frac{\partial \vec{A}}{\partial t}$$

$$\vec{B} = \nabla^2 \vec{A}$$

and V and $\vec{A}$ are the solutions to the partial derivative equations:

$$\nabla^2 V - \mu'\varepsilon'\frac{\partial^2 V}{\partial t^2} = -\frac{\rho}{\varepsilon}$$

$$\nabla^2 \vec{A} - \mu'\varepsilon'\frac{\partial^2 \vec{A}}{\partial t^2} = -\mu'\vec{j} \qquad (42)$$

when the supplementary condition below is met:

$$\nabla \bullet \vec{A} + \mu'\varepsilon'\frac{\partial V}{\partial t} = 0$$

In a stationary regime, the solutions for equation (42) are:

$$V = \frac{1}{4\pi\varepsilon'}\iiint\limits_V \frac{\rho}{r} dV \quad \vec{A} = \frac{\mu'}{4\pi}\iiint\limits_V \frac{\vec{j}}{r} dV$$

and in a nonstationary regime:

$$V = \frac{1}{4\pi\varepsilon'}\iiint\limits_V \frac{\rho\left(t - \dfrac{r}{v}\right)}{r} dV \quad \vec{A} = \frac{\mu'}{4\pi}\iiint\limits_V \frac{\vec{j}\left(t - \dfrac{r}{v}\right)}{r} dV$$

Poynting's Vector. From (34) and (35),

$$\nabla \bullet \left(\vec{E} \times \vec{H}\right) + \frac{\partial}{\partial t}\left(\frac{\varepsilon'E^2}{2} + \frac{\mu'H^2}{2}\right) = -\vec{E} \times \vec{j} \qquad (43)$$

If E' is the impressed electric field and since:

$$\vec{E} + \vec{E}' = \frac{\vec{j}}{\sigma},$$

(43) can be written:

$$\nabla \bullet \left(\vec{E} \times \vec{H} \right) + \frac{1}{2} \frac{\partial}{\partial t} \left(\varepsilon' E^2 + \mu' H^2 \right) + \frac{j^2}{\sigma} = \vec{j} \times \vec{E}' \tag{43a}$$

Integrating (43a) on the volume V bordered by surface Σ, we have:

$$\iiint_V \vec{j}\, \vec{E}'\, dV = \iiint_V \frac{j^2}{\sigma}\, dV + \frac{\partial}{\partial t} \iiint_V \frac{1}{2} \left(\varepsilon' E^2 + \mu' H^2 \right) dV + \iint_\Sigma \left(\vec{E} \times \vec{H} \right) \tag{44}$$

Physically, (44) expresses the fact that the energy per unit of time (i.e., power) due to the emf impressed in volume V is equal to the sum of the power developed through Joule effect, the variation of electric and magnetic field power, and the power exiting the surface Σ.

The vector $\vec{S} = \vec{E} \times \vec{H}$ (W/m^2) is Poynting's vector, which describes the phenomena of electromagnetic energy propagation. Its flux through a given area is used to calculate the power radiated by an antenna.

PROBLEM 7:

Calculate the magnetic induction B at a distance R from an infinitely long straight wire carrying a current I. Refer to the accompanying figure.

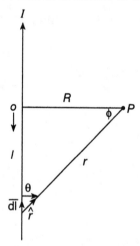

Figure 10

SOLUTION:

The Biot-Savart law is:

$$\vec{B} = \frac{\mu_0}{4\pi} \oint \frac{I \times d\vec{l} \times \hat{r}}{r^2}$$

where $\hat{r}$ is a unit vector pointing from the current element $I \times dl$ to point P. $\vec{B}$ is in the direction of $dl \times \hat{r}$, which is perpendicular to the plane of the paper and points into the paper.

$$B_p = \frac{\mu_0 I}{4\pi} \oint \frac{\vec{dl} \times \sin\theta}{r^2}$$

In order to integrate, express all the variables in terms of a single variable. Here ϕ will be used.

$$\sin\theta = \cos\phi; \quad \frac{l}{R} = \tan\phi; \quad l = R\tan\phi; \quad dl = R\sec^2\phi \, d\phi; \quad r = \frac{R}{\cos\phi}.$$

Limits of ϕ are from $-\pi/2$ to $+\pi/2$.

Therefore,

$$B = \frac{\mu_0 I}{4\pi} \int_{-\frac{\pi}{2}}^{\frac{\pi}{2}} \frac{\left(R \times \sec^2\phi \times d\phi\right)\cos^2\phi \times \cos\phi}{R^2}$$

$$= \frac{\mu_0 I}{4\pi R} \int_{-\frac{\pi}{2}}^{\frac{\pi}{2}} \cos\phi \times d\phi = \frac{\mu_0 I}{4\pi R}[\sin\phi]_{-\frac{\pi}{2}}^{\frac{\pi}{2}}$$

$$= \frac{\mu_0 I}{4\pi R} \times 2 = \frac{\mu_0 I}{2\pi R}$$

PROBLEM 8:

A circular coil of diameter 20 mm is mounted with the plane of the coil perpendicular to the direction of a uniform magnetic flux density of 100 mT. Find the total flux threading the coil.

SOLUTION:

The flux is given by $\Phi = \int B \times ds$. As the flux density is uniform, $\Phi = B \times A$.

The vector area is normal to the plane of the area so that the vector flux density is parallel to the vector area, and the required flux is the product of the flux density and the area. Therefore,

$$\Phi = 10^{-1} \times \pi \times 10^{-4} = 3.14 \times 10^{-5} \, \text{Wb} = 31.4 \mu\text{Wb}.$$

PROBLEM 9:

Find the flux density at a distance of 20 cm from a north pole of strength 550 ampere-meters in a medium with relative permeability 50. Also find the force on another north pole of equal strength at this distance. Assume that the south poles are at a large distance.

SOLUTION:

The flux density is:

$$B = \frac{\mu_0 \mu_r Q_m}{4\pi r^2} = \frac{4\pi \times 10^{-7} \times 50 \times 550}{4\pi \times (0.2)^2} = 6.875 \times 10^{-2} \, \text{newton/ampere-meter}.$$

Since the pole is positive, the direction of B is radially away from the pole. Another pole of equal strength at this point is acted on by a force of magnitude,

$$F = Q_m B = 550 \times 6.875 \times 10^{-2} = 37.8 \, \text{N}.$$

The direction of the force F is the same as for the flux density B.

PROBLEM 10:

If the mean radius of a toroidal coil is 10 cm and it has 1,500 turns, find the average self-inductance with (a) an air core, (b) and an iron core having an average relative incremental permeability of 100.

SOLUTION:

(a)   The self-inductance is $L = \dfrac{N^2 \mu A}{l}$ where, for this problem, $N = 1500$ turns, $\mu = 4\pi \times 10^{-7}$ H/m (air core), and $A = \pi \times (10^{-1})^2$.

Therefore,

$$L = \frac{(1,500)^2 \times 4\pi \times 10^{-7} \times \pi \times (10^{-1})^2}{2\pi \times (10^{-1})} = 141.37 \, \text{mH}.$$

(b)   Here $\mu = 100 \times 4\,\pi \times 10^{-7}$ H/m. Therefore,

$$L = \frac{(1,500)^2 \times 100 \times 4\pi \times 10^{-7} \times \pi \times (10^{-1})^2}{2\pi \times (10^{-1})^2} = 14.137 \text{ H.}$$

PROBLEM 11:

A single turn loop is situated in air, with a uniform magnetic field normal to its plane. The area of the loop is 5 m^2. What is the emf appearing at the terminals of the loop, if the rate of change of flux density is 2 Wb/m^2/s?

SOLUTION:

According to Faraday's law for a loop of N turns, where all turns are linked by the same flux Φ_m, the emf is:

$$E = -N \frac{d\phi_m}{dt}$$

Thus,

$$E = -\frac{d\phi_m}{dt} = -\frac{d(B_m \times area)}{dt} = -\frac{dB_m}{dt} \times area = -2 \times 5 = -10 \text{ V.}$$

PROBLEM 12:

Given an electric field:

$$\vec{E} = \vec{j}A \times \cos \omega \left(t - \frac{z}{c} \right),$$

determine the time-dependent magnetic intensity $\vec{H}$ in free space.

SOLUTION:

Use Maxwell's equation:

$$\nabla \times \vec{E} = -\frac{\partial \vec{B}}{\partial t} = -\mu_0 \frac{\partial \vec{H}}{\partial t}$$

where $\vec{B}$ is the magnetic induction and μ_0 is the permeability of free space. Expanding the $\nabla \times \vec{E}$ in rectangular coordinates:

$$\vec{i}\left(\frac{\partial E_z}{\partial y} - \frac{\partial E_y}{\partial z}\right) + \vec{j}\left(\frac{\partial E_x}{\partial z} - \frac{\partial E_z}{\partial x}\right) + \vec{k}\left(\frac{\partial E_y}{\partial x} - \frac{\partial E_x}{\partial y}\right) = -\mu_0 \frac{\partial \vec{H}}{\partial t}$$

$E_z = E_x = 0$, $E_y = f(t, z)$ only.

$$-\vec{i}\,\frac{\partial E_y}{\partial z} = -\mu_0 \frac{\partial \vec{H}}{\partial t}.$$

Therefore,

$$\frac{\partial E_y}{\partial z} = \frac{\partial}{\partial z}\left[A \times \cos\omega\left(t - \frac{z}{c}\right)\right] = \frac{\omega}{c} A \times \sin\omega\left(t - \frac{z}{c}\right)$$

$$H_x = \frac{\omega A}{c\mu_0}\int \sin\omega\left(t - \frac{z}{c}\right) dt = -\frac{A}{c\mu_0}\cos\omega\left(t - \frac{z}{c}\right) + C_1$$

$$\vec{H} = -\frac{\vec{i}A}{c\mu_0}\cos\omega\left(t - \frac{z}{c}\right)$$

The constant C_1 can be set equal to zero since fields that are constant in time do not influence the time varying part.

PROBLEM 13:

Consider a simple magnetic field that increases exponentially with time, as described by the function: $\vec{B} = B_0 e^{bt}\,\vec{a}_z$, where B_0 is constant. Find the electric field produced by this varying field $\vec{B}$.

SOLUTION:

Choose a circular path of radius a in the $z = 0$ plane, along which E_ϕ must be constant by symmetry.

$$\text{emf} = \oint \vec{E} \times d\vec{l} = -\int_s \frac{\partial \vec{B}}{\partial t} d\vec{s}; \quad \text{emf} = 2\pi a E_\phi = -b \times B_0 e^{bt}\pi a^2$$

The emf around this closed path is $-b \times B_0\, e^{bt}\, \pi\, a^2$. It is proportional to a^2, since the magnetic flux density is uniform and the flux passing through the surface at any instant is proportional to the area. The emf is evidently the same for any other path in the $z = 0$ plane enclosing the same area. Replacing a by r, the electric field intensity at any point is thus

$$\vec{E} = -\frac{1}{2} b \times B_0 e^{bt} r \vec{a}_\phi.$$

Alternatively,

$$\left(\nabla \times \vec{E}\right) = -\frac{\partial \vec{B}}{\partial t}$$

which becomes:

$$\left(\nabla \times \vec{E}\right)_z = -b \times B_0 e^{bt} = \frac{1}{r}\frac{\partial(r \times E_\phi)}{\partial r}.$$

Rearranging the equation and integrating from 0 to r (treating t as a constant, since the derivative is a partial derivative),

$$\frac{1}{2} b \times B_0 e^{bt} r^2 = r \times E_\phi + K$$

or, once again,

$$\vec{E} = -\frac{1}{2} b \times B_0 e^{bt} r \vec{a}_\phi.$$

PROBLEM 14:

If 5 W/m² is the Poynting vector of a plane wave travelling in free space, what is its average energy density?

SOLUTION:

The Poynting vector, energy density, and the velocity are related by:

$$\frac{\text{Poynting vector}}{\text{Velocity}} = \text{Energy density, i.e., } \frac{S_{av}}{v} = w_{av}.$$

Here
$$v \text{ (in free space)} \approx 3 \times 10^8 \text{ m/s}$$
$$S_{av} = 5 \text{ W/m}^2 \text{ (given)}$$

Therefore,

$$w_{av} = \frac{5}{3 \times 10^8} = \frac{5 \times 10^{-8}}{3} \text{ J/m}^3.$$

PROBLEM 15:

Consider a straight wire of radius r_o oriented along the Z-axis carrying a steady current I. Determine the total power entering a unit length of wire.

SOLUTION:

First, find the electric and magnetic fields of this configuration. The magnetic field at the surface of the wire is:

$$\vec{H} = \frac{1}{2\pi r_0} \vec{a}_\phi.$$

The electric field is in the Z-direction and it is equal to:

$$\vec{E} = \frac{\vec{J}}{\sigma} = \frac{J\vec{a}_z}{\sigma} = \frac{I}{\pi r_0^2 \sigma} \vec{a}_z.$$

Hence, the Poynting vector at the surface of the wire is equal to:

$$\vec{S} = \vec{E}_z \times \vec{H}_\phi = -\frac{I^2}{2\pi^2 r_0^3 \sigma} \vec{a}_r$$

The total power entering a unit length of wire is:

$$\oint_s \vec{S} \times d\vec{s} = \frac{I^2}{2\pi^2 r_0^3 \sigma} \times 2\pi r_0 = I^2 \frac{1}{\pi r_0^2 \sigma} = I^2 \times R$$

The resistance of a conductor is $R = l/s\sigma$ where l is the conductor length, $s = \pi r_o^2$ is the conductor cross-section area, σ is the material conductivity, and r_o is the conductor radius. This indicates that the field supplies the energy to balance out the $I^2 R$ (Joule) heat losses in the wire. The contribution to the surface integral is only from the cylindrical part of the surface. The contribution from the top and the bottom surfaces is zero since $\vec{E}_z \times \vec{H}_\phi$ is perpendicular to $d\vec{s}$.

FE/EIT

FE: PM Electrical Engineering Exam

CHAPTER 10

Instrumentation

CHAPTER 10

INSTRUMENTATION

VOLTMETER LOADING EFFECTS

When using a voltmeter to measure the voltage across a circuit component, the resistance of the voltmeter itself is in parallel with the circuit component which results in a lesser total resistance value. The voltage across the component is, thus, less when the voltmeter is connected.

PROBLEM 1:

A voltmeter is used to measure the voltage across the load resistor R_L in the circuit below.

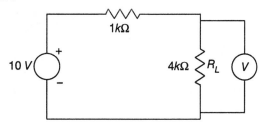

Figure 1

The voltmeter has a sensitivity of $S = 20 \; k\Omega/V$ in its $10V$ range.

Calculate the percentage error.

SOLUTION:

The actual voltage across the load resistor is:

$$V_L = 10 \; V \left[\frac{4k\Omega}{4k\Omega + 1k\Omega} \right] = 8 \text{ volts}$$

The resistance of the meter in its $10V$ range is:

$$R_m = 20k\Omega / V \times 10V = 200\,k\Omega$$

The load resistance with the meter connected is:

$$R_{Lm} = \frac{(4k\Omega)(200k\Omega)}{4k\Omega + 200k\Omega} = 3.92k\Omega$$

The measured voltage across the load resistor is:

$$V_{Lm} = 10V\left[\frac{3.92k\Omega}{3.92k\Omega + 1k\Omega}\right] = 7.97V$$

The percentage error is:

$$\frac{(8V - 7.97V)}{8V} \times 100\% = 0.38\%$$

AMMETER LOADING EFFECT

All ammeters contain some internal resistance. When an ammeter is inserted in a circuit, the resistance of the circuit is increased and therefore reduces the circuit current.

PROBLEM 2:

An ammeter with an internal resistance of 50 ohms is used to measure the current through the load resistor R_L of the circuit below.

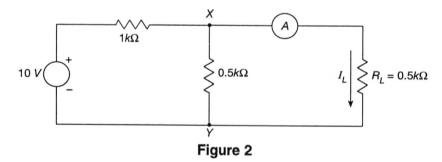

Figure 2

Calculate the percentage of error due to ammeter loading.

SOLUTION:

First, calculate the actual load current without the meter.

$$V_{xy} = 10V\left[\frac{0.25k\Omega}{0.25k\Omega + 1k\Omega}\right] = 2.0V$$

$$I_L = \frac{2.0V}{0.5k\Omega} = 4mA$$

With the meter connected, we have the internal resistance of the meter in series with the load resistance: $0.5\ k\Omega + 0.05\ k\Omega = 0.55\ k\Omega$.

$0.5\ k\Omega$ in parallel with $0.55\ k\Omega$ gives:

$$\frac{(0.5k\Omega)(0.55k\Omega)}{0.5k\Omega + 0.55k\Omega} = 0.26k\Omega$$

$$V_{xyM} = 10V\left[\frac{0.26k\Omega}{0.26k\Omega + 1k\Omega}\right] = 2.06V$$

The measured load current is:

$$I_{LM} = \frac{2.06V}{0.55k\Omega} = 3.75mA$$

The percentage error is:

$$\frac{4.0 - 3.75}{3.75} \times 100\% = 6.67\%$$

SUMMING AMPLIFIER

Inverting Configuration

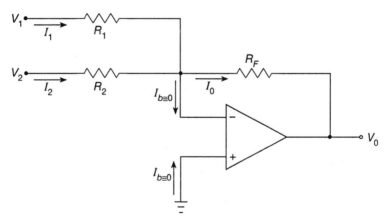

Figure 3

For an ideal operational amplifier, such as would be applied in instrumentation, the input bias current $I_b = 0$ and $V_i = 0$. Using Kirchhoff's current law, we have:

$$I_1 + I_2 = I_0$$

$$\frac{V_1}{R_1} + \frac{V_2}{R_2} = -\frac{V_0}{R_F}$$

If we select $R_1 = R_2 = R_F$, then:

$$V_0 = -(V_1 + V_2)$$

This can be extended to any number of inputs:

$$V_0 = -(V_1 + V_2 + ... + V_n)$$

This circuit is called an inverting summing amplifier.

PROBLEM 3:

The inverting summing amplifier can also be used as a scaling or weighted amplifier by choosing different values for the input resistors. Consider the following circuit:

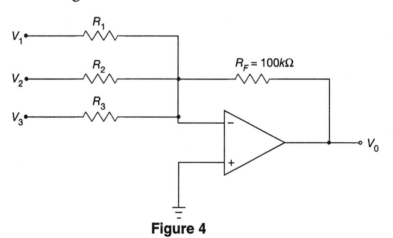

Figure 4

Determine the values for R_1, R_2, and R_3 so that:

$$V_0 = -(5V_1 + 2V_2 + 4V_3).$$

SOLUTION:

Using Kirchhoff's current law, we have:

$$\frac{V_1}{R_1} + \frac{V_2}{R_2} + \frac{V_3}{R_3} = \frac{-V_0}{R_F}$$

Solving for V_0:

$$V_0 = -\left(\frac{R_F}{R_1} \times V_1 + \frac{R_F}{R_2} \times V_2 + \frac{R_F}{R_3} \times V_3\right)$$

Hence:

$$\frac{R_F}{R_1} = 5; \quad \frac{R_F}{R_2} = 2; \quad \frac{R_F}{R_3} = 4$$

for $R_F = 100 \text{ k}\Omega$.

Solving for R_1, R_2, and R_3, we obtain:

$$R_1 = 20k\Omega; \quad R_2 = 50k\Omega; \quad R_3 = 25k\Omega$$

Non-inverting Configuration

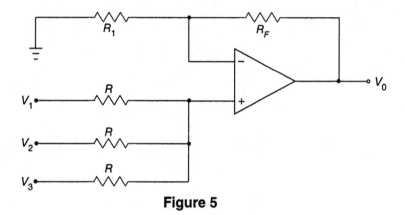

Figure 5

Using the superposition theorem, the output voltage V_0 is:

$$V_0 = \left(1 + \frac{R_F}{R_1}\right)\left(\frac{V_1 + V_2 + V_3}{3}\right)$$

If we select

$$\left(1 + \frac{R_F}{R_1}\right) = 3$$

then:

$$V_0 = V_1 + V_2 + V_3$$

This circuit is called a non-inverting summing amplifier.

INSTRUMENTATION AMPLIFIER

The figure below shows a simplified differential instrumentation amplifier using a transducer bridge. A resistive transducer whose resistance changes as a function of some physical energy is connected in one arm of the bridge and is denoted as $R_T \pm \Delta R$. ΔR is the change in the resistance R_T. Commonly used resistive transducers are thermistors, photoconductive cells, and strain gages.

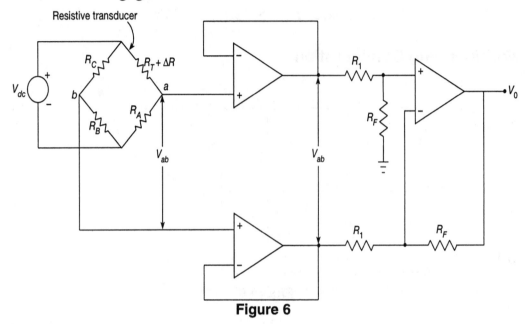

Figure 6

For a balanced bridge:

$$V_a = V_b$$

or:

$$\left(\frac{R_A}{R_A + R_T}\right)V_{dc} = \left(\frac{R_B}{R_B + R_C}\right)V_{dc}$$

$$\Rightarrow \frac{R_C}{R_B} = \frac{R_A}{R_T}$$

R_A, R_B, and R_C are selected to be equal to R_T at some reference condition. As the physical quantity to be measured changes, the resistance of the transducer changes, which causes the bridge to become unbalanced.

Let ΔR be the change in the resistance of the transducer. Selecting $R_A = R_B = R_C = R_T = R$, we have:

$$V_{ab} = -\frac{\Delta R \times V_{dc}}{2(2R + \Delta R)}$$

The two voltage follower circuits (unity gain) are connected ahead of the differential amplifier circuit to help eliminate the loading of the bridge circuit.

$$V_0 = V_{ab} \times \frac{(R_F)}{R_1} = -\frac{\Delta R \times V_{dc}}{2(2R + \Delta R)} \times \frac{R_F}{R_1}$$

Note that the output voltage is a function of the change in resistance, ΔR, of the transducer.

PROBLEM 4:

In the instrumentation amplifier circuit, $R_1 = 1\ k\Omega$, $R_F = 5\ k\Omega$, R_A, R_B, and R_C are equal to 400 $k\Omega$. $V_{dc} = 5V$. The transducer is a thermistor with the following data:

$R_T = 400\ k\Omega$ at a reference temperature of 25°C.

The temperature coefficient of the resistance is $-10\ k\Omega/\ °C$.

Determine the output voltage at 0°C and at 75°C.

SOLUTION:

At 25°C, R_A, R_B, R_C, and R_T are equal to 400 $k\Omega$.

The bridge is balanced, $V_{ab} = 0 \Rightarrow V_0 = 0$.

At 0°C, the change in the resistance of the thermistor is:

$$\Delta R = (0°C - 25°C)(-10k\Omega/°C) = 250k\Omega.$$

$$V_0 = V_{ab} \times \frac{(R_F)}{R_1} = -\frac{\Delta R \times V_{dc}}{2(2R + \Delta R)} \times \frac{R_F}{R_1}$$

$$V_0 = -\frac{(250k\Omega)(5V)}{2(800k\Omega + 250k\Omega)} \times \frac{5k\Omega}{1k\Omega} = -2.98V$$

Similarly, at 75°C, the change in the resistance of the thermistor is:

$$\Delta R = (75°C - 25°C)(-10k\Omega/°C) = -500k\Omega.$$

$$V_0 = -\frac{(-500k\Omega)(5V)}{2(800k\Omega - 500k\Omega)} \times \frac{5k\Omega}{1k\Omega} = 20.83V$$

FE/EIT

FE: PM Electrical Engineering Exam

CHAPTER 11

Network Analysis

CHAPTER 11

NETWORK ANALYSIS

BASIC CIRCUIT LAWS

Ohm's Law

Ohm's Law is the relationship between voltage (V), current (i), and resistance (R):

$$V = Ri \ \text{ or } \ i = GV$$

where $G = \dfrac{1}{R}$ is the conductance measured in siemens (S).

The power delivered to a resistor is:

$$p = vi = \frac{V^2}{R} = i^2 R$$

Kirchhoff's Laws

Kirchhoff's Voltage Law (KVL) states that the algebraic sum of the voltages around any closed loop in a network is equal to zero. $\Sigma V = 0$.

Kirchhoff's Current Law (KCL) states that the algebraic sum of all the currents entering or sum of all the currents leaving a node is equal to zero. $\Sigma i = 0$.

Series and Parallel Circuits

Circuit elements connected in series carry the same current. If n resistances are connected in series, the equivalent resistance is given by:

$$R_{es} = R_1 + R_2 + R_3 + ... + R_n = \Sigma R_k$$

Circuit elements that are connected in parallel have the same voltage across them. For n resistances connected in parallel, the equivalent resistance is:

$$\frac{1}{R_{ep}} = \frac{1}{R_1} + \frac{1}{R_2} + ... + \frac{1}{R_n} = \Sigma \frac{1}{R_k}$$

Voltage and Current Divider Circuits

The voltage, V_k, across the kth resistor of n resistors connected in series is:

$$V_k = \frac{R_k}{R_{es}} V_s = \frac{R_k}{R_1 + R_2 + ... + R_n} V_s$$

The current, I_k, in the kth resistor of n resistors connected in parallel is:

$$I_k = \frac{R_{ep}}{R_k} I_p$$

CIRCUIT ANALYSIS METHODS

Nodal Analysis

The nodal method of circuit analysis is based on writing Kirchhoff's current equations. The steps involved in solving a circuit with n major nodes are as follows:

1. Select one major node as the reference node.

2. Write Kirchhoff's current equation at each of the $n-1$ nodes.

3. Solve for the unknown node voltages from the set of simultaneous equations.

PROBLEM 1:

Solve for the current i_x.

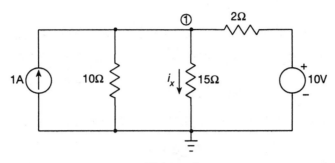

Figure 1

SOLUTION:

This circuit has two major nodes. Choose one node as the reference node. Hence, we need only one current equation to solve this problem. Writing the KCL equation at node ①, we have:

$$1 - \frac{V_1}{10} - \frac{V_1}{15} + \frac{10 - V_1}{2} = 0$$

$$V_1 = 9V; \; i_x = \frac{9V}{15 \, \Omega} = 0.6 \, A$$

Mesh Analysis

Mesh analysis is based on Kirchhoff's voltage equations. The number of meshes in a circuit is determined from the following equation:

$$m = b - n + 1$$

m = number of meshes

b = number of branches

n = number of nodes

The steps involved in solving a circuit using mesh analysis are as follows:

1. Determine the number of meshes.

2. Write Kirchhoff's voltage equation for each mesh.

3. Solve for the unknown mesh currents from the set of simultaneous voltage equations.

PROBLEM 2:

Find the mesh currents I_1 and I_2.

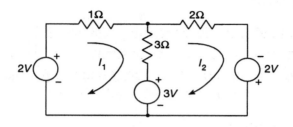

Figure 2

SOLUTION:

Applying KVL around mesh 1:

$$-2 + 1I_1 + 3(I_1 - I_2) + 3 = 0$$
$$4I_1 - 3I_2 = -1$$

Applying KVL around mesh 2:

$$-2 - 3 + 3(I_2 - I_1) + 2I_2 = 0$$
$$-3I_1 + 5I_2 = 5$$

Rearranging the equations in matrix form:

$$\begin{bmatrix} -1 \\ 5 \end{bmatrix} = \begin{bmatrix} 4 & -3 \\ -3 & 5 \end{bmatrix} \times \begin{bmatrix} I_1 \\ I_2 \end{bmatrix}$$

Solving for I_1 and I_2, we obtain $I_1 = \dfrac{10}{11} A$ and $I_2 = \dfrac{17}{11} A$.

NETWORK THEOREMS

The Superposition Theorem

The superposition theorem states that for a *linear* circuit containing independent sources, the voltage across or the current through any element can be obtained by adding algebraically all the individual voltages or currents contributed by each independent source acting alone, with all other independent sources reduced to zero (i.e., replacing the non-acting independent voltage sources by short circuits and non-acting independent current sources by open circuits).

Thevenin's Theorem

Any two-terminal network containing voltage or current sources can be replaced by an equivalent circuit consisting of a voltage equal to the open circuit voltage E_{th} in series with the resistance R_{th} looking back into the original circuit measured at the identified terminal pair.

E_{th} = open-circuit voltage E_{oc}

R_{th} = Thevenin resistance looking back into the original circuit with the sources removed (open circuit for current sources and short circuits for voltage sources)

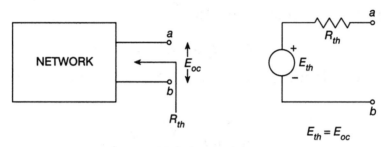

Figure 3

Norton's Theorem

Any two-terminal network containing voltage or current sources can be replaced by an equivalent circuit consisting of a current source equal to the short circuit current, I_N, in parallel with the resistance R_N ($R_N = R_{th}$) looking back into the original circuit measured at the identified terminal pair.

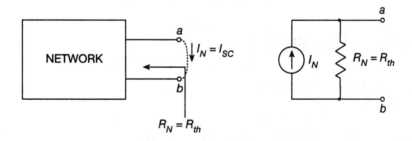

Figure 4

Maximum Power Transfer Theorem

The maximum power delivered by a source represented by its Thevenin equivalent circuit is achieved when the load R_L is equal to R_{th}.

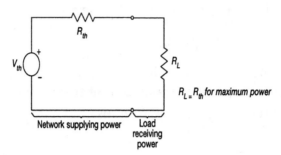

Figure 5

Power delivered to the load is:

$$P_L = \left[\frac{V_{th}}{R_{th} + R_L} \right]^2 R_L$$

PROBLEM 3:

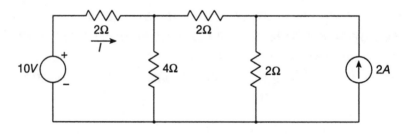

Figure 6

Determine the current I using the superposition principle.

SOLUTION:

With the 10 V source acting alone, we have:

$$I_1 = \frac{10V}{2\Omega + \dfrac{(4\Omega)(4\Omega)}{4\Omega + 4\Omega}}$$

$$I_1 = \frac{10V}{4\Omega} = 2.5A$$

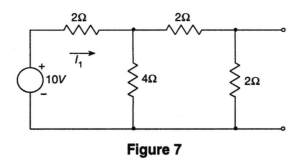

Figure 7

With the 2*A* current source acting alone, we have:

$$I_T = -\frac{2\Omega}{\dfrac{(2\Omega)(4\Omega)}{2\Omega + 4\Omega} + 2\Omega + 2\Omega}$$

$$I_T = -\left[\frac{2}{\dfrac{8}{6} + 2 + 2}\right](2A) = -\left[\frac{12}{8 + 24}\right](2A) = -0.75A$$

$$I_2 = -\frac{0.75A(4)}{4 + 2} = -0.5A$$

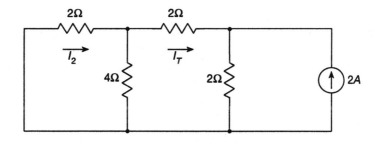

Figure 8

By superposition:

$$I = I_1 + I_2 = 2.5A - 0.5A = 2.0A$$

PROBLEM 4:

Find the Thevenin equivalent circuit at terminal $a - b$ for the circuit shown.

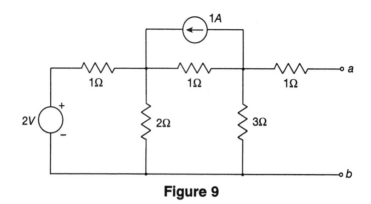

Figure 9

SOLUTION:

Using source transformation, we have the following circuit:

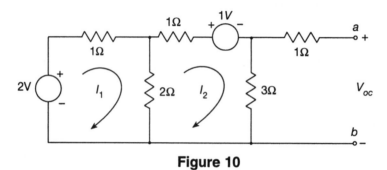

Figure 10

Applying KVL around meshes 1 and 2, respectively, we obtain:

$$3I_1 - 2I_2 = 2$$

$$-2I_1 + 6I_2 = -1$$

Solving for I_2, we find $I_2 = \dfrac{1}{14} A$

$$V_{th} = V_{oc} = (3)(I_2) = \frac{3}{14} V$$

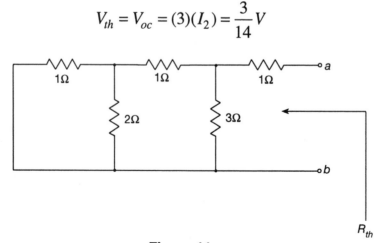

Figure 11

$$R_{th} = \left\{ \left[\frac{2}{3} + 1 \right] // 3 \right\} + 1$$

$$= \frac{\left(\frac{5}{3} \right) 3}{\left(\frac{5}{3} \right) + 3} + 1 = \frac{15}{14} + 1 = \frac{29}{14} \Omega$$

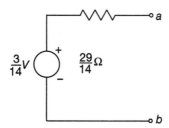

Figure 12

TRANSIENT ANALYSIS

Capacitors

The capacitor is an energy storage device that is represented by the following:

The relationship between the voltage and current is:

$$i = C \frac{dv}{dt}$$

where C is the capacitance in farads (F).

The voltage across a capacitor can be found by integration.

$$v = v(t_o) + \frac{1}{C} \int_{t_o}^{t} i \; dt$$

where $v(t_o)$ is the voltage at t_o.

The energy stored in the capacitor is:

$$W_c = \frac{1}{2}Cv^2$$

Inductors

The inductor is an energy storage device that is represented by the following:

The relationship between the voltage and current is:

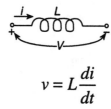

$$v = L\frac{di}{dt}$$

where L is the inductance in henrys (H).

The integral relationship between the voltage and current can be derived from the above differential relationship and is equal to:

$$i = \frac{1}{L}\int_{t_o}^{t} v \ dt + i(t_o)$$

where $i(t_o)$ is the current at t_o.

The energy stored in the inductor is:

$$W_L = \frac{1}{2}Li^2$$

The Natural Response of an RL or RC Circuit

The natural response of a circuit depends only on the internal energy storage of the circuit and not on the external sources.

For an RL circuit:

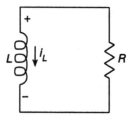

Figure 13

The natural response is $i_L = I_o e^{(-R/L)t}$ where $i_L(0) = I_o$ is the initial inductor current.

For an RC circuit:

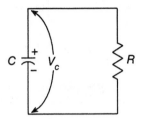

Figure 14

The natural response is $v_c(t) = V_o e^{-t/RC}$ where $v_c(0) = V_0$ is the initial voltage on the capacitor.

The Step Response of an RL or RC Circuit

The response of a circuit to a sudden application of an external constant voltage or current source is referred to as the step response of the circuit.

The step response of an RL circuit is:

$$i_L(t) = i_L(\infty) + [i_L(0) - i_L(\infty)] \, e^{-t/\tau}$$

where:

$\tau = \dfrac{L}{R}$ is the time constant

$i_L(\infty)$ is the steady-state current value at $t = \infty$

$i_L(0)$ is the initial current value at $t = 0$

The step response of an RC circuit is:

$$v_c(t) = v_c(\infty) + [v_c(0) - v_c(\infty)] \, e^{-t/T}$$

where:

$\tau = RC$ is the time constant

$v_c(\infty)$ is the steady-state voltage value at $t = \infty$

$v_c(0)$ is the initial voltage value at $t = 0$

PROBLEM 5:

After it is closed for a long time, the switch of the circuit shown is opened at $t = 0$.

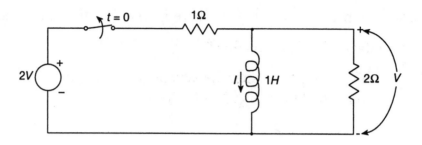

Figure 15

(a) Find the current I at $t = 0^-$.

(b) Find the voltage V across the 2 ohm resistor at $t = 0^+$.

SOLUTION:

(a) Since the switch has been closed for a long time,

$$V_L = L\frac{di}{dt} = 0,$$

the inductor is a short and the current I at $t = 0^-$ is:

$$I(0^-) = \frac{2\,V}{1\,\Omega} = 2\,A$$

(b) After the switch is open, we have:

$$I(0^+) = I(0^-) = 2\,A$$

since the inductor current cannot change instantaneously.

$$V = -(2\,A)(2\,\Omega) = -4\,V$$

PROBLEM 6:

The switch is closed at time $t = 0$. Find $v_c(t)$ for the following circuit:

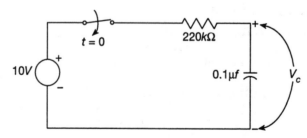

Figure 16

SOLUTION:

$$v_c(t) = v_c(\infty) + [v_c(0) - v_c(\infty)]e^{-t/RC}$$

$V_c(\infty) = 10\ V$ (a long time after the switch is closed, the capacitor voltage will be charged to $10V$)

$V_c(0) = 0$

$V_c(t) = 10 - 10e^{-t/0.022}$

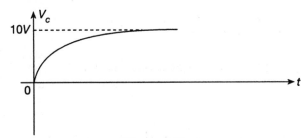

Figure 17

The Natural Response of a RLC Circuit

Consider the parallel RLC circuit:

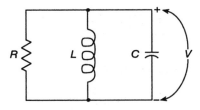

Figure 18

The time domain equation is:

$$\frac{d^2V}{dt^2} + \frac{1}{RC}\frac{dv}{dt} + \frac{V}{LC} = 0$$

The characteristic equation is:

$$s^2 + 2\alpha s + \omega_0^2 = 0$$

where:

$$2\alpha = \frac{1}{RC} \quad \text{or} \quad \alpha = \frac{1}{2RC}$$

$$\omega_0^2 = \frac{1}{LC} \quad \text{or} \quad \omega_0 = \sqrt{\frac{1}{LC}}$$

The roots of the characteristic equation are:

$$s_1 = -\alpha + \sqrt{\alpha^2 - \omega_0^2}$$

$$s_2 = -\alpha - \sqrt{\alpha^2 - \omega_0^2}$$

Three possible conditions:

1. $\alpha^2 > \omega_0^2$:　　　　　　　　　　Two real distinct roots

   $v = K_1 e^{+s_1 t} + K_2 e^{+s_2 t}$　　　　(overdamped natural response)

2. $\alpha^2 = \omega_0^2$:　　　　　　　　　　Two real equal roots

   $v = e^{-\alpha t} (K_1 t + K_2)$　　　　　(critically damped response)

3. $\alpha^2 < \omega_0^2$:　　　　　　　　　　Two complex roots

   $v = e^{-\alpha t} (C_1 \cos\omega_d t + C_2 \sin\omega_d t)$　(underdamped response)

   where:

$$\omega_d = \sqrt{\omega_0^2 - \alpha^2} \text{ is the damped resonant frequency.}$$

Consider the series RLC circuit:

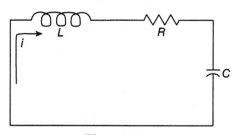

Figure 19

The time domain equation is:

$$\frac{d^2 i}{dt^2} + \frac{R}{L}\frac{di}{dt} + \frac{i}{LC} = 0$$

The characteristic equation is:

$$s^2 + 2\alpha s + \omega_0^2 = 0$$

where:

$$2\alpha = \frac{R}{L} \text{ or } \alpha = \frac{R}{2L}$$

$$\omega_0^2 = \frac{1}{LC} \text{ or } \omega_0 = \sqrt{\frac{1}{LC}}$$

The series RLC circuit is the dual of the parallel RLC circuit and the analysis is similar.

PROBLEM 7:

Find the current $i(t)$.

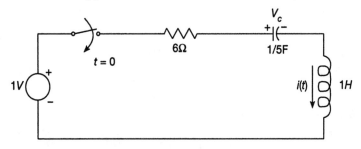

Figure 20

SOLUTION:

The characteristic equation is:

$$s^2 + 2\alpha s + \omega_0^2 = 0$$

$$\alpha = \frac{R}{2L} = \frac{6}{(2)(1)} = 3$$

$$\omega_0^2 = \frac{1}{LC} = \frac{1}{(1)\left(\frac{1}{5}\right)} = 5$$

$$s^2 + 6s + 5 = 0$$
$$s_1 = -1; \quad s_2 = -5$$
$$i(t) = K_1 e^{-t} + K_2 e^{-5t}$$

The initial conditions are: $i(0) = 0 => K_1 + K_2 = 0$

$$6i(0) + v_c(0) + \frac{di}{dt}\bigg|_{t=0} = 1$$

Since $i(0) = 0$ and $v_c(0) = 0$,

$$\left.\frac{di}{dt}\right|_{t=0} = 1$$

$$\frac{di}{dt} = -K_1 e^{-t} - 5K_2 e^{-5t}$$

$$\left.\frac{di}{dt}\right|_{t=0} = -K_1 - 5K_2 = 1$$

Thus, we have $K_1 + K_2 = 0$ and $-K_1 - 5K_2 = -1$

Solving for K_1 and K_2, we obtain $K_1 = {}^1/_4$ and $K_2 = -{}^1/_4$.

Thus,

$$i(t) = \frac{1}{4}e^{-t} - \frac{1}{4}e^{-5t}$$

SINUSOIDAL ANALYSIS

Consider the following *sinusoidal* voltage signal:

$$v(t) = V_m \cos(\omega t + \theta)$$

where:

$$\omega = 2\pi f = \frac{2\pi}{T} \text{(rad/sec)}$$

ω = angular frequency of the sinusoidal function

f = frequency or the number of cycles per second

T = period of the sinusoidal function

The phasor representation of $v(t)$ is represented by:

$$\vec{V} = V_m \angle\theta$$

$v(t)$, which is an explicit function of time, is in the *time domain*, whereas the phasor representation $\vec{V}$ is in the frequency domain.

Phasor transforms allow sinusoidal circuits to be analyzed in the frequency domain in a similar manner as resistive circuits by using the same basic tools of nodal analysis, mesh analysis, Thevenin-Norton equivalent, and the superposition principle.

To summarize, we have the following equations:

Time Domain	Frequency Domain
$v(t) = V_m\cos(\omega t + \theta)$	$\vec{V} = V_m\angle\theta$
$v = iR$	$\vec{V} = \vec{I}R$
$v = L\dfrac{di}{dt}$	$\vec{V} = (j\omega L)\vec{I}$
$v = \dfrac{1}{C}\int i\,dt$	$\vec{V} = \dfrac{1}{j\omega C}\vec{I}$

Table 1. Time Domain vs. Frequency Domain

PROBLEM 8:

Find the current $i(t)$ by means of frequency domain analysis.

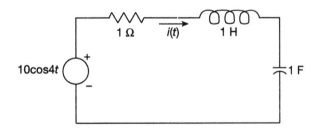

Figure 21

SOLUTION:

We have:

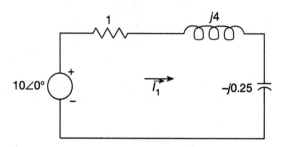

Figure 22

$$\omega = 4; \quad j\omega L = j4$$

$$\frac{1}{j\omega c} = \frac{1}{j4} = -j0.25$$

$$\vec{I} = \frac{10\angle 0°}{1 + j4 - j0.25} = 2.58 \angle -75.07°$$

$$\rightarrow i(t) = 2.58\cos(4t - 75.07°)$$

FE/EIT

FE: PM Electrical Engineering Exam

CHAPTER 12

Power Systems

CHAPTER 12

POWER SYSTEMS

THREE-PHASE POWER

The following power equations are associated with a balanced three-phase circuit connected either in wye ("Y") or delta ("Δ") configuration:

$$P = \sqrt{3}.\ V_L I_L \cos\theta$$

$$Q = \sqrt{3}.\ V_L I_L \sin\theta$$

$$S = \sqrt{3}.\ V_L I_L$$

where:

P = real power (kW)

Q = reactive power (kVAR)

S = apparent power (kVA)

V_L = line-to-line voltage

I_L = line current

$\cos\theta$ = power factor

θ = power factor angle

Expressed as a power triangle:

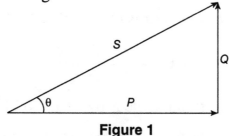

Figure 1

We have:

$$\tan\theta = \frac{Q}{P};$$

and

$$\cos\theta = \frac{P}{S} = \frac{P}{\sqrt{3}V_L I_L}$$

PROBLEM 1:

A 480-Vac three-phase source supplies power to the following two loads: a 10 kVA load at 0.8 power factor lagging, and a 20 kVA load at unity power factor ($\cos\theta = 1$).

(a) What is the total real power delivered to the two loads?

(b) What is the overall power factor?

(c) What is the line current drawn by the two loads?

SOLUTION:

(a) Load 1: $P_1 = (10)(0.8) = 8$ kW

$\qquad\quad\; Q_1 = (10)(0.6) = 6$ kVAR

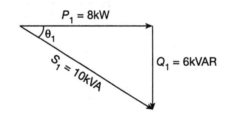

Figure 2

Load 2: $P_2 = 20$ kW $\qquad P_2 = 20$ kW

$\qquad\quad\; Q_2 = 0 \qquad\qquad\quad Q_2 = 0$

Note: Since $Q_2 = 0$, we do not have the vertical component.

The total real power delivered to the two loads is $P_T = 8$ kW $+ 20$ kW $= 28$ kW.

(b) The total reactive power is $Q_T = 6$ kVAR $+ 0 = 6$ kVAR.

$$\tan\theta_T = \frac{Q}{P} = \frac{6}{28} = 0.214$$

The overall power factor angle is $\theta_T = \tan^{-1}(0.214) = 12.09°$.

The overall power factor is $\cos\theta_T = \cos(12.09°) = 0.98$ lagging.

(c) The line current drawn by the two loads is:

$$I_L = \frac{P_T}{\sqrt{3} \times V_L \times \cos\theta_T} = \frac{28 \text{ kW}}{\sqrt{3} \times 480 \times 0.98} = 34.44 \text{ A}$$

IDEAL TRANSFORMER

An equivalent circuit of an ideal transformer is shown below:

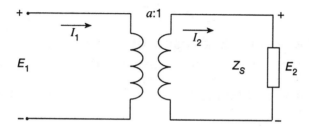

Figure 3

We have the following relationships for an ideal transformer:

$$\frac{E_1}{E_2} = \frac{I_2}{I_1} = a$$

where:

E_1 = primary applied voltage

E_2 = secondary induced voltage

I_1 = primary current

I_2 = secondary current

a = turns ratio

It can be shown that if an impedance, Z_S, is connected to the secondary, the impedance, Z_P, seen at the primary has the following relationship:

$$\frac{Z_P}{Z_S} = a^2$$

PROBLEM 2:

Consider the following transformer:

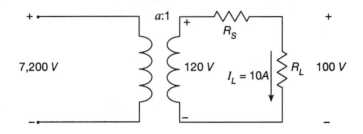

Figure 4

(a) If the resistive load draws $10A$, determine the value of the series resistance, R_S, so that we have $100V$ across this load.

(b) What would be the value of R_S if it were located in the primary winding?

SOLUTION:

(a) $R_S = \dfrac{120V - 100V}{10A} = 2$ ohms

(b) The turns ratio is $a = \dfrac{7200}{120} = 60$.

$R_S(\text{primary}) = (a^2)(2 \text{ ohms}) = (3{,}600)(2 \text{ ohms}) = 7{,}200$ ohms.

NON-IDEAL TRANSFORMER

When the effects of winding resistances, leakage reactances, magnetizing reactance, and core losses are taken into consideration, we have the following non-ideal transformer model:

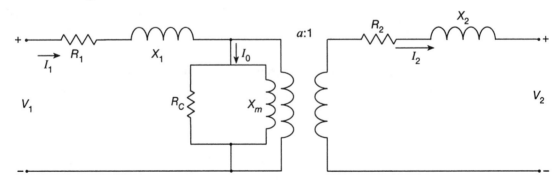

Figure 5. Non-ideal Transformer Model

where:

R_1 = resistance of the primary winding

R_2 = resistance of the secondary winding

X_1 = primary leakage reactance

X_2 = secondary leakage reactance

V_1 = primary terminal voltage

V_2 = secondary terminal voltage

X_m = magnetizing reactance

R_C = resistance accounting for the core losses

I_O = no-load (primary) current

Transformer equivalent circuits can be referred to either the primary or secondary as shown below:

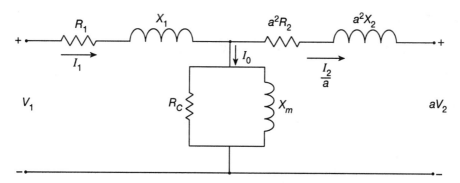

Figure 6. Transformer Equivalent Circuit Referred to the Primary

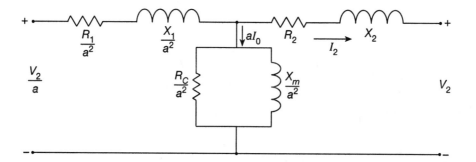

Figure 7. Transformer Equivalent Circuit Referred to the Secondary

PROBLEM 3:

A single-phase transformer has the following data on its nameplate:

$a = 10$

$x_1 = 5$ ohm

$x_2 = 0.5$ ohm

$x_m = 0$ (negligible)

$r_1 = 1$ ohm

$r_2 = 0.5$ ohm

$r_c = 0$ (negligible)

A resistive load of 0.8 ohm is connected to the secondary. A voltage of 2,400V is applied to the primary terminal. Calculate the secondary voltage.

SOLUTION:

The transformer equivalent circuit referred to the primary is shown below:

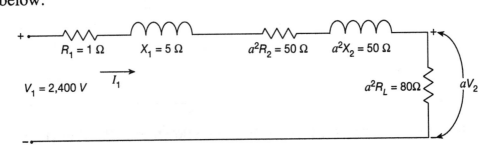

Figure 8

$$I_1 = \frac{2,400}{131 + j55} = \frac{2,400}{142.08 \angle 22.77} = 16.89 \angle -22.77°$$

$$aV_2 = (16.89 \angle -22.77°)(80 \text{ ohms}) = 1,351.2 \angle -22.77°$$

$$V_2 = 135.12 \angle -22.77° \text{ volts}$$

POLYPHASE INDUCTION MOTORS

The induction motor consists of a stator and a rotor, which is mounted on bearings and separated from the stator by an air gap. When AC power is supplied to the stator windings, an electric magnetic field that rotates around the stator at synchronous speed is established. Synchronous speed is determined by the following equation:

$$\text{Synchronous speed} = n_s = \frac{120f}{p} = (\text{rpm})$$

where:

f = stator current frequency (Hz)

p = number of poles

The actual speed of the rotor, n, is related to the synchronous speed, n_s, by:

$$s = \frac{n_s - n}{n_s}$$

where s is defined as the slip.

The equivalent circuit per-phase of the induction motor is shown below:

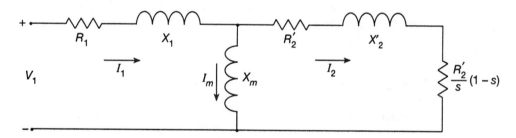

Figure 9. Per-phase Equivalent Circuit of a Poly-Phase Induction Motor

where:

R_1 = stator resistance

R'_2 = rotor standstill resistance referred to the stator

$\dfrac{R'_2}{s}(1-s)$ = rotor dynamic resistance referred to the stator depends on the rotor speed and corresponds to the load.

X_1 = stator leakage reactance

X'_2 = rotor leakage reactance referred to the stator

I_1 = stator current

I_2 = rotor current

X_m = magnetizing reactance

I_m = magnetizing current

We have the following power equations on a *per-phase basis* for an induction motor:

Input power (P_{in}): $P_{in} = V_1 \times I_1 \times \cos\theta_1$ (1)

Power crossing the air gap (P_g): $P_g = P_{in} - I^2 \times R_1$ (2)

P_g is the difference between P_{in} and the stator resistive loss.

Developed power (P_d): $P_d = (1 - s)P_g$ (3)

sP_g is the rotor resistive loss.

Output power (P_{out}): $P_{out} = P_d - P_m$ (4)

P_m is the mechanical loss.

Motor efficiency (η): $\eta = \dfrac{P_{out}}{P_{in}}$ (5)

PROBLEM 4:

The per-phase parameters of an induction motor are given below:

R_1 = 0.25 ohm

R'_2 = 0.10 ohm

X_1 = 0.5 ohm

X'_2 = 0.20 ohm

X_m = 20 ohms

The motor is three-phase, four-pole, 460 Vac, 60 Hz and operates at a speed of 1,754 rpm. The total mechanical loss at this speed is 1 kW.

Calculate:

(a) Synchronous speed

(b) Slip

(c) Input current

(d) Input power

(e) Output power

(f) Efficiency

SOLUTION:

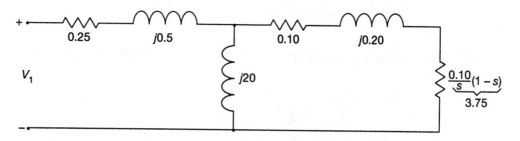

Figure 10

(a) Synchronous speed, n_s, is:

$$n_s = \frac{120 \times f}{p} = \frac{120 \times 6}{4} = 1{,}800 \ \text{rpm}.$$

(b) Slip: $s = \dfrac{n_s - n}{n_s} = \dfrac{1{,}800 - 1{,}754}{1{,}800} = 0.026$

(c) The equivalent impedance is:

$$Z_e = (0.25 + j0.5) + \frac{(j20)(3.85 + j0.20)}{j20 + 3.85 + j0.20}$$

$$Z_e = 0.25 + j0.5 + \frac{-4 + j77}{3.85 + j20.2}$$

$$Z_e = 3.89 + j1.39 = 4.13 \angle 19.66°$$

The input current is:

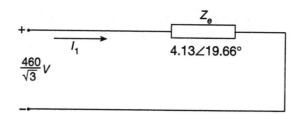

Figure 11

$$I_1 = \frac{265.6}{4.13 \ <19.66°} = 64.31 < -19.66°$$

(d) Input power per-phase:

$$P_{\text{in per-phase}} = V_1 \times I_1 \times \cos\theta_1$$

$$= (265.6)(64.31) \times \cos(19.66°)$$

$$= 16.09 \text{ kW}$$

Total input power (three-phase):

$$P_{\text{in total}} = (16.09 \text{ kW})(3) = 48.27 \text{ kW}$$

(e) Power crossing the air-gap per-phase:

$$P_{g \text{ per-phase}} = 16.09 \text{ kW} - (64.31)^2 \times (0.25) = 15.06 \text{ kW}$$

The total power crossing the air-gap is:

$$15.06 \text{ kW} \times 3 = 45.18 \text{ kW}$$

The developed electromagnetic power is:

$$45.18 \text{ kW}(1-0.026) = 44.01 \text{ kW}$$

The output power is:

$$P_{\text{output}} = 44.01 \text{kW} - 1 \text{ kW} = 43.01 \text{ kW}$$

(f) The efficiency is:

$$\eta = \frac{43.01}{48.27} \times 100\% = 89.1\%$$

FE/EIT

FE: PM Electrical Engineering Exam

CHAPTER 13

Signal Processing

CHAPTER 13

SIGNAL PROCESSING

CONTINUOUS-TIME SIGNAL ANALYSIS

Periodic and nonperiodic signals will be analyzed using Fourier series and Fourier transform. These transformations are used to look at frequency spectra of signals.

Periodic Signal and Fourier Series

A periodic function $f(t)$ is defined by $f(t) = f(t + T)$, where T is the period of $f(t)$, and can be represented by the infinite Fourier series.

$$f(t) = a_v + \sum_{n=1}^{n=\infty} a_n \cos(n\omega_o t) + b_n \sin(n\omega_o t)$$

where:

$\omega_0 = \dfrac{2\pi}{T}$ is the fundamental frequency (rad/sec).

$n\omega_o$ is the nth harmonic of ω_o.

a_n and b_n are the Fourier coefficients and can be determined from the following equations:

$$a_n = \frac{2}{T} \int_0^T f(t) \cos(n\omega_0 t)dt;$$

$$n = 1, 2, 3,\ldots$$

$$b_n = \frac{2}{T}\int_0^T f(t)\,\sin(n\omega_o t)dt;$$

$$n = 1, 2, 3, \ldots$$

a_v is the average value or the *dc* component of $f(t)$.

$$a_v = \frac{1}{T}\int_0^T f(t)\,dt$$

PROBLEM 1:

Obtain the expressions for a_v, a_n, and b_n for the following periodic voltage signal:

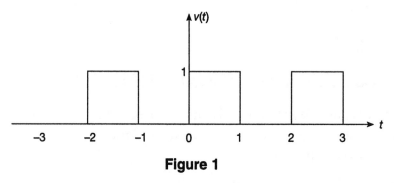

Figure 1

SOLUTION:

This voltage waveform is a square-wave function with period $T = 2$ seconds.

$$\omega_o = \frac{2\pi}{T} = \pi$$

$$a_v = \frac{1}{T}\int_0^T v(t)\,dt = \frac{1}{2}\left[\int_0^1 1\,dt + 0\right] = \left[\left(\frac{1}{2}\right)t\right]_0^1 = \frac{1}{2}$$

$$a_n = \frac{2}{T}\int_0^T v(t)\,\cos(n\omega_o t)dt = \frac{2}{2}\int_0^T v(t)\,\cos(n\pi t)dt = \frac{2}{2}\int_0^1 \cos(n\pi t)\,dt$$

$$a_n = \left[\frac{\sin(n\pi t)}{n\pi}\right]_0^1 = 0$$

$$b_n = \frac{2}{T}\int_0^T v(t)\,\sin(n\omega_o t)dt = \frac{2}{2}\int_0^1 v(t)\,\sin(n\pi t)dt = \frac{2}{2}\int_0^1 \sin(n\pi t)\,dt$$

$$b_n = \left[\frac{-\cos(n\pi t)}{n\pi}\right]_0^1 = \frac{1 - \cos(n\pi)}{n\pi}$$

Thus,

$$b_1 = \frac{1-(-1)}{\pi} = \frac{2}{\pi}$$

$$b_2 = \frac{1-1}{2\pi} = 0$$

$$b_3 = \frac{1-(-1)}{3\pi} = \frac{2}{3\pi}$$

or,

$$b_n = \frac{2}{n\pi};$$

$$n = 1, 3, 5, \ldots$$

$$b_n = 0;$$

$$n = 2, 4, 6, 8, \ldots$$

Hence,

$$f(t) = \frac{1}{2} + \frac{2}{\pi}\sum_{n=1}^{n=\infty} \frac{\sin(n\pi t)}{n}; \quad n \text{ is odd}$$

Periodic waveforms with various symmetries will simplify the problem of obtaining the Fourier coefficients.

Even-Function Symmetry

A function is defined as even if $f(t) = f(-t)$. For even periodic functions, the equations for Fourier coefficients are reduced to:

$$a_n = \frac{4}{T}\int_0^{T/2} f(t) \cos(n\omega_o t)dt;$$

$$n = 1, 2, 3, \ldots$$

$$b_n = 0;$$

$$n = 1, 2, 3, \ldots$$

$$a_v = \frac{2}{T}\int_0^{T/2} f(t)\, dt$$

Odd-Function Symmetry

A function is defined as odd if $f(t) = -f(-t)$. For odd periodic functions, the equations for Fourier coefficients are reduced to:

$$a_n = 0;$$

$$n = 1, 2, 3, \ldots$$

$$a_v = 0$$

$$b_n = \frac{4}{T} \int_0^{T/2} f(t) \sin(n\omega_o t)dt;$$

$$n = 1, 2, 3, \ldots$$

Exponential Form of the Fourier Series

The Fourier series can be expressed in the concise exponential form:

$$f(t) = \sum_{n=-\infty}^{n=\infty} C_n \times e^{jn\omega^o t}$$

where:

$$C_n = \frac{1}{T_o} \int_0^T f(t) \times e^{-jn\omega^o t} dt$$

The amplitude of the component of the exponential Fourier series at $\omega_n = n\omega_o$ is C_n, where $n = 0, \pm 1, \pm 2, \ldots$

The function C_n of the discrete variable ω_n is called the frequency spectrum. We have the following relationships:

$$C_n = C_{-n}$$

$$C_n = \frac{\sqrt{a_n^2 + b_n^2}}{2}$$

$$C_o = a_v \text{ (dc component)}$$

PROBLEM 2:

Consider the following periodic voltage signal:

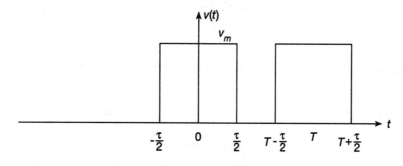

Figure 2

(a) Obtain the exponential Fourier series.

(b) Sketch the frequency spectrum of C_n.

SOLUTION:

(a)

$$C_n = \frac{1}{T}\int_0^T v(t) \times e^{-jn\omega^o t}dt = \frac{1}{T}\int_{-\tau/2}^{\tau/2} V_m e^{-jn\omega_o t}dt$$

$$C_n = \frac{V_m}{T}\left[\frac{e^{-jn\omega_o t}}{jn\omega_0}\right]_{-\tau/2}^{\tau/2}$$

$$C_n = \frac{jV_m}{n\omega_0 T}\left[e^{-jn\omega_o\tau/2} + e^{jn\omega_o\tau/2}\right]$$

Using the Euler's identity:

$$\sin x = \frac{e^{jx} - e^{-jx}}{2j},$$

we obtain:

$$C_n = \frac{2V_m}{n\omega_0\tau}\sin(n\omega_0\tau/2)$$

By rewriting C_n as:

$$C_n = \frac{V_m \tau}{T} \frac{\sin(n\omega_o \tau/2)}{n\omega_o \tau/2},$$

we see that the amplitude of C_n follows a $\dfrac{\sin x}{x}$ distribution.

The exponential series representation of $v(t)$ is therefore equal to:

$$v(t) = \sum_{n=-\infty}^{n=\infty} \frac{V_m \tau}{T} \frac{\sin(n\omega_o \tau/2)}{n\omega_o \tau/2} e^{jn\omega_o t}$$

(b) The magnitude of C_n is:

$$|C_n| = \frac{V_m \tau}{T} \left| \frac{\sin(n\omega_o \tau/2)}{n\omega_o \tau/2} \right|$$

Substituting $\omega_o = 2\pi f_o$, we have:

$$|C_n| = \frac{V_m \tau}{T} \left| \frac{\sin(n\pi f_o \tau)}{n\pi f_o \tau} \right|$$

The plot of $|C_n|$ is shown below.

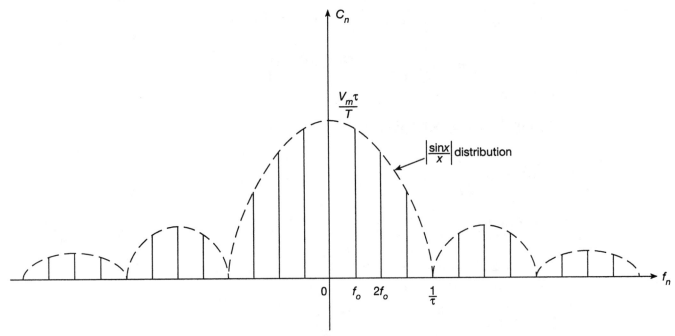

Figure 3

Non-periodic Signal and Fourier Transform

Frequency domain description of nonperiodic signals can be obtained using the Fourier transform. The function $F(j\omega)$ is the Fourier transform of $f(t)$ and can be expressed as $F[f(t)] = F(jw)$.

The inverse Fourier transform can be written as: $F^{-1}[F(j\omega)] = f(t)$.

The Fourier transform pair that establishes these two transformations are:

$$F(j\omega) = \int_{-\infty}^{\infty} f(t) \times e^{-j\omega t} dt$$

$$f(t) = \frac{1}{2\pi} \int_{-\infty}^{\infty} F(j\omega) \times e^{j\omega t} d\omega$$

PROBLEM 3:

Consider the following voltage pulse:

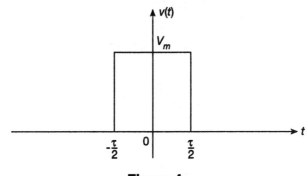

Figure 4

(a) Obtain the Fourier transform for $v(t)$.

(b) Plot the graph of $|V(j\omega)|$.

SOLUTION:

(a)

$$V(j\omega) = \int_{-\infty}^{\infty} v(t) \times e^{-j\omega t} dt = \int_{-\tau/2}^{\tau/2} V_m \times e^{-j\omega t} dt = V_m \left[\frac{e^{-j\omega t}}{j\omega} \right]_{-\tau/2}^{\tau/2}$$

$$V(j\omega) = \frac{V_m}{-j\omega} \left[e^{-j\omega\tau/2} - e^{j\omega\tau/2} \right]$$

Using the Euler's identity:

$$\sin x = \frac{e^{jx} - e^{-jx}}{2j},$$

we obtain:

$$V(j\omega) = \frac{V_m}{-j\omega} \left[-2j \sin(\omega T/2) \right]$$

This can be put in the form of $\dfrac{\sin x}{x}$:

$$V(j\omega) = V_m \tau \times \frac{\sin(\omega\tau/2)}{\omega\tau/2}$$

(b) The magnitude of $V(j\omega)$ is:

$$|V(j\omega)| = V_m \tau \times \left| \frac{\sin(\omega\tau/2)}{\omega\tau/2} \right|$$

The graph of $|V(j\omega)|$ is shown below:

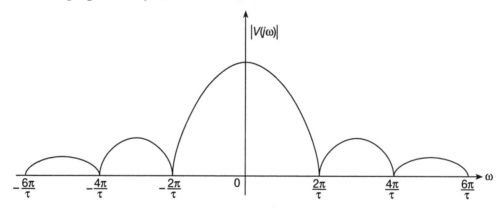

Figure 5

The magnitude of $V(j\omega)$ yields the continuous frequency spectrum. Hence, we can see clearly that as the time domain function changes from a periodic waveform (Problem 2) to a nonperiodic pulse, the frequency spectrum goes from a discrete line spectrum to a continuous spectrum.

Parseval's Theorem

The energy absorbed by a 1-ohm resistor with a voltage $v(t)$ across it is:

$$W = \int_{-\infty}^{\infty} v^2(t) dt$$

Parseval's theorem states that this same energy in the time domain can be calculated in the frequency domain by the following equation:

$$W = \frac{1}{2\pi} \int_{-\infty}^{\infty} |V(j\omega)|^2 \, d\omega$$

Hence:

$$W = \int_{-\infty}^{\infty} v^2(t) \, dt = \frac{1}{2\pi} \int_{-\infty}^{\infty} |V(j\omega)|^2 \, d\omega$$

PROBLEM 4:

Consider the following circuit:

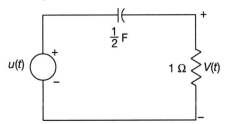

u (t): Unit Step Voltage Function

Figure 6

(a) Determine the total energy that is delivered to the 1-ohm resistor.

(b) What percentage of the total energy absorbed by the 1-ohm resistor can be associated with the frequency band $0 < \omega < \pi/2$ rad/sec?

SOLUTION:

(a) The voltage across the 1-ohm resistor is:

$$v(t) = e^{-2t} u(t)$$

$$V(j\omega) = \int_{-\infty}^{\infty} v(t) \times e^{-j\omega t} \, dt = \int_{-\infty}^{\infty} e^{-2t} u(t) \times e^{-j\omega t} \, dt$$

$$V(j\omega) = \int_{0}^{\infty} e^{-(2+j\omega)t} \, dt = -\left[\frac{1}{2+j\omega} e^{-(2+j\omega)t} \right]_{0}^{\infty}$$

$$V(j\omega) = \frac{1}{2+j\omega}$$

The magnitude of $V(j\omega)$ is:

$$|V(j\omega)| = \frac{1}{\sqrt{\omega^2 + 4}}$$

The total energy is:

$$W = \frac{1}{2\pi} \int_{-\infty}^{\infty} |V(j\omega)|^2 \, d\omega$$

$$W = \frac{1}{2\pi} \int_{-\infty}^{\infty} \frac{1}{\omega^2 + 4} \, d\omega$$

Using the integral formula:

$$W = \int \frac{1}{\omega^2 + a^2} d\omega = \frac{1}{a} \tan^{-1}\left(\frac{\omega}{a}\right)$$

we have:

$$W = \frac{1}{\pi} \int_{0}^{\infty} \frac{1}{\omega^2 + 4} \, d\omega = \frac{1}{2\pi} \left[\tan^{-1}\left(\frac{\omega}{2}\right) \right]_{0}^{\infty} = \frac{1}{2\pi} \frac{[\pi - 0]}{2}$$

$$W = \frac{1}{4} J = 0.250 \, J$$

(b) The energy associated with the frequency band $0 < \omega < \pi/2$ rad/sec is:

$$W = \frac{1}{\pi} \int_{0}^{\frac{\pi}{2}} \frac{1}{\omega^2 + 4} \, d\omega = \frac{1}{2\pi} \left[\tan^{-1}\left(\frac{\omega}{2}\right) \right]_{0}^{\pi/2} = \frac{1}{2\pi} \left[\tan^{-1}\left(\frac{\pi}{4}\right) - 0 \right]$$

$$W = \frac{1}{2\pi}[0.666 - 0] = 0.106 \, J$$

The percentage of total energy in this frequency band is:

$$\frac{0.106}{0.250} \times 100\% = 42.4\%$$

DISCRETE-TIME SIGNAL ANALYSIS

Z-Transform

The Z-transform provides a frequency domain description for discrete-time signals, and it is a basic tool for digital filter design. The Z-transform of a real-value sequence $\{f(n), n = 0, \pm 1, \pm 2, ...\}$ is defined as:

$$F(z) = [f(n)] = \sum_{n=-\infty}^{n=\infty} f(n)z^{-n}$$

where z is the complex variable.

PROBLEM 5:

Consider the positive-time sequence defined by:

$$f(n) = a^n; \ n = 0, 1, 2, ...$$

$$f(n) = 0; \ n < 0$$

where a is a real or complex number and $a < 1$.

Find the Z-transform for this function.

SOLUTION:

$$F(z) = [f(n)] = \sum_{n=0}^{n=\infty} f(n)z^{-n},$$

where $f_n = 0$ for $n < 0$

Thus,

$$F(z) = \sum_{n=0}^{n=\infty} a^n z^{-n} = \sum_{n=0}^{n=\infty} (az^{-1})^n = \frac{1}{1 - az^{-1}} = \frac{z}{z - a}$$

The Inverse Z-Transform

The determination of $\{f(n)\}$ from its Z-transform $F(z)$ and appropriate conversion tables is called the inverse Z-transform denoted by Z^{-1}. There are three methods of performing the inverse transformation: inversion formula, direct division, and partial-fraction. The method most widely used is partial-fraction expansion and is illustrated in Problem 6.

PROBLEM 6:

Obtain the inverse Z-transform of:

$$F(z) = \frac{1}{(1 - z^{-1})(1 - 0.25z^{-1})}$$

SOLUTION:

First, multiply both the numerator and denominator by z^2 to eliminate the negative powers of z.

$$F(z) = \frac{z^2}{(z - 1)(z - 0.25)}$$

Dividing $F(z)$ by z, we have:

$$\frac{F(z)}{z} = \frac{z}{(z - 1)(z - 0.25)} = \frac{A}{z - 1} + \frac{B}{z - 0.25}$$

Solving for A and B, we get $A = 4/3$ and $B = -1/3$:

$$\frac{F(z)}{z} = \frac{z}{(z - 1)(z - 0.25)} = \frac{\dfrac{4}{3}}{z - 1} - \frac{\dfrac{1}{3}}{z - 0.25}$$

$$F(z) = \frac{\dfrac{4}{3}z}{z - 1} - \frac{\dfrac{1}{3}z}{z - 0.25}$$

Using an inverse Z-transform table, we obtain:

$$f(n) = \frac{4}{3} - \frac{1}{3}(0.25)^n$$

FE/EIT

FE: PM Electrical Engineering Exam

CHAPTER 14

Solid-State Devices

$$i_D = I_S \left[e^{v_D/nV_T} - 1 \right]$$

CHAPTER 14

SOLID-STATE DEVICES

DIODE AND DIODE CIRCUITS

Diode Characteristics

The schematic symbol of a semiconductor diode is shown below:

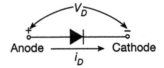

Figure 1

When $V_D \geq 0$, the diode is said to be forward-biased or "on." For a negative value of V_D, the diode is reversed-biased or "off."

The current i_D is related to the voltage V_D by the following equation:

$$i_D = I_s [e^{V_D / \eta V_T} - 1]$$

where:

I_S = saturation current

η = emission coefficient (η = 1 for Si)

V_T = thermal voltage, at room temperature

$V_T = 26 \, mV \, (T = 300°K)$

Diode Approximations

Ideal diode: An ideal diode acts like a switch. When the diode is forward-biased, it is like a closed switch, and if the diode is reverse-biased, the switch opens.

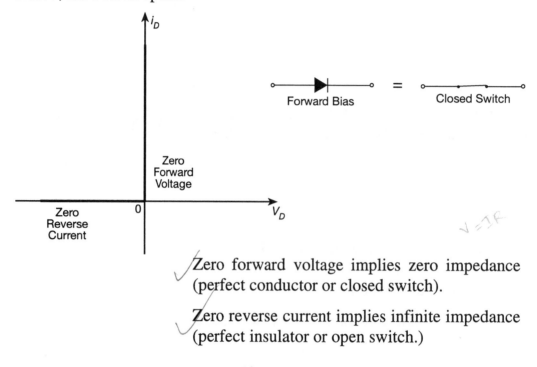

Zero forward voltage implies zero impedance (perfect conductor or closed switch).

Zero reverse current implies infinite impedance (perfect insulator or open switch.)

Figure 2

PROBLEM 1:

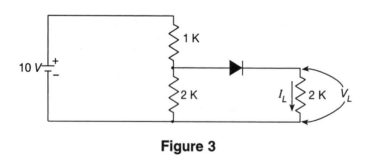

Figure 3

Find the load current I_L. Assume that the diode is ideal.

SOLUTION:

We have the following equivalent circuit for the ideal diode circuit.

$$2 \text{ K} \mathbin{//} 2 \text{ K} = 1 \text{ K}$$

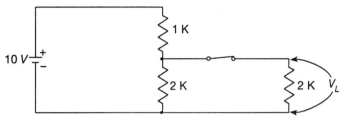

Figure 4

$$V_L = \left[\frac{1K}{1K+1K}\right](10V) = 5V$$

$$I_L = \frac{5V}{2K} = 2.5 \ mA$$

Diode approximation: It takes about $V_D = 0.7 \ V$ for the diode to fully conduct; therefore, we have the following equivalent circuit:

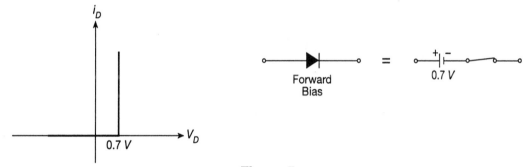

Figure 5

For most practical work, this diode approximation is used.

PROBLEM 2:

Find the load current in Problem 1, using $V_D = 0.7 \ V$.

SOLUTION:

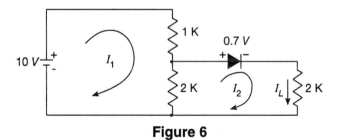

Figure 6

Writing the KVL for meshes 1 and 2, we have:

$$10 = 3I_1 - 2I_2$$

$$-0.7 = -2I_1 + 4I_2$$

The load current is equal to the mesh current I_2. Solving for I_2, we obtain:

$$I_L = I_2 = 2.24 \text{ mA.}$$

Analog Diode Circuits

Common diode circuits are shown below:

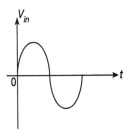 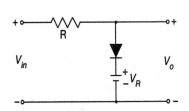 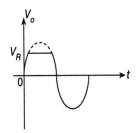

Figure 7a. Diode Clipping Circuit

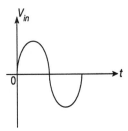 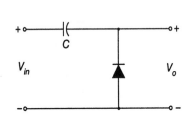 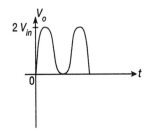

Figure 7b. Diode Clamping Circuit

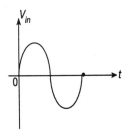 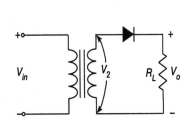 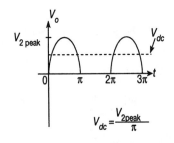

Figure 7c. The Half-Wave Rectifier

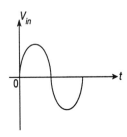 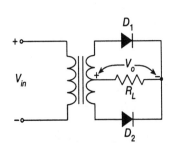 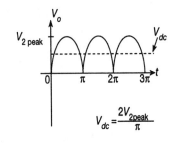

Figure 7d. The Full-Wave Rectifier

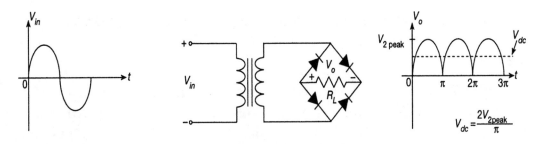

Figure 7e. The Bridge Rectifier

PROBLEM 3:

Consider the following bridge rectifier circuit:

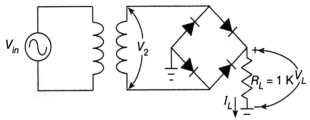

Figure 8

The secondary voltage V_{2RMS} = 24 Vac.

Calculate:

    (a)   the DC load voltage V_L,

    (b)   the DC load current I_L,

    (c)   the diode current, and

    (d)   the PIV across each diode.

SOLUTION:

$$V_2 \text{ peak} = \sqrt{2}V_{2RMS} = (\sqrt{2})(24 \text{ Vac}) = 33.94 \text{ Vac}$$

(a) $V_L = \dfrac{2V_2\text{peak}}{\pi} = 21.61 \text{ V}$

(b) $I_L = \dfrac{21.61 \text{ V}}{1 \text{ } k\Omega} = 21.61 \text{ mA}$

(c)   Since each diode conducts for only $^1/_2$ cycle, the diode current is therefore $^1/_2$ of the load current:

$$I_D = \frac{I_L}{2} = 10.8 \text{ } mA$$

265

(d)   The PIV across each diode is equal to V_2 peak = 33.94 Vac

Zener Diode

The Zener diode is designed for operation in the breakdown region. As shown in the I-V curve below, the voltage V_z in the breakdown region is almost constant. Zener diodes are the backbone of voltage regulators, i.e., circuits that hold the load voltage approximately constant for any changes in the supply voltage and load impedance.

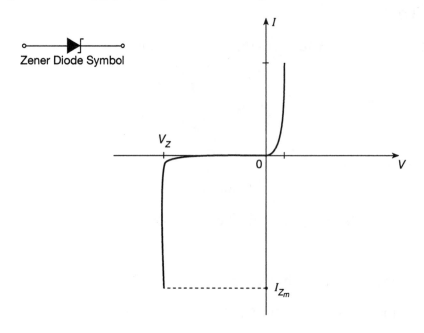

Figure 9

I_{zm} = maximum rated Zener current

V_z = Zener voltage

PROBLEM 4:

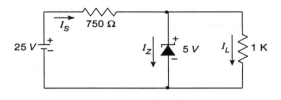

Figure 10

(a)   Verify that the Zener diode is in the breakdown region mode.

(b)   Calculate the load current and the Zener current.

SOLUTION:

(a)   The voltage across the Zener is:

$$25\,V\left[\frac{1\,\text{K}}{1\,\text{K}+0.75\,\text{K}}\right]=14.29\,V$$

Since this voltage is greater than the Zener voltage, there is breakdown.

(b)   The load current:

$$I_L=\frac{5\,V}{1\,\text{K}}=5\,\text{mA}$$

$$I_s=\frac{25\,V-5V}{750\Omega}=26.67\,\text{mA}$$

The Zener current $I_z=I_S-I_L=26.67\,\text{mA}-5\,\text{mA}=21.67\,\text{mA}$

TRANSISTORS AND TRANSISTOR BIASING CIRCUITS

Symbol and Equivalent Circuit for a Transistor

A transistor is a three-terminal device that is made of three p and n type elements, which make up two pn junctions when connected together. The three transistor elements are emitter (E), base (B), and collector (C). There are two types of transistors, *npn* and *pnp*:

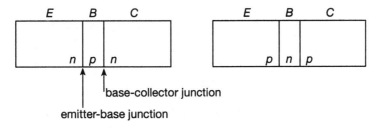

Figure 11

For normal operation of a transistor, the emitter-base junction is forward-biased and the collector-base junction is reversed-biased. Because the emitter-base junction is forward-biased, electrons are forced into the base region. Since the base region is thin and lightly doped, most of the free electrons diffuse through the base into the collector.

The schematic symbol and equivalent circuit for an *npn* transistor are shown below:

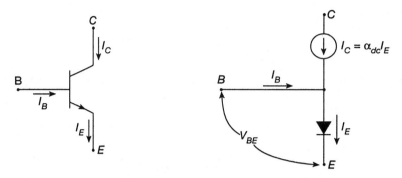

Figure 12

We have the following transistor equations:

$$I_E = I_C + I_B$$

$$\beta_{dc} = h_{FE} = \frac{I_C}{I_B} \quad \text{(the DC current gain)}$$

$$\alpha_{dc} = \frac{I_C}{I_E}$$

For practical transistor circuit analysis, treat I_C as equal to I_E since α_{dc} approaches unity, and let V_{BE} equal 0.7 V for silicon transistors (0.3 V for germanium).

DC Load Lines

Consider the following circuit, which uses base-bias:

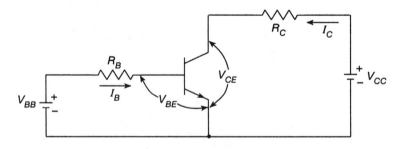

Figure 13

Applying KVL around the collector loop:

$$-V_{CC} + I_C R_C + V_{CE} = 0$$

$$\rightarrow I_C = \frac{V_{CC} - V_{CE}}{R_C}$$

This is the DC load line equation and can be drawn on the collector curves to see how a transistor works and what region it operates in.

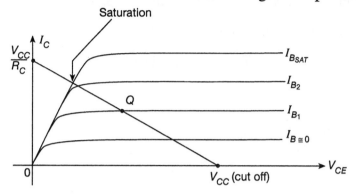

Figure 14

The two end points of the DC load line are:

$$I_C = \frac{V_{CC}}{R_C} \text{ (Transistor is ON and saturated.)}$$

$$I_C = 0 \ (V_{CC} = V_{CE}) \text{ (Transistor is cut-off.)}$$

The intersection of the DC load line with the calculated base current is the Q-point (also called the operating point or quiescent point).

For linear operation, the Q-point should be designed to be in the middle of the DC load line to ensure an AC input signal will be amplified and reproduced with minimal distortion.

Transistor Biasing Circuits

There are a number of different ways to bias a transistor for linear operation, i.e., setting up the Q-point near the middle of the DC load line. These techniques are illustrated below.

PROBLEM 5:

The circuit shown incorporates emitter-feedback bias:

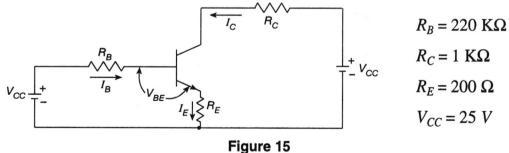

$R_B = 220 \ \text{K}\Omega$

$R_C = 1 \ \text{K}\Omega$

$R_E = 200 \ \Omega$

$V_{CC} = 25 \ V$

Figure 15

269

(a) Calculate the collector current; the transistor has an β_{dc} of 80.

(b) Calculate the voltage between the collector and ground (V_C).

(c) Draw the DC load line.

(d) For what value of β_{dc} does the circuit saturate?

SOLUTION:

(a) Applying KVL around the base loop:

$$-V_{CC} + I_B R_B + V_{BE} + I_E R_E = 0$$

Since $I_E \cong I_C = \beta_{dc} I_B$, we have:

$$-V_{CC} + \frac{I_C R_B}{\beta_{dc}} + V_{BE} + I_C R_E = 0$$

$$I_C \left(R_E + \frac{R_B}{\beta_{dc}} \right) = V_{CC} - V_{BE}$$

$$\rightarrow I_C \cong \frac{V_{CC} - V_{BE}}{R_E + \dfrac{R_B}{\beta_{dc}}} = \frac{25 - 0.7}{0.2\ K + \dfrac{220\ K}{80}}$$

$$I_C = 8.24\ mA$$

(b) $V_C = V_{CC} - I_C R_C = 25\ V - (8.24\ mA)(1\ K)$

$V_C = 16.76\ V$

(c) Applying KVL around the collector loop:

$$-V_{CC} + I_C R_C + V_{CE} + I_E R_E = 0$$

Since $I_E \cong I_C$, we have:

$$V_{CE} = V_{CC} - I_C (R_C + R_E)$$

$$V_{CE} = 25 - 8.24\ mA\ (1.2\ K)$$

$$V_{CE} = 15.11\ V$$

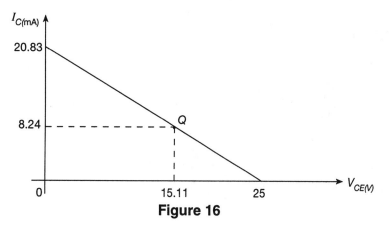

Figure 16

(d) I_C (saturation) $= \dfrac{V_{CC}}{R_C + R_E} = \dfrac{25\text{ V}}{1\text{ K} + 0.2\text{ K}} = 20.83$ mA

$$I_C\text{ (saturation)} = \dfrac{25 - 0.7}{0.2\text{ K} + \dfrac{220\text{ K}}{\beta_{dc}}} = 20.83 \text{ mA}$$

$$0.2 + \dfrac{220}{\beta_{dc}} = 1.17$$

$$\beta_{dc} = 228$$

PROBLEM 6:

The figure below shows the collector-feedback bias circuit.

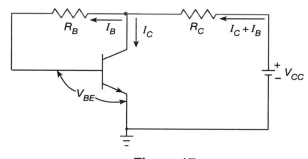

Figure 17

(a) Derive the equation for I_C.

(b) For what value of R_B is the Q-point near the middle of the load line?

SOLUTION:

(a) $I_B R_B + (I_C + I_B) R_C - V_{CC} + V_{BE} = 0$

Substituting $I_B = \dfrac{I_C}{\beta_{dc}}$,

$$\frac{I_C}{\beta_{dc}} R_B + I_C R_C - V_{CC} + V_{BE} \cong 0 \quad (I_C + I_B \cong I_C)$$

$$I_C = \frac{V_{CC} - V_{BE}}{R_C + \dfrac{R_B}{\beta_{dc}}}$$

(b) $R_B = \beta_{dc} R_C$

PROBLEM 7:

The figure below shows a voltage divider bias circuit. This is the most widely used bias technique in linear circuits and sometimes is also called universal bias. The term "voltage divider" comes from the voltage divider formed by R_1 and R_2.

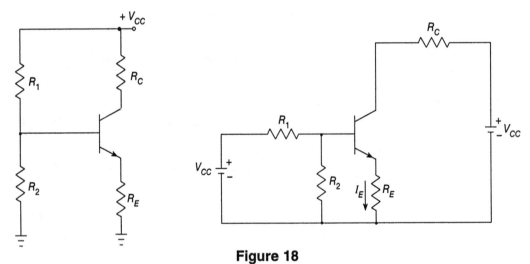

Figure 18

Simplified Schematic   **Complete Schematic**

(a) Derive the equation for I_E.

(b) For $R_1 = 6.8$ K

$R_2 = 1$ K

$R_C = 2.7$ K

$R_E = 1$K

$$\beta_{dc} = 100$$

$$V_{CC} = 25 \; V_{DC},$$

calculate the collector-emitter voltage V_{CE}.

SOLUTION:

(a)   Thevenizing the base circuit, we have:

$$V_{TH} = V_{CC}\left[\frac{R_2}{R_1 + R_2}\right]$$

$$R_{TH} = R_1 \; / /R_2 = \frac{R_1 R_2}{R_1 + R_2}$$

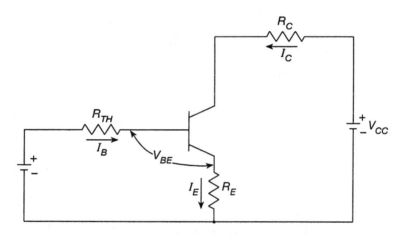

Figure 19
(Thevenin equivalent circuit for the voltage divider bias circuit.)

Applying KVL around the base loop:

$$-V_{TH} + I_B R_{TH} + V_{BE} + I_E R_E = 0$$

Substituting $I_B = \dfrac{I_C}{\beta_{dc}} \cong \dfrac{I_E}{\beta_{dc}}$, we have:

$$-V_{TH} + \frac{I_E}{\beta_{dc}} R_{TH} + V_{BE} + I_E R_E = 0$$

Rearranging and solving for I_E:

$$I_E \left[\frac{R_{TH}}{\beta_{dc}} + R_E \right] = V_{TH} - V_{BE}$$

$$I_E = \frac{V_{TH} - V_{BE}}{\dfrac{R_{TH}}{\beta_{dc}} + R_E}$$

(b)

$$V_{TH} = 25 \left[\frac{1\,K}{6.8\,K + 1\,K} \right] = 3.21\,V$$

$$R_{TH} = 0.87\,K$$

$$I_E = \frac{3.21 - 0.7}{\dfrac{0.87\,K}{100} + 1\,K} = 2.49\,mA$$

$$I_C \cong I_E = 2.49\,mA$$

$$V_{CE} = 25 - 2.49\,mA\ (2.7K + 1K) = 15.79\,V$$

JFETS AND APPLICATIONS

JFET Symbol and Operating Characteristics

There are two basic types of field-effect transistors, the junction JFET and the MOSFET (Metal Oxide Semiconductor Field-Effect Transistor). The schematic symbol for an *n*-channel JFET is shown below.

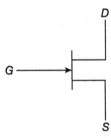

Figure 20

The source (*S*) and drain (*D*) perform the same functions as the Emitter (*E*) and collector (*C*) of a transistor, while the gate (*G*) performs the same function as the base (*B*). The JFET functions by responding to voltage at gate (*G*) terminal, unlike the transistor which functions by responding to current at the base (B). We have the following relationship between the drain current (i_D) and the gate-source voltage (V_{GS}):

$$i_D = I_{DSS}\left[1 - \frac{V_{GS}}{V_{GS(OFF)}}\right]^2$$

where:

I_{DSS} = Drain saturation current

$V_{GS(OFF)}$ = Gate-source cut-off voltage

The values of I_{DSS} and $V_{GS(OFF)}$ are shown on the JFET data sheets. The plot of I_D versus V_{GS}, called the transconductance curve, is shown below:

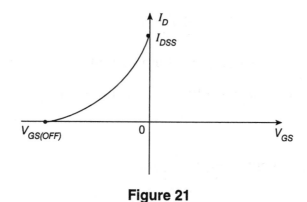

Figure 21

JFET Biasing Circuits

There are a number of ways to bias a JFET. They are:

(a) gate bias, which is similar to base bias of a bipolar transistor.

(b) self-bias, where a supply voltage is applied only to the drain.

(c) voltage-divider bias, which is similar to the voltage-divider bias used with a bipolar transistor.

(d) source-bias, which is similar to emitter bias, and

(e) current-source bias.

PROBLEM 8:

The figure below shows an example of voltage-divider bias.

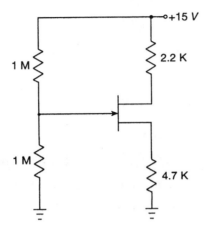

Figure 22

(a)   If $V_{GS} = -1V$, what is the drain current?

(b)   Calculate the voltage between the drain and ground.

SOLUTION:

(a)   The equivalent Thevenin voltage is:

$$V_{TH} = 15 \, V \left[\frac{1 \, M\Omega}{1 \, M\Omega + 1 \, M\Omega} \right] = 7.5 \, V$$

The drain current is equal to:

$$i_D = \frac{V_{TH} - V_{GS}}{4.7 \, K} = \frac{7.5 - (-1)}{4.7 \, K} = 1.81 \, \text{mA}$$

(b) $V_D = 15 \, V - (1.81 \, \text{mA})(2.2 \, K) = 11.02 \, V$

PROBLEM 9:

This circuit below called current-source bias is used to set up a constant drain current.

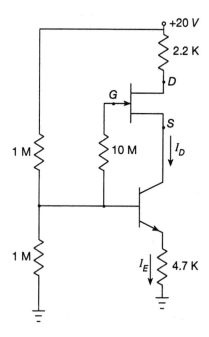

Figure 23

If $V_{GS} = -2\ V$, calculate I_D, V_D, V_G, and V_S.

SOLUTION:

The Thevenin equivalent voltage is:

$$V_{TH} = 20\,V\left[\frac{1\,M}{1\,M + 1\,M}\right] = 10\,V$$

The emitter current is:

$$I_E = \frac{10\,V - 0.7\,V}{4.7\,K} = 1.98\ mA$$

$I_D = I_E = 1.98\ mA$

$V_D = 20\ V - 1.98\ mA\ (2.2\ K) = 15.64\ V$

$V_G = V_{TH} = 10\ V$ (since the gate current is very small)

$V_S = V_G - V_{GS} = 10 - (-2) = 12\ V$

FE/EIT

FE: PM Electrical Engineering Exam

Practice Test 1

FUNDAMENTALS OF ENGINEERING EXAMINATION

TEST 1

(Answer sheets appear in the back of this book.)

TIME: 4 Hours
60 Questions

DIRECTIONS: For each of the following questions and incomplete statements, choose the best answer from the four answer choices. You must answer all questions.

Questions 1–4 are based on the following:

A resistor network is connected in a star pattern as shown below. The resistors R_1–R_{10} are all equal to 1Ω. The current source I_{s1} is set equal to 1A.

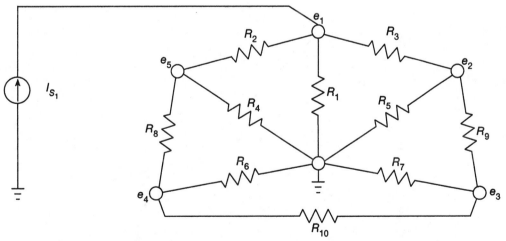

Figure 1. Resistor Network Pattern

1. The equivalent network resistance (R_{1eq}) from node e_1 to ground is

   (A) $1/10\Omega$

   (B) $10/11\Omega$

   (C) $5/11\Omega$

   (D) $1/2\Omega$

2. The voltage from node e_2 to ground is equal to

   (A) $1V$

   (B) $10/11V$

   (C) $2/11V$

   (D) $1/2V$

3. The voltage between node e_3 and node e_4 is

   (A) $1V$

   (B) $0V$

   (C) $10/11V$

   (D) $2/11V$

4. The equivalent resistance from node e_4 to ground is

   (A) $1/2\Omega$

   (B) $34/55\Omega$

   (C) $17/55\Omega$

   (D) $2/11\Omega$

Questions 5 and 6 are based on the following:

For the RLC network in the following diagram, compute the parameters listed in Questions 5 and 6. The answers for the questions require the generalized Laplace notation(s) for the reactive elements. The network parameters are as follows:

$$R_1 = 1\Omega$$

$$L_1 = L_2 = 1H$$

$$C_1 = 1F$$

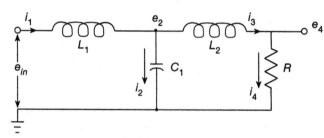

Figure 2

5. The transfer function e_4/e_{in} for the network is

   (A) $1/(s^2 + 2s + 1)$

(B) $s/(s^3 + s^2 + 2s + 1)$

(C) $1/(s^3 + s^2 + 2s + 1)$

(D) $2s/(s^2 + 2s + 1)$

6. The input impedance (Z_{in}) for the network is

(A) $2s/(s^2 + 2s + 1)$

(B) $(s^3 + s^2 + 2s + 1)/(s^2 + s + 1)$

(C) $(s^3 + s^2 + 2s + 1)/(s^2 + 2s + 1)$

(D) $1/(s^2 + 2s + 1)$

Questions 7–9 are based on the following:

The transformer-coupled, single-phase, full-wave rectifier circuit is connected to a resistive load (Figure 3a). The source driving the transformer is 120V RMS at 60Hz. The turns ratio is 1:1 between the primary and secondary windings.

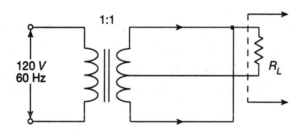

Figure 3a

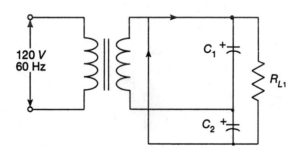

Figure 3b

7. The DC voltage across the load resistor (R_L) in Figure 3a is

    (A) 120V (C) 27V

    (B) 54V (D) 108V

8. The RMS value of the ripple voltage across the load resistor (R_L) is

    (A) 120V (C) 84V

    (B) 60V (D) 169V

9. The DC voltage across the load resistor (R_{L1}) in Figure 3b is

    (A) 120V (C) 339V

    (B) 108V (D) 216V

Questions 10–13 are based on the following:

The active second order low- and high-pass filters shown in Figure 4a and 4b are configured with the following parameters: In the low-pass filter, $R_1 = R_2 = R$. In the high-pass, filter $C_1 = C_2 = C$, and $R_2 = 2R_1$.

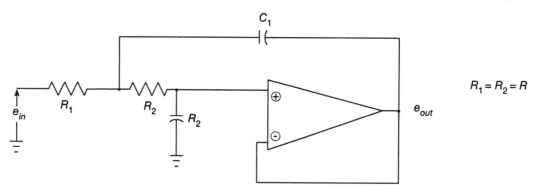

Figure 4a

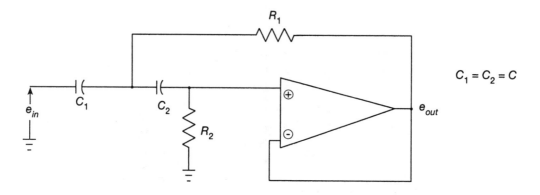

Figure 4b

10. For the low-pass filter with $R = 10K$, $C_1 = 0.022\mu F$, and $C_2 = 0.011\mu F$, what is the filter cutoff frequency, f_n?

(A) 2kHz   (C) 1kHz

(B) 4kHz   (D) 3kHz

11. What is the damping factor for the low-pass filter if the components have the values indicated in Question 10?

(A) 0.5   (C) 1.0

(B) 0.7071   (D) 1.731

12. Which equation represents the cutoff frequency (f_n) for the high-pass filter?

(A) $\dfrac{1}{(\pi\sqrt{2}\ R_1 C)}$ (C) $\dfrac{\sqrt{2}}{(\pi\ R_1 C)}$

(B) $\dfrac{1}{(2\pi\sqrt{2}\ R_1 C)}$ (D) $\dfrac{1}{(2\pi\ R_2 C)}$

13. What is the high-pass filter cutoff frequency (f_n) if $C = 0.01\mu F$, $R_1 = 5K$, and $R_2 = 10K$?

(A) 2.25kHz   (C) 1kHz

(B) 5kHz   (D) 2.05kHz

Questions 14 and 15 refer to the dual operational amplifier shown below.

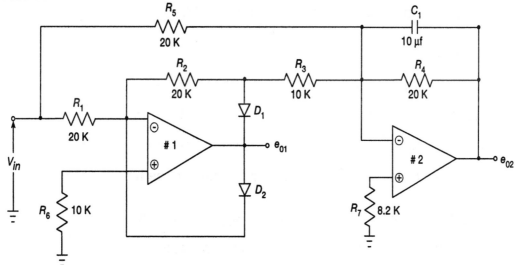

Figure 5

14. The voltage e_{01} at the output of amplifier 1 is

    (A) $-V_{in}$ when $V_{in} = +$ and 0 if $V_{in} = -$

    (B) $2V_{in}$ when $V_{in} = -$ and 0 when $V_{in} = +$

    (C) V_{in}

    (D) $-2V_{in}$

15. The voltage e_{02} at the output of amplifier 2 is

    (A) V_{in} (C) $-|2V_{in}|$

    (B) $2V_{in}$ (D) $|V_{in}|$

16. _____ memory is located between 640K and 1MB of RAM and is used for programs that control input and output devices as well as other computer hardware.

    (A) Conventional   (C) Extended

    (B) Upper   (D) Expanded

17. Interlaced monitors _____

    (A) are used only with active matrix LCD displays using separate transistors to control each crystal cell.

    (B) display every other scan line on the screen and then rescan the screen from top to bottom with the position of each scan line placed between the previous scan lines.

    (C) scan the entire screen in a single pass.

    (D) are only used with SVGA (super VGA) computer displays.

18. Magnetic tape density is considered _____.

    (A) the width of the tape

    (B) the length of the tape that is on the reel or cartridge

    (C) the number of bits that can be stored on an inch of tape

    (D) the number of rows or channels that run the length of the tape

19. System software consists of which of the following?

    (A) Business, scientific, and educational programs

(B) Programs that are related to the control of the computer equipment operation

(C) Procedures used for computer operations as well as other related requirements

(D) Programs that enable the computer to produce usable information

20. Many computers use a method defined as the _____ that works with the operating system in order to simplify interfacing to the computer.

(A) software package

(B) software system

(C) operating application

(D) operating environment

21. The value of _____ software is that it provides a method for businesses to control and administer processes that help to ensure their timely completion at a defined budget level.

(A) project management

(B) spreadsheet

(C) database management

(D) presentation graphics

22. Algorithms developed for computers to generate trigonometric functions such as $\sin(x)$, $\cos(x)$, and $\tan(x)$ use _____ to produce precise numerical values.

(A) curve fitting techniques

(B) table lookup

(C) polynomial approximation

(D) estimated values and interpolation

23. The major limitation to the methods used to determine which procedure to use in the numerical approximation of a selected function is _____.

(A) the speed of computer computation

(B) the precision required

(C) its monotonic characteristics

(D) its regions of convergence

24. The method of successive approximation in the evaluation of algebraic and transcendental functions relies on an initial value in the region of interest and a(n) _____ to generate an accurate answer.

(A) Taylor series approximation

(B) Tschebycheff polynomial

(C) interval halfing and iteration

(D) least squares fitting

Questions 25–28 are based on the following:

The block diagram of a proportional error second order servo system is shown in Figure 6. The components in the system are assumed to be linear. The parameters are defined as follows:

θ_o = output variable

J = inertia of the load

K = gain constant of controller–power device combination

f = viscous damping coefficient of the system

ε = instantaneous error = $(\theta_I - \theta_o)$

The overall error transfer function θ_i/ε_i is also shown in Figure 6.

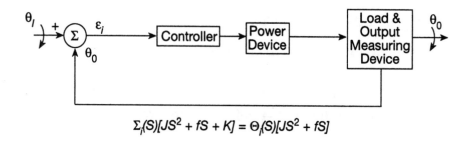

$$\Sigma_i(S)[JS^2 + fS + K] = \Theta_i(S)[JS^2 + fS]$$

Figure 6

25. For an initial steady-state system, the output is subject to a load torque T_L. What is the final steady-state error, ε_{SS}?

    (A) T_L (C) T_L/K

    (B) K/J (D) $\sqrt{1/JK}$

26. If the input to the servo is a step velocity with a value $\theta_I = \omega_I t$, what is the final steady-state error?

    (A) K/J (C) $f/2[\sqrt{KJ}]$

    (B) $f\,\omega_I/K$ (D) KJ

27. For the above system, if $J = 3$ slug-ft^2, $f = 21.2$ lb-ft/radian/sec, and $K = 104$ lb-ft/radian, what is the value of the dimensionless damping ratio, ξ?

    (A) 1.0   (C) 0.6

    (B) 0.7071   (D) 0.86

28. Using the parameters defined in Question 27, calculate the time constant of the servo system where $\tau = 1/\xi\omega_n$.

    (A) 0.636 sec   (C) 1.0 sec

    (B) 0.283 sec   (D) 0.5 sec

Questions 29 and 30 are based on the following:

The figure below indicates a second order proportional error servo-mechanism where integral error control has been added to the system forward loop.

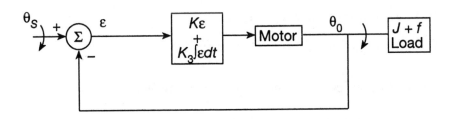

Figure 7

29. What effect does the integral control have on the steady-state error, ε_{SS}?

   (A) It increases the proportional servo error.

   (B) It reduces the error to zero.

   (C) It reduces the proportional servo error to a value > 0.

   (D) It has no effect on the proportional servo error.

30. What effect can we estimate for the system transient performance for integral control?

   (A) It increases system response time.

   (B) It improves system response time.

   (C) It improves system response time with a decreased system stability.

   (D) It gives no change to system response time.

31. Semiconductor material is generally considered an element that primarily contains

   (A) a completed outer electron shell.

   (B) two valence electrons.

   (C) four valence electrons.

   (D) eight valence electrons.

32. The addition of controlled impurities, called doping, to pure semiconductor crystals results in

   (A) the removal of excess electrons.

   (B) the completion of the outer valence shell.

   (C) the removal of excess holes.

   (D) the addition of excess electrons or holes.

33. Majority carriers and minority carriers refer to

   (A) stable electrons and holes.

   (B) n-type material conduction.

(C) holes and electrons or electrons and holes.

(D) *p*-type material conduction.

34. Placing together *p* and *n*-type materials to form a junction creates a region that has

   (A) an excess amount of holes.

   (B) an excess amount of electrons.

   (C) a reduced amount of holes and electrons.

   (D) no holes or electrons.

35. The barrier potential of a *p-n* junction diode has been created due to

   (A) a battery voltage across the junction.

   (B) a junction depletion region.

   (C) an excess amount of electrons.

   (D) an excess amount of holes.

36. The *I-V* curve for a diode is nonlinear because of

   (A) the conductivity of the *p* material.

   (B) the conductivity of the *n* material.

   (C) the junction barrier potential.

   (D) the width of the junction.

37. Calculate the division of the two hexidecimal numbers ($1A8E \div 21$).

   (A) $30FC$ (C) CE_{16}

   (B) $1E7F$ (D) CB

38. Calculate the multiplication of the two octal numbers ($775_O \times 56_O$).

   (A) $4,761_8$ (C) $55,566_8$

   (B) $5,756_8$ (D) $67,546_8$

39. The main property of cyclic codes is that successive numbers differ by only one binary bit position. Converting from binary to Gray is given by the Boolean equation (a_j is the binary bit position)

(A) $g_j = a_j \bar{a}_{j+1} + \bar{a}_j a_{j+1}$ (C) $g_j = a_j \bar{a}_{j+1}$

(B) $g_j = \bar{a}_j \bar{a}_{j+1} + a_j a_{j+1}$ (D) $g_j = \bar{a}_j a_{j+1}$

40. What is the minimum number of operations (shifts, additions, and subtractions) needed to square the binary number 0011111?

    (A) 7   (C) 5

    (B) 8   (D) 3

41. Compared to EPROM memories, PROM devices differ because

    (A) PROMs mask is programmed by the chip manufacturer.

    (B) PROMs permit only changes to unprogrammed bits.

    (C) PROMs are electrically eraseable.

    (D) PROMs are optically eraseable.

42. Direct memory access (DMA) in a microcomputer is useful because it

    (A) allows access to memory address

    (B) allows data transfer to I/O devices

    (C) allows access to memory without the involvement of the CPU

    (D) allows data transfer to RAM

43. Communications as defined in a technical sense refers to the

    (A) transmission of digital data

    (B) transmission of analog and digital data

    (C) transmission of data and information over a selected medium

    (D) modulation of a baseband carrier

44. Analog modulation in terms of communication refers to the

    (A) continuity of the carrier amplitude

    (B) continuity of the carrier

    (C) continuity of a carrier parameter

    (D) sinusoidal character of the carrier amplitude

45. Pulse modulation differs from CW modulation with respect to the

   (A) periodicity of the carrier

   (B) continuity of the carrier

   (C) periodicity of the carrier amplitude

   (D) shape of the carrier amplitude

46. Pulse Code Modulation (PCM) has a digital format in terms of the

   (A) number of pulses/unit time

   (B) number of discrete amplitude levels/pulse

   (C) number of carrier frequency shifts/unit time

   (D) number of carrier phase shifts/unit time

47. An AM modulated signal is represented as follows: $S(t) = A_C [1 + m(t)] \cos \omega_C t$, where A_C is the carrier amplitude and ω_C is the carrier frequency. The modulation positive peak is A_{max} and the modulation negative peak is A_{min}. What is the overall percent modulation?

   (A) $(A_{max}/A_{min}) \times 100^2$

   (B) $((A_C - A_{min})/A_C) \times 100$

   (C) $((A_{max} - A_{min})/A_C) \times 100$

   (D) $((A_{max} - A_C)/A_C) \times 100$

48. If the modulation signal in Question 47 contains no dc level (average of $m(t) = 0$), what is the normalized average power in the AM signal?

   (A) $<S^2(t)> = \frac{1}{2}(A_C)^2[1 + <m^2(t)>]$

   (B) $<S^2(t)> = \frac{1}{2}(A_C)^2$

   (C) $<S^2(t)> = \frac{1}{2}(A_C)^2 + \frac{1}{4}(A_C)_2[<m^2(t)>]$

   (D) $<S^2(t)> = (A_C)$

49. The ultimate ability of a receiver in the electromagnetic spectrum to detect signals is limited by

   (A) the type of electronic hardware design

   (B) the bandwidth of the receiver

(C) the noise energy within the frequency spectrum of the received signal

(D) the amplitude of the received signal

50. A matched filter receiver design is used in statistical signal processing to

(A) filter the incoming noise

(B) set a threshold to incoming noise signals

(C) maximize output peak–signal to average noise (power) ratio

(D) preserve the shape of the incoming signal waveform

51. The Fourier transform of a square pulse of unit amplitude, which varies in time from $-T/2$ to $T/2$, is given by $S(\omega) = T\sin(\omega T/2)/(\omega T/2)$. Use Parseval's theorem to obtain the energy within the spectral content of the pulse:

$$E = \frac{1}{2}\pi\int|S(\omega)|^2\,d\omega \qquad -\infty \le \omega \le \infty$$

(A) $\dfrac{1}{2}\pi$

(C) $\dfrac{T}{4}\pi$

(B) $\dfrac{T}{2}\pi$

(D) T

52. An electron of charge -1.60×10^{-19} coulombs and mass of 9.0×10^{-31}kg starts from rest and is accelerated by a uniform electric field of intensity 10,000 volts/m. How long does it take the electron to move a distance of 10 cm?

(A) 10.6×10^{-9} sec

(C) 160×10^{-9} sec

(B) 16.5×10^{-9} sec

(D) 9×10^{-9} sec

53. A dipole having charges of $\pm q$ are separated by a distance of $2d$. The dipoles located about the origin in the X-Y plane produce a potential at some distance r from the origin that is represented in polar coordinates as: $V = (2dq \cos \theta)/4\pi\varepsilon_0 r^2$. What is the magnitude of the force lines along the equipotential lines?

(A) $|F| = dq^2 \cos \theta/2\pi\varepsilon_0 r$

(B) $|F| = dq^2 (1 + 3\cos^2 \theta)^{1/2}/2\pi\varepsilon_0 r^3$

(C) $|F| = dq^2 \cos^2 \theta/2\pi\varepsilon_0 r^2$

(D) $|F| = dq^2 \cos^2 \theta/2\pi\varepsilon_0 r^3$

54. For the dipole described in Question 53, what is the radial ε_r and polar ε_θ components of the electric field intensity?

(A) $\varepsilon_r = dq \cos \theta/\pi\varepsilon_0 r^3$; $\varepsilon_\theta = dq \sin\theta/2\pi\varepsilon_0 r^3$

(B) $\varepsilon_r = dq \cos^2 \theta/2\pi\varepsilon_0 r^2$; $\varepsilon_\theta = dq \sin\theta/4\pi\varepsilon_0 r^2$

(C) $\varepsilon_r = dq \cos \theta/\pi\varepsilon_0 r$; $\varepsilon_\theta = dq \sin\theta/2\pi\varepsilon_0 r$

(D) $\varepsilon_r = dq \cos^2 \theta/2\pi\varepsilon_0 r^3$; $\varepsilon_\theta = dq \sin^2\theta/4\pi\varepsilon_0 r^3$

55. A capacitor consists of a metallic cylinder of radius a and a concentric hollow cylinder of inner radius b surrounding the cylinder of radius a. If the length l of the cylinders is large compared to their separation, find the capacitance/unit length of configuration.

(A) $C' = 4\pi\varepsilon_0 [(1/a) - (1/b)]$

(B) $C' = 4\pi\varepsilon_0 ab$

(C) $C' = 2\pi\varepsilon_0 [1/ln(b/a)]$

(D) $C' = 2\pi\varepsilon_0 a/b$

56. The magnetic force on a moving charge q (where B is the magnetic field vector, and v is the charge velocity) is defined as

(A) $F = vB \sin \theta$ (θ is the angle between v and B)

(B) $F = qvB \cos \theta$

(C) $F = q(v \times B)$ (Cross product)

(D) $F = q(v \cdot B)$ (Dot product)

57. The magnetic intensity H due to a current i in a wire at a perpendicular distance d from the wire is

(A) $H = \dfrac{i}{2\pi d}$

(C) $H = \dfrac{i}{2}\pi\mu_0 d$

(B) $H = \dfrac{i}{4}\pi\mu_0 d^2$

(D) $H = \dfrac{i}{4}\pi\mu_0 d$

58. For an instrumentation system as applied to the process control industry, powerful tools for the control of batch processes usually consist of which of the following?

    (A) Control computer and sensors

    (B) Control computer, sensors, data acquisition hardware, PLC, and control system

    (C) Control computer, pressure, temperature, and flow sensors

    (D) Control computer and data interface hardware

59. The manufacture of steel requires a complex interaction of raw materials and thermochemistry. One of the processes uses high purity oxygen. The pure oxygen introduced into the process results in the formation of iron oxide, carbon monoxide, and carbon dioxide. Elimination of the carbon compound is essential to the production of the high purity steel. On-line measurement instrumentation to monitor the carbon compound gases is readily achieved using

    (A) gas chromatography

    (B) infrared (IR) reference gas analyzer

    (C) chemical analysis of sample batches of steel

    (D) ultraviolet (UV) measurement system

60. The manufacture of conventional electrical pressure transducers use many different types of pressure elements to satisfy the large variety of specific applications. If a fiber optic bifurcated transmissive/reflective probe is applied to the sensor for pressure measurements, what physical parameter will be converted by the instrumentation to yield pressure measurements?

    (A) Direct force measurement of a diaphragm converted to an optical signal with overall calibration

    (B) Calibrated optical transmission through a diaphragm

    (C) Calibration of displacement for a diaphragm with an optically reflecting surface

    (D) Measurement of fiber optic cladding signal

TEST 1

ANSWER KEY

1.	(C)	16.	(B)	31.	(C)	46.	(B)
2.	(C)	17.	(B)	32.	(D)	47.	(C)
3.	(B)	18.	(C)	33.	(C)	48.	(A)
4.	(B)	19.	(B)	34.	(D)	49.	(C)
5.	(C)	20.	(D)	35.	(B)	50.	(C)
6.	(C)	21.	(A)	36.	(C)	51.	(D)
7.	(B)	22.	(C)	37.	(C)	52.	(A)
8.	(B)	23.	(D)	38.	(C)	53.	(B)
9.	(C)	24.	(C)	39.	(A)	54.	(A)
10.	(C)	25.	(C)	40.	(B)	55.	(C)
11.	(B)	26.	(B)	41.	(B)	56.	(C)
12.	(B)	27.	(C)	42.	(C)	57.	(A)
13.	(A)	28.	(B)	43.	(C)	58.	(B)
14.	(A)	29.	(B)	44.	(C)	59.	(B)
15.	(D)	30.	(C)	45.	(B)	60.	(C)

DETAILED EXPLANATIONS
OF ANSWERS

TEST 1

1. **(C)**

Note that the star network is symmetrical about a vertical center line through node e_1 and resistor R_1. This symmetry results in equal voltages from e_4 to ground and e_3 to ground. The resistor R_{10}, thus, has no effect on the equivalent network resistance. In addition, the reader can easily see that the combination of R_1 (1Ω) is in parallel with the collection of resistors R_2 - R_4 - R_6 - R_8 on one side and R_3 - R_5 - R_7 - R_9 on the other side. R_1 is in parallel with two equivalent resistor networks. Each network is a simple unbalanced ladder network. (See figure below.) Using one section of the network, the following equivalent resistance is obtained: combining R_6 and $R_8 = 2Ω$. This equivalent resistor is in parallel with R_4. The resultant equivalent resistance is equal to 2/3Ω. Combining this resistance with R_2, we obtain 5/3Ω. This 5/3Ω resistance is in parallel with the resistance R_1 (1Ω). Since there are two identical networks in parallel with R_1, the following is the equivalent value for the network, $R_{1eq} = 5/11Ω$.

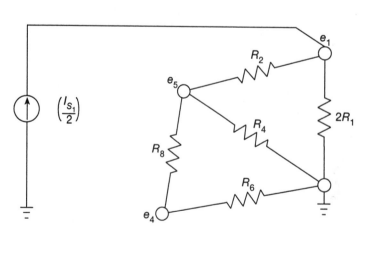

2. **(C)**

With the circuit's total equivalent resistance equal to $5/11\Omega$ (determined in Question 1), the voltage between node e_1 and ground is $E = IR = (1)(5/11) = 5/11$ volt. This voltage divides proportionally across resistor R_3 and the equivalent parallel resistance of R_5, R_7, and R_9. The equivalent parallel resistance of R_5, R_7, and R_9 is $(1)(2)/(1 + 2) = 2/3\Omega = R_x$. Thus, the voltage at node e_2 is $E(R_x)/(R_3 + R_x) = (5/11)(2/3)/(1 + 2/3) = 2/11$ volt.

3. **(B)**

Since the network is symmetrical, the voltages e_3 and e_4 with respect to ground are equal. Therefore, the voltage between node e_3 and node e_4 is 0 volts.

4. **(B)**

Using the unbalanced ladder network shown, each section or one-half of the symmetrical network has an equivalent resistance of $10/11\Omega$. This equivalent resistance is in parallel with $2R_1$. Calculating the effective overall resistance by using series parallel resistance combinations, the equivalent resistance from node e_4 to ground is $34/55\Omega$. Or,

$$2R_1 \parallel 10/11 = 5/8\Omega$$

$$5/8 + R_2 = 13/8\Omega$$

$$13/8 \parallel R_4 = 13/21\Omega; \ 13/21 + R_8 = 34/21\Omega$$

$$34/21 \parallel R_6 = 34/55\Omega =$$

the equivalent resistance from node e_4 to ground.

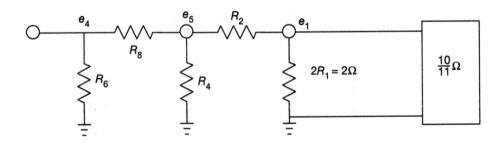

5. **(C)**

For this linear network, assume that the voltage across the output resistor $e_4 = 1$ volt. Then $i_4 = i_3 = 1$ amp.

The voltage across $L_2 = s$ volts.

The voltage $e_2 = e_4 + e_{L2} = 1 + s$.

The current in capacitor $C_1 = s + s^2$.

The current $i_1 = i_3 + i_{C1} = 1 + s + s^2$.

The voltage across $L_1 = s + s^2 + s^3$.

The input voltage $e_{in} = e_{L1} + e_2 = s^3 + s^2 + 2s + 1$.

The transfer function is $e_4/e_{in} = 1/(s^3 + s^2 + 2s + 1)$.

6. **(C)**

The input impedance of the RLC network is:

$$\frac{e_{in}}{i_1} = Z_{in} = \frac{(s^3 + s^2 + 2s + 1)}{(s^2 + 2s + 1)}.$$

7. **(B)**

The RMS AC voltage on the secondary winding of the transformer between one side and the center tap is $60V$. The DC voltage across the load resistor R_L is obtained from the average value of the full wave rectified sinusoidal voltage. The peak voltage E_p is $E_{RMS} \times \sqrt{2} = 84V$.

Thus,

$$V_{DC} = \left(\frac{2E_P}{T}\right) \int_0^{T/2} \sin\left[\left(\frac{2\pi}{T}\right)t\right] dt = \frac{2E_P}{\pi} = 54V.$$

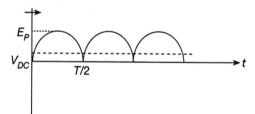

Voltage across R_L

V_{DC} = Average value of waveform

The ripple voltage is the AC value of the above waveform.

8. **(B)**
    The RMS value of the ripple voltage is:

$$V_{RMS} = \sqrt{(2E_p^2 / T)} \int_0^{T/2} \sin^2 [(2\pi/T)t]\, dt = E_p/\sqrt{2} = E_{RMS} = 60V$$

9. **(C)**
    Figure 3b is a so-called "voltage doubler" network. During an AC cycle, each capacitor charges to the peak input voltage, $E_P = \sqrt{2}\,E_{rms}$, with E_{rms} in this case representing the voltage across the entire secondary winding, or 120V. The DC output voltage is thus (ideally) the summed voltage across capacitors C_1 and C_2, or $2E_P = 2\sqrt{2}=E_{rms} = 339V$. In practical applications, the value of the load resistance R_{L1} and output capacitors (the combination of which basically acts as a filter), and any resistors placed in series with the diodes to limit input-surge currents will reduce the DC output voltage from a maximum of 339V down to approximately $2E_{rms}$.

10. **(C)**
    Using the generalized filter circuit as shown below, the overall transfer function can easily be derived.

$$e_O/e_{in} = 1/[1+ (Z_1 + Z_2)/Z_3 + Z_1 Z_2/Z_3 Z_F].$$

If we substitute the component values in the low pass filter, we obtain:

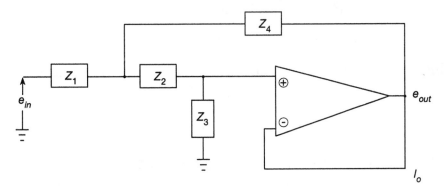

$$(e_O/e_{in})_{LP} = (1/R_1 R_2 C_1 C_2)/[S^2 + (R_1 + R_2)S/R_1 R_2 C_1 + (1/R_1 R_2 C_1 C_2)] .$$

The standard form for a second-order equation yields the following:

$$f_n^2 = (1/4\pi^2\, R_1 R_2 C_1 C_2)$$

Since

$$R_1 = R_2 = R = 10\text{K}; \; C_1 = 0.022\mu\text{F}; \text{ and } C_2 = 0.011\mu\text{F}$$

$$f_n = 1\text{kHz}$$

11. **(B)**

$$\xi = (\sqrt{(C_1/\,C_2)}[(R_1 + R_2)\,/\,2\sqrt{(R_1 R_2)}]. \quad \xi = 1/\sqrt{2} = 0.7071$$

12. **(B)**

The high-pass filter parameters yield the following:

$$\left(\frac{e_o}{e_{in}}\right)_{HP} = \frac{\left(\dfrac{S^2}{C_2}\right)}{\left[S^2 + \left(\dfrac{1}{R_2 C_2}\right)\left(\dfrac{1}{C_1 C_2}\right)S + \left(\dfrac{1}{R_1 R_2 C_2^2}\right)\right]}.$$

From the standard form for a second-order equation, we obtain:

$$f_n = 1/(2\pi C_2 \sqrt{(R_1 R_2)})$$

Since $\quad C_1 = C_2 = C$

and $\quad R_2 = 2R_1$, then $f_n = 1/(2\pi \sqrt{2} R_1 C)$

13. **(A)**

Inserting the parameters indicated yields the cutoff frequency,

$$f_n = 2.25\text{kHz}.$$

14. **(A)**

The diodes in the feedback loop of amplifier 1 determine the availability of the signal at the output terminal, as well as at the junction of resistors R_2 and R_3.

If V_{in} is positive, the amplifier will serve as an inverter and $e_{01} = -V_{in}$. If V_{in} has a negative polarity with respect to ground, inverting amplifier 1 output, e_{01} initially goes positive. Therefore, diode D_1 is back biased and nonconducting. Diode D_2 is forward biased and conducting. Assume "perfect" diodes, that is the forward resistance for D_2 is zero. Since the feedback resistance for amplifier 1 is zero, its gain is zero. Therefore, for a negative input voltage, $e_{01} = 0V$.

15. **(D)**

The voltage introduced to amplifier 2 via R_5 from V_{in} is inverted and filtered by capacitor C_1. The DC gain of amplifier 2 is $-(R_4/R_5) = -1$. Therefore, $e_{02} = |\,V_{in}\,|$.

When the input voltage is negative, there is no output from amplifier 1. If V_{in} has a positive polarity, then the output voltage of amplifier 1 is negative. Diode D_1 is forward biased and conducting. Diode D_2 is back biased and nonconducting. The inverting gain of amplifier 1 is then:

$$-(R_2/R_1) = -1.$$

Therefore,
$$e_{01} = -V_{in}.$$

Since the forward resistance of diode D_1 is zero, the voltage at the junction of resistors R_2 and R_3 is $-V_{in}$.

The output voltage e_{02} from amplifier 2 due to the voltage at the junction of resistors R_2 and R_3 is:

$$-V_{in}\,(-R_4/R_3) = 2V_{in}.$$

The voltage at the output of amplifier 2 due to the input voltage via R_5 is:

$$-(R_4/R_5)\,V_{in} = -V_{in}.$$

The resultant voltage at the amplifier output summing the two input values is thus equal to V_{in}. The output voltage e_{02} is always positive.

16. **(B)**

Memory (RAM) for personal computers is segmented into four areas. Conventional memory is located in the first 640K of RAM and is used temporarily to store the operating system, user programs, and required data. Upper memory is located between 640K and 1MB of RAM and is used for programs that control input and output devices and other computer hardware. Extended memory consists of all memory above 1MB and is used for programs and data. Not all programs are written to make use of extended memory. Expanded memory consists of up to 32MB of memory on a memory expansion board. These boards were used on some of the older computers. Most present-day computers use only extended memory and do not use expanded memory.

17. **(B)**

Interlaced monitors usually refer to computer displays that utilize a CRT (cathode ray tube). An electron gun at the rear of the tube generates a stream of electrons that is directed and accelerated toward the front screen of the tube. A magnetic coil device (or Yoke) or electrostatic deflection plates create an electromagnetic, or electrostatic field, respectively, within the device. These fields deflect the electron beam across and down scanning the CRT screen in two separate passes. Scanning on the second pass is interspersed between the first set of scan lines.

18. **(C)**

Magnetic tape density refers to the number of bits that can be stored on an inch of tape (bpi).

19. **(B)**

System software consists of programs related to the control of the computer's equipment operation. Within the system software is a set of programs called the operating system. Instructions within the operating system enable the computer to perform its basic tasks such as loading, storing, and executing programs. In order for a computer to operate, the operating system software must be stored and accessible from the system's memory. Each time the computer is started (boot operation) or restarted, the operating system software is loaded into the computer's main memory.

20. **(D)**

Many present-day computers use an operating environment that works with the operating system. This environment simplifies the process of computer utilization by a given user.

21. **(A)**

Project management software allows the user to plan, schedule, track, and analyze the events, resources, and costs of a project. The software provides a method to control and manage the variables of a project enabling the project to be completed on time and within budget.

22. **(C)**

With the speed and algorithm-development capability of present-day computers, optimized best fit polynomials are used to develop accurate and precise trigonometric functions. Computer storage would only require the program and algorithm to develop the numeric values.

23. **(D)**

Mathematically, the approximation technique for any selected function must be evaluated to determine if the numerical method used results in a process that oscillates and converges; oscillates and diverges; converges monotonically; or diverges monotonically. Each of these factors impact the speed of computation, accuracy, and precision over the region where these values are computed.

24. **(C)**

Interval halfing and iteration result in the accurate representation of algebraic and transcendental functions. Successive approximation starts with an initial estimate of the answer within a selected region. When this estimated value is inserted into the function, the result is calculated. If the answer to this calculation results in a value that is too large, half the estimated value is taken and subtracted from the original estimate. If the value is too small, half the estimated value is taken and added to the original estimate. The problem of solving an equation $F(x) = 0$ is finding a value or root x_i such that $F(x_i) = 0$. The iteration process for the successive approximation proceeds using this half interval approach until the answer results in some selected error that is less than or equal to some preassigned value.

25. **(C)**

The generalized transfer function for the second order proportional servomechanism with a disturbance torque T_L (step function T_L/s) at the output shaft is given by:

$$\varepsilon(s) = T_L/s[s^2 J + sf + K].$$

The steady-state value is $s\,\varepsilon(s)$ when $s = 0$.

Therefore, $\varepsilon_{ss} = T_L/K$.

26. **(B)**

Given a step of velocity input, the transfer function of the error signal is given by:

$$\varepsilon(s) = (sJ + f)\,\omega_I/s[s^2 J + sf + K].$$

The steady-state value is $s\,\varepsilon(s)$ when $s = 0$.

Therefore, $\varepsilon_{ss} = f\,\omega_I/K$

27. **(C)**

The standard form for a second order polynomial representing the poles and first or 0 order for the zeros is as follows:

$$\varepsilon(s) = T_L/Js\,[s^2 + 2\xi\omega_n s + (\omega_n)^2].$$

The damping ratio is:

$$\xi = f/2[\sqrt{KJ}] = 0.6.$$

28. **(B)**

The natural frequency of the servo $\omega_n = [\sqrt{K/J}] = 5.89$ radians/sec.

since $t = 1/\xi\omega_n = 0.283$ sec

29. **(B)**

The transfer function for the proportional servo with integral error control is:

$$\varepsilon(s) = \frac{\left(\dfrac{T_L}{J}\right)}{\left[\dfrac{s^3 + 2\xi\omega_n s^2 + (\xi\omega_n)^2 s + K_3}{J}\right]}.$$

The result is zero for the steady-state error.

30. **(C)**

If integral control is added to the proportional servo-mechanism, the system improves the steady-state performance but impairs the transient performance since the error becomes more oscillatory. The cubic denominator has three roots. In servo work there is usually one real root and two complex conjugate roots resulting in an exponentially weighted oscillatory term.

31. **(C)**

Semiconductors generally refers to a class of resistive crystalline material that contains only four valence electrons in its outer shell. Usually eight electrons are required to complete the outer shell. Semiconductors contain half the required number.

32. **(D)**

The process of doping an intrinsic semiconductor material adds a controlled amount of impurities to a pure crystalline structure. Depending on the dopant used as the impurity, an excess amount of electrons (*n*-type doping) or excess amount of holes (*p*-type doping) is contributed to the resultant material. Donor or acceptor atoms modify the electrical behavior of the intrinsic semiconductor.

33. **(C)**

If the dopant added to the semiconductor is *n*-type, then the majority carriers are free electrons and the minority carriers are the holes.

In *p*-type doping, the majority carriers are holes and the minority carriers are free electrons.

34. **(D)**

The area where *p* and *n* material are in contact is called the junction. In the vicinity of the junction between the two materials, there is a small area where the holes from the *p*-type material have been filled with electrons from the *n*-type material. This small region around the junction is called the depletion region because it has neither holes nor electrons.

35. **(B)**

As a result of the junction depletion region, a barrier potential has been created at the *pn* interface resulting in a semiconductor device called a diode.

36. **(C)**

If we place an external voltage across the diode *pn* junction and vary its magnitude, the electric field strength in the material begins to increase. As the potential increases, its value is sufficiently high to overcome the barrier potential at the junction depletion region. Standard ohmic conduction begins and current flows. The barrier potential creates the nonlinearity in the diode or *pn* junction I-V curve.

37. **(C)**

The hexidecimal numbers, base 16 (16^N), when converted to decimal numbers base 10 are given by:

$$1A8E_{16} = 6{,}798_{10} \; ; \; 21_{16} = 33_{10}.$$

The ratio of $\dfrac{1A8E}{21} = \dfrac{6{,}798}{33} = 206_{10} = CE_{16}.$

38. **(C)**

The octal numbers, base 8, when converted to decimal numbers base 10 are given by:

$$775_8 = 509_{10}; \; 56_8 = 46_{10}.$$

The product of $775 \times 56 = 509 \times 46 = 23{,}414_{10} = 55{,}566_8.$

39. **(A)**

The family of cyclic codes have the property that successive numbers differ by only a single bit position. The codes can be derived from the corresponding binary numbers as follows:

If a_j is a *binary* digit (0, 1) at bit position j as indexed from right to left ($j = 1...n$ from least significant to most significant bits), then the jth bit of the *cyclic* (e.g., Gray) code can be found from the a_j plus a_{j+1} bits of the binary code by means of the exclusive-OR (XOR) function:

$$g_j = a_j\,a_{j+1} + a_j\,a_{j+1}\,.$$

40. (B)

The binary number 0011111 can be written as:

$$2^5 - 2^0 = 100000 - 000001 = 31.$$

If we square the value of 31 using $2^5 - 2^0$, we obtain

$$2^{10} - 2^6 + 2^0 = 1{,}024 - 64 + 1 = 961.$$

Using this method we have one addition, one subtraction, and the rest of the operations are just six left shifts (multiplication by two for each shift). There are thus eight operations to achieve this rapid multiplication.

41. (B)

EPROMs or erasable PROMs are memory devices whose contents are programmed by a user and can be subsequently erased. This permits the memory device to be reprogrammed should changes be desired in the original stored program. PROMs or field programmable ROMs (Read Only Memory devices) only permit unprogrammed bits to be programmed at a later date.

42. (C)

Direct memory access (DMA), when it is an available resource of a µp (microprocessor), permits the accessing of memory without having the CPU involved. It is typically used to transfer data into or out of RAM from a device outside the µp. A typical computer application occurs in the transfer of records between the µp and a magnetic disk storage unit.

43. (C)

Communications refers to the transmission of data and information over a communications channel such as wire, optical, microwave, and RF links. These links allow wired and wireless connections enabling communications between a transmitting source and a receiving site.

44. (C)

Analog modulation refers to the property or parameter of a carrier wave (typically a fixed frequency sinusoid upon which the signal information $S(t)$ is impressed) that is proportional to the instantaneous value of the message and varies continuously within a predetermined range. Such is not the case for digital modulation.

45. (B)

Pulse modulation differs from continuous wave (CW) modulation (carrier is most frequently a fixed frequency sinusoid) in that the carrier signal is discontinuous and exists in a series of pulses, with some characteristic of the pulses modified in accordance with the modulating signal. The carrier in this case consists most often of a periodic sequence of pulses that is on only during a portion of the cycle.

The signal $S(t)$ is used to vary some parameter of the pulse such as amplitude (pulse amplitude modulation, or PAM), its duration (pulse duration modulation, or PDM), or its displacement from a reference point on the time scale (pulse position modulation, or PPM).

In PAM, which is the pulse analog of AM, the signal is impressed on the amplitude of the pulse. In PDM, the duration of the pulse is proportional to the signal amplitude during the instant when the pulse is on. In PPM, the delay of the pulse is proportional to the signal amplitude.

46. (B)

Pulse code modulation (PCM) takes the input analog amplitude (PAM) at a given instant and assigns it one of N preselected levels. The preselected levels are assigned numerical values referencing a defined code. This coded information is then transmitted over the communications channel. Generation of PCM requires sampling the modulated waveform, quantizing, and coding. Sampling is done by using a periodic sequence of pulses on a carrier. Quantizing generates a finite set of amplitude levels representing a continuous set of amplitude values. Each of the discrete amplitude levels values is assigned a code (typically a binary number representing the sampled amplitude at a given instant).

47. (C)

The percentage of modulation for an AM signal is defined in terms of positive modulation, negative modulation, and overall modulation.

$$\% \text{ positive modulation} = \left(\frac{(A_{\max} - A_c)}{A_c} \right) \times 100$$

$$\% \text{ negative modulation} = \left(\frac{(A_c - A_{min})}{A_c} \right) \times 100$$

$$\% \text{ overall modulation} = \left(\frac{(A_{max} - A_{min})}{A_c} \right) \times 100$$

48. **(A)**

The normalized average power of an AM signal

$$<S^2(t)> = <(A_c)^2[1 + m(t)]^2 \cos^2\omega_c t>$$

$$= \frac{1}{2}(A_c)^2 <[1 + m(t)]^2> + \frac{1}{2}(A_c)^2 <[1 + m(t)]^2 \cos 2\omega_c t>$$

$$[<S^2(t)> = \frac{1}{2}(A_C)^2 + \frac{1}{2}(A_C)^2 <m^2(t)>]$$

$$= \text{carrier power} + \text{sideband power}$$

49. **(C)**

The ultimate ability of a receiver to detect weak signals is limited by the noise energy that occupies the same portion of the frequency spectrum as does the signal energy. The weakest signal that a receiver can detect is called the minimum detectable signal.

50. **(C)**

A receiver whose spectrum or frequency response function maximizes the output peak-signal to mean noise (power) ratio is called a matched filter. The matched filter is an optimum method for the detection of signals in noise.

51. **(D)**

Parseval's theorem states:

$$\int | S(t)|^2 \, dt \, (-\infty \le t \le \infty) = \frac{1}{2}\pi\int | S(\omega) |^2 \, d\omega \, (-\infty \le \omega \le \infty).$$

The unit amplitude pulse has a total time duration of T sec. Therefore, $E = T$.

52. **(A)**

In a uniform field the electric intensity is the same everywhere, and the force acting on an electron is constant in magnitude and direction. Newton's law of motion gives $F = q\varepsilon = m \, dv/dt$. Integrating the velocity is given by:

$$v = v_0 + q\varepsilon t/m.$$

Since, $$v = dx/dt$$

$$x = v_0 t + q\varepsilon t^2/2m.$$

If, $$x = 10 \text{ cm} = 0.10 \text{m and the initial velocity } v_0 = 0$$

$$x = 0.10 = \frac{1}{2}[(1.60 \times 10^{-19}) \times 10^4/(9.0 \times 10^{-31})] \, t^2$$

$$t^2 = (9/8) \times 10^{-16}$$

Therefore, $$t = 10.6 \times 10^{-9} \text{ sec.}$$

53. **(B)**

For the dipole described, the potential energy is given by:

$$V = \frac{(2dq\cos\theta)}{4\pi\varepsilon_0 r^2}.$$

The radial and tangential force components relate to the rate of distance and angular change of the potential energy $F_r = q\varepsilon_r = -\dfrac{\partial V}{\partial \rho}$

$$F_\theta = q\varepsilon_\theta = -\frac{(1)}{r} \frac{\partial V}{\partial \theta}$$

Therefore, we obtain the following:

$$F_r = (4dq^2 \cos \theta)/4\pi\varepsilon_0 r^3$$

$$F_\theta = (2dq^2 \sin \theta)/4\pi\varepsilon_0 r^3$$

$$F^2 = (F_r)^2 + (F_\theta)^2$$

$$|F| = (dq^2/2\pi\varepsilon_0 r^3) \times (1 + 3\cos^2\theta)^{1/2}$$

54. **(A)**

Since $$V = (2dq\cos\pi\varepsilon)/4pe_0 r^2$$

then $$\varepsilon_r = (1/q)(-\partial V/\partial r) = dq\cos\theta/\pi\varepsilon_0 r^3$$

and $$\varepsilon_\theta = -(1/qr)\,\partial V/\partial\theta = dq\sin\theta/2\pi\varepsilon_0 r^3$$

55. **(C)**

The capacitance is defined as:

$$C' = q/(V_b - V_a).$$

The electric field due to a line of charges along the length of the cylinder is given by $\varepsilon = q/2\pi\varepsilon_0 r$. The potential difference $(V_b - V_a)$ is derived from the electric field as:

$$(V_b - V_a) = -\int \varepsilon_r \, dr \; (a \leq r \leq b)$$

$$(V_b - V_a) = (q/2\pi\varepsilon_0) \, [ln \, (b/a)].$$

$$C' = 2\pi\varepsilon_0/(ln \, (b/a)$$

56. (C)

Due to the solenoidal nature of the magnetic induction vector B, the force vector for a moving charge, similar to the cross product of a torque vector, is given by:

$$F = q(v \times B).$$

57. (A)

The contribution to H at a given point in space due to a current element ids along the length of the wire is:

$$dH = \frac{i \, ds \, \sin\alpha}{4\pi r^2}.$$

The angle α is obtained at the intersection of the distance vector r to a point in space and the current element ids. Integrating along the length of the wire (x axis):

$$H = \frac{i}{4\pi} \int dx \, \sin \frac{\alpha}{r^2}$$

$$H = \frac{i}{2\pi d}$$

58. (B)

A personal computer coupled to a programmable logic controller (PLC) as applied to distributed process control systems is extremely popular in the chemical process industry. Applications to many batch processes are currently applied to automating the instrumentation required to generate closed loop solutions to complex problems.

The typical instrumented configuration to automate this process consists of the personal computer coupled to a touch screen monitor and ruggedized line printer; the PLC supplies relay ladder logic with its own interface functioning as an I/O controller to many of the high-power motor drives and power supply hardware; and the array of sensors required to monitor the physical parameters associated with the batch process. The data acquisition equipment converts the sensor signals into a format required by the PC software for analysis and the implementation of the appropriate decision.

59. (B)

Basically the on-line instrumentation consists of a dual chamber IR gas analyzer. This instrumentation, defined as NDIR, is used with a suitable extractive sampling probe and sample gas conditioning system. The NDIR has found acceptance in the steel-making industry as a gas monitoring instrument. Conventional dispersive methods as applied to gas chromatography are generally suited for laboratory use because of cost and fragility. Nondispersive methods are in widespread use as applied to on-line measurements. For many years absorption of radiation at certain wavelengths by gases has been used as a means of identifying and quantifying them. The type of phenomena and their corresponding wavelength absorption are electronic transitions, 0-1.5 microns; bond vibration 1.5-30 microns; and srotation of molecules, 30-1,000 microns. In the case of gases, the vibration spectra are of the most practical interest.

60. (C)

A bifurcated fiber optic probe enables the transmission and reception, in a single cable, of the energy required to impinge on a diaphragm and the reflected energy from the diaphragm's deflecting surface. Calibration of this deflection enables a direct measure of pressure. In a basic pressure transducer a flat diaphragm is normally "bowed" or displaced from its nominal rest position as pressure is applied by the fluid or gas impinging on the transducer. Relating to the cross-sectional area of the diaphragm, sensors monitor this surface displacement. If the surface of the diaphragm is coated with an optically reflecting material, this displacement can be measured using optical means. That is, if there is a source (transmitter) of optical energy and a receiver of optical energy, the transducer could be calibrated in terms of the required physical parameter.

FE/EIT

FE: PM Electrical Engineering Exam

Practice Test 2

FUNDAMENTALS OF ENGINEERING EXAMINATION

TEST 2

(Answer sheets appear in the back of this book.)

TIME: 4 Hours
60 Questions

DIRECTIONS: For each of the following questions and incomplete state-ments, choose the best answer from the four answer choices. You must answer all questions.

Questions 1 and 2 are based on the following:

For the RLC network indicated in the diagram below, compute the parameters listed in Questions 1 and 2. (The answers for the ques-tions require the generalized Laplace notation (s) for the reactive elements.) Use the following generalized formulas to compute the instantaneous energy stored in the inductive and capacitive elements.

The s terms in the equations should be replaced by $s = j\omega$. Assume that the voltage and current in the system are sinusoids, and the voltage across $R_1 = 1$ volt and $\omega = 1$ radian/sec.

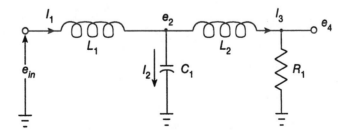

Figure 1

The network parameters are as follows:

$R_1 = 1\Omega$

$L_1 = L_2 = 1\text{H}$

$C_1 = 1\text{F}$

Instantaneous stored magnetic energy:

$$T = {}^1\!/_4 \Sigma\, L_K |I_K|^2 + {}^1\!/_4 Re[e^{2st}\Sigma\, L_K I_K^2]$$

$$= {}^1\!/_4 \Sigma\, L_K |I_K|^2 + {}^1\!/_4 Re\,[\cos(2t) + j\sin(2t)]\Sigma\, L_K I_K^2 \text{ joules}$$

Instantaneous stored electric energy:

$$V = (-1/4s^2)\Sigma|I_K|^2/C_K + (1/4s^2)Re[e^{2st}\,\Sigma\, I_K^2/C_K]$$

$$= (-1/4s^2)\Sigma|I_K|^2/C_K + {}^1\!/_4 Re\,[\cos(2t) + j\sin(2t)]\,\Sigma\, I_K^2/C_K \text{ joules}$$

1. The magnetic energy T stored in the inductors is

   (A) $^1\!/_2 + ^1\!/_2 \cos(2t)$ (C) $^1\!/_4 + ^1\!/_4 \cos(2t)$

   (B) $^1\!/_2$ (D) $^1\!/_4$

2. The energy V stored in the capacitor is

   (A) $^1\!/_2 + ^1\!/_2 \sin(2t)$ (C) $^1\!/_2 - ^1\!/_2 \sin(2t)$

   (B) $^1\!/_2$ (D) $^1\!/_4$

Questions 3 and 4 are based on the following:

For the given networks below, indicate which network or networks result in the required driving point impedance, $Z(s) = s(s^2 + 4)/(s^2 + 1)(s^2 + 9)$.

(a)

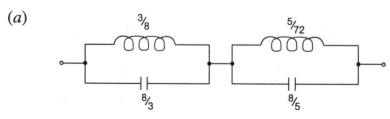

(b)

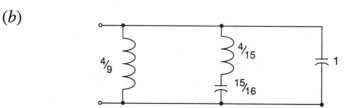

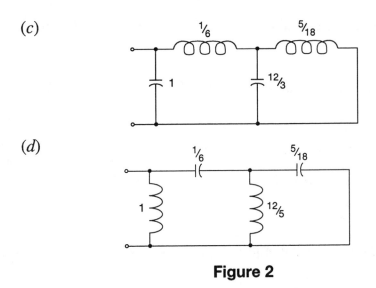

(c)

(d)

Figure 2

3. The required driving point impedance is satisfied by

   (A) network *a*.   (C) networks *a, b*, and *c*.

   (B) networks *a* and *b*.   (D) networks *c* and *d*.

4. Which network has a Cauer synthesized format?

   (A) network *a*   (C) network *c* and *d*

   (B) networks *a* and *b*   (D) networks *a*, *b*, and *c*

Questions 5 and 6 are based on the following:

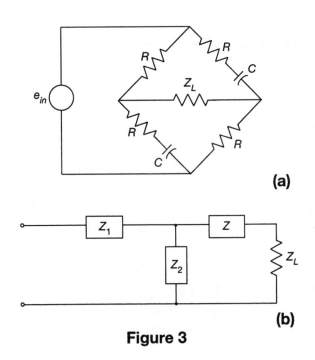

(a)

(b)

Figure 3

The Wheatstone Bridge shown in (a) can be replaced by the unbalanced T circuit in (b).

5. The series and shunt components of the T network are

    (A) $Z_1 = 2R; Z_2 = R + 1/sC$

    (B) $Z_1 = R + 1/sC ; Z_2 = 1/2sC$

    (C) $Z_1 = 2R + 2/sC; Z_2 = R$

    (D) $Z_1 = 1/sC; Z_2 = R$

6. The input impedance of the equivalent T network is

    (A) $Z_{in} = 2R$

    (B) $Z_{in} = (R + 4/3) + [(2/3)/[1 + 6/[(R + Z_L)sC]]]$

    (C) $Z_{in} = R + 2/(sC)^2$

    (D) $Z_{in} = 1/[1 + 2RsC + (RsC)^2]$

Questions 7–9 are based on the following:

Three-phase networks use combinations of Y-Delta/Delta-Y transformations to convert impedance or conductance levels, voltages, and currents to operate systems more efficiently than their single, phase counterparts. Using the following Y-Delta/Delta-Y networks, compute the following:

7. The impedance in each leg of the Delta as indicated in Figure 4a (on the next page) is

    (A) 100Ω (C) 300Ω

    (B) 173Ω (D) 260Ω

8. The impedance in each leg of the Y as indicated in Figure 4b is

    (A) 600Ω (C) 346Ω

    (B) 200Ω (D) $1,039\Omega$

9. What is the ratio of P_1/P_3? [Hint: Assume the total power P is supplied at a voltage V to both a single-phase network and a three-phase network (V is line to line), where both networks are resistive (Figure 4c), and power line losses in each network is represented by R.]

(A) 3

(C) 1/3

(B) 6

(D) 1/4

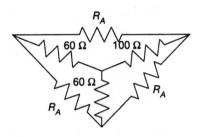

Figure 4a

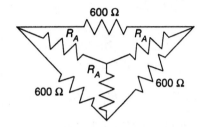

Figure 4b

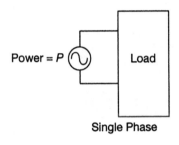

Single Phase

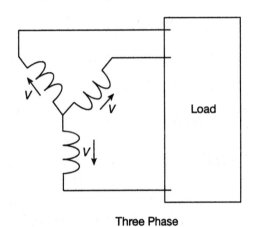

Three Phase

Figure 4c

Questions 10 and 11 are based on the following:

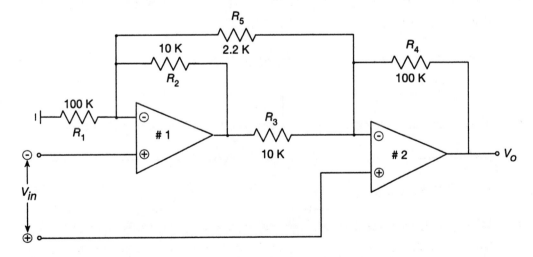

Figure 5

10. What is the gain (V_o/V_{in}) of the dual differential amplifier?

    (A) 11

    (C) 56

    (B) 25

    (D) 75

11. When is the optimum common-mode rejection for this amplifier achieved?

    (A) $R_4 = R_1$

    (C) $R_2/R_1 = R_3/R_4$

    (B) $R_1/R_2 = R_4/R_3$

    (D) $R_4 + R_5 = R_1$

Questions 12–15 are based on the following:

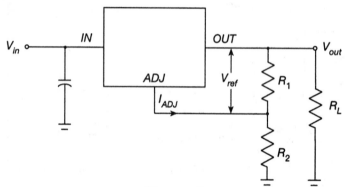

Figure 6a

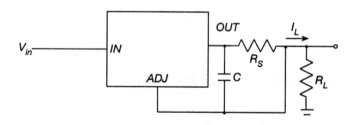

Figure 6b

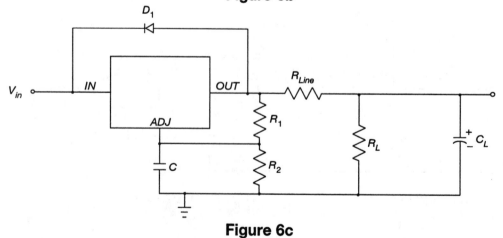

Figure 6c

12. The voltage across the load resistor R_L shown in Figure 6a is

    (A) $I_{ADJ}R_L + V_{REF} (1 + R_L/R_S)$ (C) $V_{REF} (1+ R_L/R_S)$

    (B) $I_{ADJ}R_L + V_{REF} (R_L/R_S)$ (D) $V_{REF} (R_L/R_S)$

13. The design configuration in Figure 6b defines what type of source?

    (A) Variable voltage source   (C) Variable current source

    (B) Fixed voltage source   (D) Fixed current source

14. In Figure 6c, if the distance to the load is large, where should R_1 be connected in order to maintain a fixed output voltage?

    (A) At the load terminal

    (B) Regulator terminal

    (C) It doesn't matter, at either terminal.

    (D) The load is only for a large R_L value.

15. What is the function of the diode D_1 in Figure 6c?

    (A) Protect against input terminal overvoltage

    (B) Protect against output capacitor discharge into the regulator

    (C) Protect against output terminal overvoltage

    (D) Protect against output terminal undervoltage

16. The Extended Binary Coded Decimal Interchange Code (EBCDIC) is

    (A) the most commonly used coding system to represent data.

    (B) used primarily on mainframe computers.

    (C) used on personal computers.

    (D) a seven-bit code that is expanded to an eight-bit code when representing special characters.

17. In a computer, the control unit and the ALU contain _____, which are temporary storage locations for specific types of data.

    (A) buses   (C) counters

    (B) registers   (D) clock drivers

18. A method of storing large amounts of data on tape is the application of _____, which uses helical scan technology to write data at much higher densities across the tape at an angle.

    (A) cache storage

    (B) optical methods

    (C) mass storage

    (D) digital audiotape (DAT)

19. Which is the most commonly used operating system for present-day computer workstations?

    (A) DOS

    (B) UNIX

    (C) Windows NT

    (D) Windows 95

20. The advantage of interpreters is

    (A) interpreted programs run faster than compiled programs.

    (B) the compiling process is not necessary before program changes can be tested.

    (C) the program is converted to machine language and stored in memory.

    (D) Both (A) and (C).

21. In object-oriented programming, the capability to combine methods (instructions) with objects (data) is called

    (A) inheritance

    (B) debugging

    (C) looping

    (D) encapsulation

22. Given that a function is stored in the computer in a table look-up form, which one of the following interpolation methods results in the most accurate numbers for computational purposes?

    (A) linear

    (B) quadratic

    (C) higher order polynomial

    (D) cubic

23. In order to compute the value of the error function in the computer $\left[f(x) = (2 / \sqrt{\pi}) \int_0^x e^{-t^2} dt \right]$, the method that results in the most accurate and compact representation of the integral is

    (A) integration using the Trapezoid rule.

    (B) integration using Simpson's rule.

(C) integration of Taylor series expansion.

(D) polynomial representation as $[1 - 1/(1 - a_1x + a_2x^2 + a_3x^3 + a_4x^4)^4]$.

24. Due to truncation used in the computation of infinite series representation of functions within the computer, the key issue for maximum accuracy is

(A) significant figures in arithmetic operations.

(B) round off.

(C) absolute accuracy of arithmetic operations.

(D) All of the above.

25. One of the methods that can be used to determine the stability of a servomechanism is to evaluate the coefficients of the polynomial representing the poles of the system transfer function. The method, called Routh's criterion, can be quickly used to determine if the polynomial contains positive roots or poles in the right half plane. For the following cubic equation, determine whether there are any positive roots in this cubic equation.

$$D(s) = s^3 + 2s^2 + 2.6s + 1.6$$

(A) one positive root   (C) three real negative roots

(B) none   (D) three negative complex roots

26. The general equation for the transfer function of a servomechanism can be described by the ratio of two polynomials. This transfer function can be graphically represented by the log-magnitude versus log-frequency curve and the phase angle versus log-frequency curve. The slope of the magnitude curve is usually described as $-X$db/octave, where X is usually 6, 12, 18, etc. The criteria for system stability of the transfer function is based on

(A) the phase angle is always $< 180°$.

(B) the magnitude curve is > -12 db/octave.

(C) the slope of the magnitude curve at 0 db is < -12 db/octave.

(D) the slope of the magnitude curve at 0 db is < -6 db/octave.

27. The gain margin in terms of stability for a system as defined in the log-magnitude plot is a measure of gain referenced to the gain at

    (A) low frequency when phase is $< 180°$.

    (B) 0db.

    (C) -12db.

    (D) -6db.

28. A system requiring critical damping normally has a phase margin of $60°$. This value is obtained where

    (A) the phase curve crosses the 0db gain.

    (B) the magnitude curve crosses 0db gain.

    (C) the magnitude curve $= -6$db.

    (D) the magnitude curve $= -12$db.

29. Statistical design theory as applied to control systems aims at

    (A) minimizing mean square noise in the system.

    (B) minimizing mean square error between actual and desired output.

    (C) designing nonlinear transfer functions.

    (D) optimizing system response time.

30. What method does the statistical design approach use to achieve the system response?

    (A) correlation between input and output

    (B) impulse response of output

    (C) superposition

    (D) input power density spectrum

Questions 31–34 are based on the following:

Transistor configurations can be generally described by five parameters. They are:

voltage gain $A_v = (e_{out}/e_{in})$

current gain $A_i = (i_{out}/i_{in})$

power gain $A_p = A_i A_v$

input resistance $r_{in} = (e_{in}/i_{in})$

output resistance $r_{out} = (e_{out}/i_{out})$

The common-base, common-emitter, and common-collector configurations are shown below.

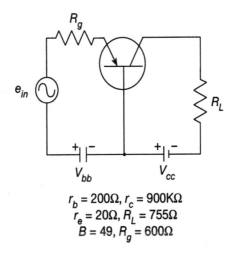

$r_b = 200\Omega,\ r_c = 900K\Omega$
$r_e = 20\Omega,\ R_L = 755\Omega$
$B = 49,\ R_g = 600\Omega$

Figure 7a

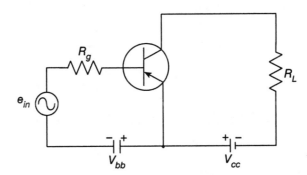

Figure 7b

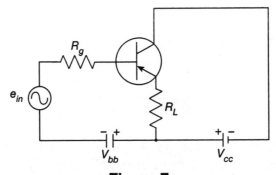

Figure 7c

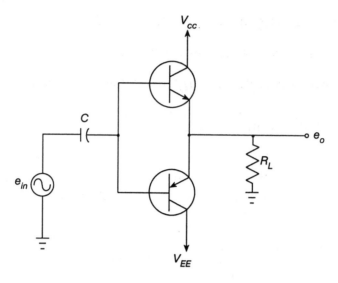

Figure 7d

31. For the common base (CB) configuration, determine r_{in} and r_{out}.

    (A) $r_{in} = 620\Omega$; $r_{out} = 900\text{K}\Omega$

    (B) $r_{in} = 624\Omega$; $r_{out} = 685\text{K}\Omega$

    (C) $r_{in} = 820\Omega$; $r_{out} = 755\Omega$

    (D) $r_{in} = 820\Omega$; $r_{out} = 754\Omega$

32. For the common emitter (CE) configuration, determine A_v and A_p.

    (A) $A_v = 20.55$; $A_p = 1{,}007$

    (B) $A_v = 61.7$; $A_p = 3{,}021$

    (C) $A_v = 1.26$; $A_p = 61.7$

    (D) $A_v = 46.2$; $A_p = 2{,}266$

33. For the common collector (CC) configuration, determine r_{in} and r_{out}.

    (A) $r_{in} = 37.6\text{K}\Omega$; $r_{out} = 755\Omega$

    (B) $r_{in} = 39.55\text{K}\Omega$; $r_{out} = 36\Omega$

    (C) $r_{in} = 1.355\text{K}\Omega$; $r_{out} = 754\Omega$

    (D) $r_{in} = 38.6\text{K}\Omega$; $r_{out} = 900\text{K}\Omega$

34. The complementary symmetry output transistor circuit shown in Figure 7d operates in a common collector configuration. This class B zero-base current bias configuration is useful because

(A) there is no nonlinearity in the output signal.

(B) it has high efficiency as a power driver.

(C) the output waveform is a good reproduction of the input waveform.

(D) it's applicable for tuned circuit loads.

35. The conduction angle for the SCR's in Figure 8 is regulated by the triggers from the sensing circuit. A small conduction angle will give a _____ output voltage, while a large conduction angle will give a _____ output voltage.

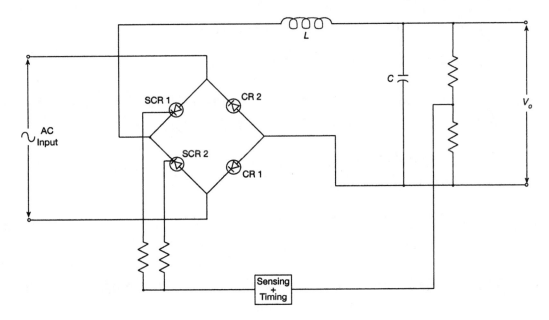

Figure 8

(A) high, low   (C) low, low

(B) low, high   (D) high, high

36. The N-channel JFET shown in Figure 9 achieves control and amplifying characteristics because of its

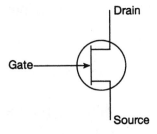

Figure 9

(A) voltage control of gate resistance.

(B) similarity to transistors.

(C) voltage control of drain to source resistance.

(D) current control of drain to source resistance.

37. Which one of the following major functions is performed by the control unit in a basic microprocessor?

(A) interprets and directs the computer program

(B) controls the signals to the I/O port

(C) controls the signals to the random access memory

(D) controls the computer timing

38. The instruction register in a basic microprocessor design is primarily used for

(A) special instructions.

(B) instructing the arithmetic unit.

(C) instructing the indexing register.

(D) I/O instructions.

39. The arithmetic unit in a basic microprocessor often employs which one of the following number of registers?

(A) 2, accumulator and instruction registers

(B) 3, accumulator, index, and instruction registers

(C) 3, accumulator, multiplier, and addend registers

(D) 4, accumulator, index, instruction, and control registers

40. The functioning of a basic computer during the execution of an instruction is defined in how many basic phases?

(A) eight phases   (C) four phases

(B) two phases   (D) three phases

41. The operations code in a computer programmed instruction performs what function?

(A) It defines the next instruction address.

(B) It defines the operation for the data specified by the address field.

(C) It is used only for indirect addressing.

(D) It is used to control the index register.

42. Address modification of a programmed instruction is normally achieved using the

(A) accumulator.   (C) instruction register.

(B) index register.   (D) current address register.

43. A standard AM signal ($v(t) = A_C[1 + m(t)]$ cos $\omega_C t$) is fed into a diode resistor/capacitor network shown below, where the diode has the following characteristics: $i_d = i_s (e^{qv/KT} - 1)$. The output waveform will be characteristic of a

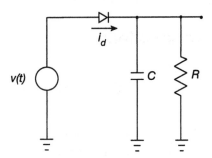

Figure 10

(A) square law envelope detector

(B) linear envelope detector

(C) complex power series detector

(D) combination linear and square law envelope detector

44. If an FM signal is represented as $v(t) = A_C \cos(\omega_C t + \delta \sin \omega_m t)$ where $\delta = k_f A_m/\omega_m$ and $\delta = \Delta\omega_C/\omega_m$ is defined as the modulation index (ratio of the maximum frequency deviation to the modulating frequency), what is the Fourier series representation of this complex waveform?

(A) $v(t) =$ (B) or (D), where $1 \le n \le \infty$; $J_\alpha(\delta)$ = Bessel function.

(B) $v(t) = A_C \Sigma(2J_{2n}(\delta) \cos (2n\omega_m t) + J_0(\delta))\cos (\omega_C t) - A_C \Sigma 2J_{2n-1}(\delta)$ $\sin((2n - 1) \omega_m t) \sin(\omega_C t)$, where $1 \le n \le \infty$; $J_\alpha(\delta)$ = Bessel function.

(C) $v(t) = A_C \Sigma(2J_{2n}(\delta) \cos (2n\omega_m t) + J_0(\delta))\cos (\omega_C t) + A_C \Sigma 2J_{2n-1}(\delta)$ $\sin((2n-1) \omega_m t) \sin(\omega_C t)$, where $1 \le n \le \infty$; $J_\alpha(\delta)$ = Bessel function.

(D) $v(t) = A_C \Sigma(J_{2n}(\delta) [\cos (\omega_C + 2n\omega_m)t + \cos (\omega_C - 2n\omega_m)t] + J_0(\delta)\cos (\omega_C t) + A_C \Sigma J_{2n-1}(\delta) [\cos (\omega_C - (2n - 1)\omega_m)t - \cos(\omega_C + (2n - 1)\omega_m)t]$.

45. The spectrum of the FM signal, which is represented by the information in Question 44, consists solely of frequencies whose spacing is determined by

   (A) the difference frequencies (C) the carrier frequency

   (B) the modulation frequency (D) the sum frequencies

46. A time function $f(t)$, which is band-limited to B Hz, is represented as follows:

$$f(t) = C_0 / T + 2/T \Sigma |C_n| \cos(\omega_n t + \theta_n)$$

   where $\omega_n = 2\pi n/T$ and $1 \le n \le BT$. How many independent samples are required to represent $f(t)$ over the interval of T seconds?

   (A) BT

   (B) $2BT$

   (C) $\omega_n T$

   (D) $4BT$

47. For the band-limited signal described in Question 46, what is the maximum channel capacity for information transmission in bits/sec?

   (A) $C = 2\pi n/T$

   (B) $C = 2B$

   (C) $C = (1/T) \log_2 n$

   (D) $C = B \log_2 n$

48. For a band-limited modulated signal whose message spectrum is limited to $|f| \le B$ and ideal filtering, what is the required bandwidth occupancy for double sideband AM using synchronous demodulation?

   (A) B

   (B) $2B$

   (C) $4B$

   (D) $3B$

49. The matched filter receiver, in order to optimize the peak-signal to noise ratio (S/N), achieves its result by

    (A) filtering the thermal noise input.

    (B) cross correlating the signal and noise.

    (C) cross correlating the signal plus noise, and signal.

    (D) determining the inverse frequency transform of the noise.

50. Given a receiver with a narrow bandwidth spectrum, the probability that the envelope of a wide-band Gaussian noise signal will exceed a threshold V_T at the output of the receiver is given by: $P_{fa} = exp\,[-(V_T)^2/2\,\psi_0]$, where ψ_0 is the mean of the noise power. P_{fa} defines the probability of a false alarm. The average time interval between crossings of the threshold by noise alone is defined as the false alarm time $T_{fa} = 1/N\,\Sigma\,T_K$, where lim $(N \to \infty)$ and T_K is the time between crossings of the threshold V_T by the noise envelope. $P_{fa} = 1/T_{fa}\,B$. B is the receiver bandwidth. For a 1 MHz bandwidth and average false alarm time of 15 minutes, what is the ratio of threshold voltage V_T to rms value of noise voltage $\sqrt{\psi_0}$?

    (A) $V_T/\sqrt{\psi_0} = 10$

    (C) $V_T/\sqrt{\psi_0} = 8.52$

    (B) $V_T/\sqrt{\psi_0} = 6.42$

    (D) $V_T/\sqrt{\psi_0} = 12.84$

51. Given that a series of 50 identical pulses are accepted at the input to a noisy receiver, what estimate can be attributed to the improvement of signal-to-noise ratio if the signals are filtered by an integrating detection system?

    (A) 50:1

    (C) $5\sqrt{2}$:1

    (B) $50/\sqrt{2}$:1

    (D) 25:1

52. Ampère's circuital law relating to electromagnetic theory can be stated as which of the following?

    (A) The magnetic intensity H due to a current in a straight wire at a point P in space is inversely related to the perpendicular distance from P to the wire.

(B) The magnetic intensity H integrated around any closed path is equal to the current crossing any surface of which this closed path is boundary.

(C) The magnetic induction field B at a point r in space due to a current in a wire is related to the volume integral of the current density and the cross product of the unit distance vector $\div r^3$.

(D) The current flow in a conductor is continuous.

53. If there is an alternating current density $J = J_0 \sin \omega t$ at some point in a dielectric medium of conductivity σ and permittivity $\in$, the displacement current J_d then equals

(A) J/σ.

(C) $J_0 \omega \in \cos \omega t$.

(B) $J_0 \in \sin \omega t$.

(D) $(J_0 \omega \in /\sigma) \cos \omega t$.

54. The relationship between the electric displacement vector D and the potential φ produced by a given charge q in space is defined as

(A) $D = \in_0 \varphi$

(B) $D = \in_0 \partial \varphi /\partial v$, where v is the vector components of the charge space coordinates.

(C) $D = \in_0 q\varphi$

(D) $D = \in_0 q\varphi^2$

55. Given the solutions to Maxwell's equations are $(\partial H_z/\partial x) = -\in_0 (\partial \varepsilon_y / \partial t)$; and given the electric vector y component is $\varepsilon_y = \varepsilon_0 \sin \omega (t - x/c)$, and the term c is the velocity of light in a vacuum. What is the wave impedance in space of a traveling plane wave?

(A) $120/\pi$ ohms

(C) 120π ohms

(B) $(\in_0 \mu_0)^{1/2}$ ohms

(D) $(\in_0 / \mu_0)^{1/2}$ ohms

56. The Poynting vector relates to the energy flow per time due to electromagnetic waves propagating in a selected medium. If the Poynting vector S is represented by the cross product $(\varepsilon \times H)$, select the equation for the time average power/area in the x-axis direction of a linearly polarized traveling plane wave with an electric field $\varepsilon_y = \varepsilon_0 \sin \omega (t - x/c)$.

(A) $S = (c/2) \in_0 (\varepsilon_0)^2$

(B) $S = (c)[\in_0 (\varepsilon_0)^2 + \mu_0 (H_0)^2]^{1/2}$

(C) $S = (c/2) \, (\in_0/\mu_0)(\varepsilon_0)^2$

(D) $S = (c/2) \, (\mu_0 \in_0) \, (H_0)^2$

57. If a dipole with a charge q and separation distance d is oscillating at a radian frequency of ω, the time average of energy flow/area across a sphere of radius r is

$$S = \left[\frac{\omega^4 (dq\varepsilon_0)^2}{32\pi^2 \in_0^3} \right] \frac{\sin^2 \theta}{r^2}$$

What is the total radiated power for the dipole?

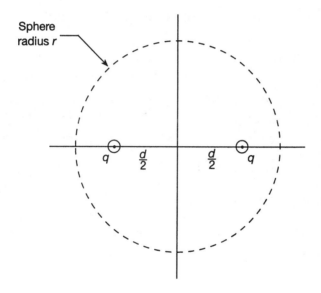

Figure 11

(A) $P = \omega^4 \, (dq\varepsilon_0)^2 / 32\pi^2 \in_0 c^3$

(B) $P = \omega^4 \, (dq\varepsilon_0)^2 / 12\pi \in_0 c^3$

(C) $P = \omega^4 \, (dq\varepsilon_0)^2 / 12\pi \in_0 c^2$

(D) $P = \omega^4 \, (dq\varepsilon_0)^2 / 12\pi c^2 \, (\in_0 \mu_0)^{1/2}$

58. Instrumentation to accurately measure flow in various fluid and gas systems covers a wide range of technologies. Which one of the following technologies will result in the most accurate measurement of liquid or gas flow?

(A) Turbine meter

(B) Venturi tube

(C) Magnetic flowmeter

(D) Vortex shedding meters

59. Noncontact temperature measurements of metal surfaces require instrumentation that reduces or eliminates the nonlinear proportionality of radiated energy with respect to radiated wavelength (λ^{-5}). Select a design approach that will result in a temperature measurement yielding the highest accuracy.

(A) Calibration for emissivity of a metal surface and calculations using Planck's black body equation

(B) Calibration and ratiometric wavelength measurements using Wien's equation

(C) Calibration and table lookup in the control computer to reference measured data

(D) Optical temperature measurement via wavelength

60. Instrumentation to monitor the vibration of machinery (possibly destructive) on the factory floor can be implemented using tuning forks or high-frequency accelerometers. Which design approach does not require actual contact with the machine to determine the vibration and is not influenced by surrounding environmental parameters?

(A) capacitance probe

(B) magnetic proximity probe

(C) optical displacement measurement probe

(D) acoustic measurement probe

TEST 2

ANSWER KEY

1.	(B)	16.	(B)	31.	(B)	46.	(B)
2.	(C)	17.	(B)	32.	(A)	47.	(D)
3.	(C)	18.	(D)	33.	(B)	48.	(C)
4.	(C)	19.	(B)	34.	(B)	49.	(C)
5.	(B)	20.	(B)	35.	(B)	50.	(B)
6.	(B)	21.	(D)	36.	(C)	51.	(C)
7.	(C)	22.	(C)	37.	(A)	52.	(B)
8.	(B)	23.	(D)	38.	(B)	53.	(D)
9.	(B)	24.	(D)	39.	(C)	54.	(B)
10.	(C)	25.	(B)	40.	(C)	55.	(C)
11.	(C)	26.	(D)	41.	(B)	56.	(A)
12.	(B)	27.	(B)	42.	(B)	57.	(B)
13.	(D)	28.	(B)	43.	(B)	58.	(A)
14.	(B)	29.	(B)	44.	(A)	59.	(B)
15.	(B)	30.	(A)	45.	(B)	60.	(C)

DETAILED EXPLANATIONS
OF ANSWERS

TEST 2

1. **(B)**
    With $s = j1$ and the given network parameters, we have $I_{RI} = I_3 = 1$, $I_1 = I_2 + I_3 = j1$, and $I_2 = j(1 + j1) = -1 + j1$. The input voltage is $E_{in} = E_1 + E_C = j1$, $E_1 = j I_1 = -1$, the voltage across L_2 is $E_{L2} = j1$, and the voltage across C is $E_C = E_{RI} + E_{L2} = 1 + j1$.

    As a result, $|i_1^2| = 1$, $|i_2^2| = 2$, and $|i_3^2| = 1$. Substituting these values in T, we obtain:

    $$T = 1/4 \, (|i_1^2| + |i_3^2|) + 0 \cos(2t) = 1/2$$

2. **(C)**
    With $|i_2^2| = 2$, the equation for V yields:

    $$V = 1/4(|i_2^2|) - 1/4 Re[\cos(2t) + j \sin(2t)][-j2]$$

    $$V = \frac{1}{2} - \frac{1}{2}\sin(2t)$$

3. **(C)**
    If we perform a partial fraction expansion for the impedance and susceptance functions, we obtain:

    $$Z(s) = (3/8s)/(s^2 + 1) + (5/8s)/(s^2 + 9) = s(s^2 + 4)/(s^2 + 1)(s^2 + 9)$$

    $$Y(s) = (9/4)/s + (15/4)s/(s^2 + 4) + s = 1/Z(s)$$

Network A impedance is:

$$[3/8s \, || \, 1/((8/3)s)] + [5/72s \, || \, 1/((8/5)s)]$$

$$= \left[\frac{\left(\dfrac{3}{8}\right)\left(\dfrac{3}{8}\right)}{\dfrac{3}{8}s + \dfrac{1}{\dfrac{8}{3}s}} \right] + \left[\frac{\left(\dfrac{5}{72}\right)\left(\dfrac{5}{8}\right)}{\left(\dfrac{5}{72}s\right) + \dfrac{1}{\left(\dfrac{8}{5}\right)s}} \right]$$

Network *B* impedance is:

$$1/[s + 1/((4/9)s) + 1/[(4/15)s + 1/((15/16)s)]]$$

Network *C* impedance is:

$$1/[1/[[(12/3)s + 1/((5/18)s)] + (1/6)s] + s]$$

Network *D* impedance is:

$$1/[1/[1/[(5/18)s + 1/((12/5)s)] + 1/((1/6)s)] + 1/s]$$

The networks *a*, *b*, and *c* satisfy the pole, zero requirements of the impedance function *Z*(*s*).

4.   **(C)**

Inverting the impedance function and dividing the numerator by the denominator, we obtain the Cauer form of network synthesis. The Cauer form of network synthesis (unbalanced network) is obtained from a continuous fraction expansion of the pertinent impedance function and removal of poles either at $s = 0$ or $s = \infty$. This is referred to as a canonic form. This results in network formats shown in (*c*) and (*d*)

$$\frac{s^3 + 4s}{\left(s^4 + 10s^2 + 9\right)}$$

The parallel series terms for the network are s, $s/6$, $12/5s$, and $5s/18$.

5.   **(B)**

The Bridge not including load impedance, Z_2, or lattice circuit can be replaced by the following *T* network using circuit symmetry. In a lattice the following equivalence is obtained:

$$Z_1 = Z_A$$

and:
$$Z_2 = (Z_B - Z_A)/2.$$

$$Z_{11} \text{ (Lattice)} = \tfrac{1}{2}(Z_B + Z_A)$$

$$Z_{12} \text{ (Lattice)} = \tfrac{1}{2}(Z_B - Z_A)$$

$$Z_{11}(T) = (Z_1 + Z_2)$$

$$Z_{12}(T) = Z_2$$

Let:
$$Z_{11} \text{ (Lattice)} = Z_{11}(T)$$

and:
$$Z_{12} \text{ (Lattice)} = Z_{12}(T)$$

Therefore:
$$Z_1 = Z_A$$

and:
$$Z_2 = (Z_B - Z_A)/2.$$

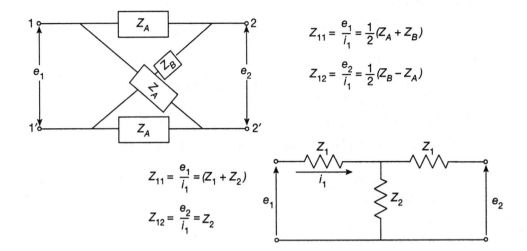

$$Z_{11} = \frac{e_1}{i_1} = \frac{1}{2}(Z_A + Z_B)$$

$$Z_{12} = \frac{e_2}{i_1} = \frac{1}{2}(Z_B - Z_A)$$

$$Z_{11} = \frac{e_1}{i_1} = (Z_1 + Z_2)$$

$$Z_{12} = \frac{e_2}{i_1} = Z_2$$

6. **(B)**

The input impedance of the unbalanced linear network is calculated by assuming one volt across the output load resistor and calculating the series/shunt voltages and current. The input impedance is:

$$E_{in}/i_1 = Z_{in}.$$

Alternatively, $\quad\quad Z_{in} = Z_1 + [(Z_1 + Z_L) \parallel Z_2]$

7. **(C)**

The conductance transformation from a Y-Delta is given by the following equations:

$$g_A = (g_a g_b)/(g_a + g_b + g_c)$$

$$g_B = (g_b g_c)/(g_a + g_b + g_c)$$

$$g_C = (g_c g_a)/(g_a + g_b + g_c)$$

where g_a, g_b, or g_c is the value of the conductances in each leg of the Y. Since the resistance value in each leg of the Y is 100Ω ($R_a = 1/g_a$, etc.), the Delta resistance values are 300Ω.

8. **(B)**

The impedance transformation from a Delta-Y is the dual of the Y-Delta transformation. Thus:

$$r_A = (r_a r_b)/(r_a + r_b + r_c)$$

$$r_B = (r_b r_c)/(r_a + r_b + r_c)$$

$$r_C = (r_c r_a)/(r_a + r_b + r_c)$$

Since the resistance value in each leg of the Delta is 600Ω, the Y resistance values are 200Ω.

9. (B)

The current in each line in the single-phase system $I = P/V$. The total line loss is $2I^2R = 2(P/V)^2R$. In the three-phase line, the current in each conductor is $I = P/3V$. Each phase transmits 1/3 the power. The total line loss is $3I^2R = (P/V)^2R/3$. The line loss for the single-phase line is six times the three-phase line.

10. (C)

The gain of amplifier 1 is $(1 + R_2/R_1)$. Now $V_{in} = V_2 - V_1$, where V_2 is the voltage at the noninverting input of amplifier 2, and V_1 is the voltage at the negative input of amplifier 1 (and thus at V_{in}'s negative terminal by virtue of the amplifier's virtual ground). Thus, the output of amplifier 1 is:

$$Vo_1 = V_1(1 + R_2/R_1)(-R_4/R_3)$$

The voltage at the output of amplifier 2 due to V_1 as applied through resistor R_5 is:

$$Vo_2 = V_1(-R_4/R_5)$$

Finally, the voltage at the output of amplifier 2 due to V_2 is approximately:

$$e_{o2} = V_2(1 + R_4/(R_3 \mathbin{\|} R_5)).$$

The summed output voltage is thus $Vo = Vo_1 + Vo_2 + e_{o2}$. With $V_{in} = V_2 - V_1$ and the given resistor values, we get:

$$Vo = V_2(1 + R_4(R_3 \mathbin{\|} R_5)) + V_1(-R_4/R_5) + V_1[1 + (R_2/R_1)(-R_4/R_3)$$

$$Vo = (1 + 100/1.8)V_2 - (100/2.2)V_1 - (1.1)(10)V_1$$

or

$$Vo \approx 56(V_2 - V_1).$$

Thus,

$$Vo/V_{in} \approx 56.$$

11. (C)

If the input voltage at the negative terminal of amplifier 1 with respect to ground is defined as V_1 and the input to the positive terminal of amplifier 2 with respect to ground is defined as V_2, then we have the following:

$$V_{CMM} \text{ (common mode voltage)} \equiv Vo \text{ when } V_2 = V_1.$$

$$V_{in} = V_2 - V_1.$$

If $V_{in} = 0$ volts, then the common mode voltage $V_{CMM} \equiv Vo$ is minimized when $R_2/R_1 = R_3/R_4$.

12. **(B)**

The figure represents the standard configuration for an adjustable three-terminal voltage regulator. The reference voltage and adjustment current help define the required output characteristics. As determined from the circuit, the output current, or load current, is:

$$I_L = V_{REF}/R_S + I_{ADJ}$$

The output voltage is:

$$I_L R_L = (V_{REF}/R_S + I_{ADJ}) \, R_L.$$

13. **(D)**

The design configuration in the figure is effectively a constant current source.

14. **(B)**

In the figure, the resistor R_1 should be connected to the regulator output terminal. If R_1 is connected to the load resistor, then the output voltage will fluctuate as the line resistance varies.

$$V_{OUT} = V_{REF} \, (1 + R_2/R_1) \, / \, (1 + R_{LINE}/R_1) + I_{ADJ} R_2$$

15. **(B)**

For a fluctuating regulator load, the charge/discharge demand on the capacitor C_L becomes important in order to sustain a fixed output voltage. Since the regulator output impedance is very low (voltage source), the load capacitor will "dump" its charge into this terminal during a discharge cycle. To prevent regulator damage, the diode D_1 is added to the circuit as indicated in the figure. The discharge current flowing in diode D_1 will bypass the output terminal and flow back to the regulator supply voltage.

16. **(B)**

The Extended Binary Coded Decimal Interchange Code (EBCDIC) is typically used for mainframe computers. The eight-bit code has similar characteristics to the standard eight-bit ASCII code used on personal computers. The lower order four bits of the EBCDIC code are similar to the low order four bits in the ASCII code. Between the numbers 0–9 and the characters A–I, the low order bits for the two codes are identical. EBCDIC only uses the binary equivalent of 0–9 for these four bits. EBCDIC as well as ASCII codes are also used to represent data on magnetic tape.

17. **(B)**

In a computer, the central processing unit (CPU) contains, among other functional units, a control unit and an arithmetic logic unit (ALU). The control unit operates by performing the machine cycle tasks of fetching, decoding, executing, and storing programs. The ALU contains the hardware required to perform arithmetic and logical operations on data. Both the control unit and the ALU contain registers, representing temporary storage locations for selective types of data.

18. **(D)**

Storing large amounts of data on tape is readily achieved using digital audiotape (DAT). Data is written on this tape using a helical scan process, rather than in precise rows along the length of the tape. This method leads to extremely high density of bit storage. The data on magnetic tape is organized in rows that run along the length of the tape. A column of data on the tape runs along the width of the tape. Each column from the rows is used to represent a character.

19. **(B)**

Workstations were initially developed to be used for intensive engineering software applications that were typically connected in a network environment. Personal computers or PC's have evolved from a single-user requirement. The required operating system that would allow great programming flexibility at the same time that the user could readily interact with other computer systems was determined to be the Bell Labs software called UNIX. This software was licensed from ATT by a number of computer hardware companies. They incorporated the UNIX operating system in various forms in their workstation type of computers.

20. **(B)**

A compiler converts an entire program into machine language that is stored in the computer memory for execution at some later time. An interpreter translates one program statement at a time and then executes the resulting machine language code before translating the next program statement. When an interpreter is used, program execution is line by line. There is no requirement to store a separate machine language or object program. The advantage of interpreters is that the compiling process is not necessary for the program process of debugging, testing, and running. The disadvantage of interpreters is that interpreted programs do not run as fast as compiled programs. Translation to machine language is performed "on the fly."

21. **(D)**

Object-oriented programs (OOP) is an approach that allows the programmer to create objects, a combination of data and instructions. Previous approaches to programming kept the data requirements separate from the programming code. Specific instructions called methods define how objects act when used by a program. The capability to combine methods (instructions) with objects (data) is called encapsulation. OOP define classes of objects. Each class contains methods unique to that class. Each class can have a number of subclasses. Each subclass contains the methods of its higher classes plus any method that is unique to that subclass. The OOP capability to pass methods from higher classes to lower classes is called inheritance.

22. **(C)**

Curve fitting techniques as applied to stored reference data in the computer indicates that using a higher order polynomial interpolation approach will result in nonstored computed values with the maximum accuracy. Linear and quadratic interpolation are just a subset of the more general higher order polynomial interpolation.

23. **(D)**

The Trapezoid rule as applied to numerical integration represents the area under the selected function using the sum of rectangular and triangular areas. Simpson's rule represents the area under the curve to be integrated by using parabolic or quadratic polynomials over selected intervals. Integration of the terms in the Taylor series expansion of the Gaussian function can result in an accurate representation of the error function. The number of terms in the series expansion will determine the final accuracy of the error function's computed value. The most accurate and compact representation of the error function, as defined by the integral, is accomplished by using the ratio of polynomials. This representation has been demonstrated by mathematicians in their research on numerical analysis.

24. **(D)**

Truncation of the series representation for Transcendental functions in the computer limit the accuracy of the computed value. Within the truncation process, precision, round-off error, and the absolute accuracy of the computer's arithmetic operations all impinge on the accuracy of computed values.

25. **(B)**

Routh's criterion as applied to the generalized cubic equation:

$$As^3 + Bs^2 + Cs + D$$

results in no positive roots if $AD < BC$.

In this problem, $AD = 1.6$ and $BC = 5.2$. The polynomial has no positive roots. This can be easily seen by factoring the cubic equations into the following terms:

$$(s + 1)(s^2 + s + 1.6).$$

26. **(D)**

The log-magnitude and phase plots for the transfer function can be easily used to determine overall system stability. Oscillation occurs in a feedback system if the loop gain ≥ 1 and the phase shift around the loop is 180°. A system with a log-magnitude gain slope at 0db of −6db/octave has a maximum phase shift of −90°. A system with a log-magnitude gain slope at 0db of −12db/octave has a maximum phase shift of 180°.

27. **(B)**

Stability for gain and phase are referenced at the 0db ($G = 1$) cross-over point for the log-magnitude plot.

28. **(B)**

The phase margin is a measure of the phase shift of the system transfer function when the log-magnitude plot crosses the 0db level. The margin for system stability is 180° minus the transfer function phase shift.

29. **(B)**

Statistical design theory as applied to control systems specifies that the mean square error between the actual system output and the desired system output should be minimized. Using the superposition integral which relates the input to the system to the unit impulse response of the system, the mean square error function results in: autocorrelation of the input signal, autocorrelation of the output signal, and cross correlation between input and desired output.

30. **(A)**

The statistical design approach achieves the system response via the superposition integral which results in cross correlation between input and output.

31. **(B)**

The input resistance of the common base (CB) circuit is:

$$r_{in} = R_g + [1/(\beta + 1)] \, r_b = 600 + 200/50 = 624\Omega.$$

The ouput resistance of the CB circuit is:

$$r_{out} = r_c \, [1 - (\beta/\beta + 1) \, r_b/(r_b + r_e + R_g)]$$

$$= 900K \times [1 - (49/50) \times 200/820] = 685K\Omega$$

32. **(A)**

The current gain:

$$A_i = \beta.$$

The voltage gain for the CE circuit:

$$A_v = \beta R_L/[r_b + (\beta +1) \, r_e + R_g].$$

The power gain is then equal to:

$$A_i \, A_v = \beta^2 \, R_L/[r_b + (\beta +1) \, r_e + R_g].$$

The voltage gain:

$$A_v = 20.55.$$

The power gain:

$$A_p = 1,007.$$

33. **(B)**

The input resistance is:

$$r_{in} = R_g + r_b + (\beta +1)(R_L + r_e)$$

$$= 600 + 200 + 50 \times 775$$

$$= 39,550\Omega$$

The output resistance is:

$$r_{out} = r_e + (R_g + r_b)/(\beta + 1)$$

$$= 20 + 800/50$$

$$= 36\Omega$$

34. **(B)**

The complementary symmetry circuit has both stages operating with zero bias, and these stages can be considered as amplifiers operating in

Class B. As such, they provide relatively high-power conversion efficiency. Both stages are emitter followers and thus will only give current (power) gain not voltage gain. Power gain is usually required in an output stage to drive low impedance devices such as loudspeakers.

35. (B)

A small conduction angle will give a low output voltage while a large conduction angle will give a high output voltage.

36. (C)

Basically, a JFET can be considered as a variable resistor. The current between the source and drain depends on the *N*-type material. One of the basic features of the JFET is the very high impedance of the device as measured between the gate and source terminal. The current between the source and drain is under the control of an electric field caused by a voltage that is applied to the gate terminal. This voltage-controlled device is similar to the grid voltage control that is present in vacuum tube technology.

37. (A)

The computer control unit must perform at least a minimum of two assigned functions. The unit must interpret the set of program instructions defined for the selected computer. Based on this interpretation, it must direct the operation of the arithmetic unit. The control function that interprets or decodes the instruction is called the instruction decoder. After the instruction has been decoded, the control unit via the instruction register tells the arithmetic unit which operation to perform.

38. (B)

The instruction register primarily directs the operation of the arithmetic unit.

39. (C)

The basic arithmetic unit in a simple microprocessor design normally employs a minimum of three registers. They are defined as the A, R, and Q registers. Register A functions as an accumulator. Register R stores the addend, subtrahend, multiplicand, and divisor. Register Q or MQ, operating as a shift register, stores the multiplier at the start of a multiplication function and the quotient at the end of a division function. This register is not used during addition and subtraction.

40. **(C)**

The functioning of a computer during the execution of an instruction is usually summarized in terms of four phases. Assuming that an instruction has been transmitted to the instruction register, phase one involves the transmission of the first argument from memory to the accumulator. During this phase the instruction decoder determines the address of the first argument from the instruction, and the control unit produces signals that enable transmission of this memory address into the accumulator. During phase two the second argument is shifted into the arithmetic unit and the operation is performed. During phase three the contents of the accumulator is transmitted into the memory address specified by the instruction. Phase four defines the address of the next instruction, and the contents of the current address register is changed to the new address. The contents of this new address is then transmitted into the instruction register as the next instruction.

41. **(B)**

The contents of the instruction register consists of two fields of data. They are the operation code field and an address field. The operation code specifies the operation to be performed on the operand in the memory address located at the address specified by the address field.

42. **(B)**

Address modification can be effectively achieved by using one or more index registers (occasionally referred to as the B registers), an index adder, and associated control circuits. The amount of change of an address, called the index value, is stored in the index register.

43. **(B)**

The process of detection or demodulation is generally accomplished by a process of rectification, which essentially requires a nonlinear circuit element. The circuit elements are usually separated into two classes: linear envelope detection and square law detection. In linear detection, the current through the detecting element is zero part of the time and flows in pulses. Square law detectors have unidirectional current flow, which is greater than zero at all times. The output of the detector in this circuit approaches the value of the input envelope of the modulated signal.

44. **(A)**

Expanding:

$$v(t) = A_C \cos(\omega_c t + \delta \sin \omega_m t)$$

we obtain the following:

$$v(t) = A_C[\cos(\omega_c t) \cos(\delta \sin \omega_m t) - \sin(\omega_c t) \sin(\delta \sin \omega_m t)]$$

The cosine and sine of trigonometric functions are related to the nth order Bessel function. Therefore:

$$v(t) = A_C \Sigma (2J_{2n}(\delta) \cos (2n\omega_m t) + J_0(\delta))\cos (\omega_c t)$$

$$- A_C \Sigma 2J_{2n-1}(\delta) \sin((2n-1) \omega_m t) \sin(\omega_c t)$$

where $1 \leq n \leq \infty$; $J_\alpha(\delta)$ = Bessel function.

This function can be expanded into sum and difference terms:

$$v(t) = A_C \Sigma (J_{2n}(\delta) [\cos(\omega_c + 2n\omega_m)t + \cos(\omega_c - 2n\omega_m)t]$$

$$+ J_0(\delta)\cos (\omega_c t) + A_C \Sigma J_{2n-1}(\delta)$$

$$[\cos(\omega_c - (2n-1)\omega_m)t - \cos(\omega_c + (2n-1)\omega_m)t]$$

45. **(B)**

Regardless of how small the modulation index δ is, the spectrum of $v(t)$ consists solely of frequencies that are separated by intervals set by the modulating frequency $\omega_m/2\pi$—not the deviation frequency.

46. **(B)**

The Nyquist sampling theorem for signals band-limited to B Hz requires a minimum of $2B$ samples/sec to completely reproduce and define $f(t)$. Thus, $2BT$ independent samples are needed to specify $f(t)$ over the interval or period of T seconds.

47. **(D)**

Shannon's theory states that the channel capacity C and bandwidth are related by: $C = B \log_2 n$ bits/sec, where $2\pi B = 2\pi n/T$. B is the channel bandwidth in Hertz.

48. **(C)**

Perfect reproduction of a band-limited double sideband ($\pm B$ band spread) AM signal using synchronous or envelope demodulation requires a bandwidth of $(2 \times 2B) = 4B$. This is consistent with the Nyquist sampling theorem.

49. **(C)**

The output of the matched filter is not a replica of the input signal. The output is proportional to the input signal cross-correlated with a replica of the transmitted signal except for a time delay t_d. The cross-correlation function $R(t)$ of two signals $y(\lambda)$ and $s(\lambda)$ is defined as:

$$R(t) = \int y(\lambda)\, s(\lambda - t)\, d\lambda$$

$$-\infty \leq t \leq \infty$$

The output $y_0(t)$ of a filter with an impulse response $h(t)$ when the input is:

$$y_{in}(t) = s(t) + n(t)$$

is:

$$y_0(t) = \int y_{in}(\lambda)\, h(t - \lambda)\, d\lambda - \infty \leq \lambda \leq \infty.$$

For the matched filter $h(\lambda) = s(t_d - \lambda)$. Then

$$y_0(t) = \int y_{in}(\lambda)\, s(t_d - t + \lambda)\, d\lambda = R(t - t_d).$$

The matched filter cross correlates the received signal corrupted by noise and a replica of the transmitted signal.

50. **(B)**

The probability of false alarm:

$$P_{fa} = 1/\, T_{fa}\, B$$

$$= 1/(10^6 \times 15 \times 60)$$

$$= 1.1111 \times 10^{-9}$$

$$= exp\, [-\,(V_T)^2\, /\psi_0].$$

Therefore, using natural logs, we have the ratio:

$$(V_T)^2\, /2\; \psi_0 = 20.6179$$
$$V_T\, /\sqrt{\psi_0} = 6.42$$

51. **(C)**

If n pulses of all the same signal-to-noise ratio were integrated by an ideal coherent detector, the resulting signal-to-noise ratio would be n times that of a single pulse. However, when a large number of pulses are integrated for small signal-noise ratio per pulse, the resulting signal-noise ratio approaches $n^{1/2}$. For the 50 pulses in the example, the improvement is $5\sqrt{2}:1$.

52. **(B)**

Ampère's circuital law relates to the solenoidal nature of a magnetic field. The integral of the magnetic intensity $\int H_s \, ds$ around any closed path is equal to the current crossing any surface of which the closed path is a boundary.

$$\int H_s \, ds = \int J_n \, dS = i.$$

53. (D)

Ampère's law enables us to relate the displacement current across a closed surface.

$$\int J_n \, dS + \partial q / \partial t = 0; \int D_n \, dS = q$$

$$\int (J_n + \partial D_n / \partial t) dS = 0 = \int (J_n + J_{dn}) dS$$

$$J_d = \partial D_n / \partial t = \epsilon \, \partial e / \partial t = (\epsilon / \sigma) \, \partial J / \partial t = \omega(\epsilon / \sigma) \, J_0 \cos \omega t$$

54. (B)

From the auxiliary relationships needed to define the quantities in Maxwell's equations, $B = \mu_0 H$ and $D = \epsilon_0 \varepsilon$. Therefore, $\int \varepsilon_s \, dS = - \int (\partial B_n / \partial t) \, dS$. $\varepsilon = \partial \varphi / \partial v$, where v is the coordinates of the space components.

55. (C)

Using Maxwell's equations, we have:

$$(\partial H_z / \partial x) = - \epsilon_0 \, (\partial \varepsilon_y / \partial t)$$

where $$\varepsilon_y = \varepsilon_0 \sin \omega \, (t - x/c).$$

Therefore, $$(\partial H_z / \partial x) = - \omega \, \varepsilon_0 \cos \omega \, (t - x/c).$$

$$H_z = c \epsilon_0 \varepsilon_0 \sin \omega \, (t - x/c).$$

In addition,

$$(\mu_0)^{1/2} H_0 = (\epsilon_0)^{1/2} \varepsilon_0.$$

Therefore, the wave impedance $= \varepsilon_0 / H_0 = (\mu_0 / \epsilon_0)^{1/2} \approx 377$ ohms $\approx 120\pi\Omega$.

56. (A)

The Poynting vector $S = (\varepsilon \times H)$. For the linearly polarized traveling plane waves, we have:

$$(\mu_0)^{1/2} H_z = (\epsilon_0)^{1/2} \varepsilon_y.$$

Also,

$$S = c \epsilon_0 \, (\varepsilon_y)^2.$$

Thus, the time average power/area is equal to:

$$c\epsilon_0 (\epsilon_{rms})^2 = (c/2)\epsilon_0(\epsilon_0)^2$$

57. (B)

Integrating the radiated power over the surface of a sphere of radius $r \int S\, dA$, we have the following:

$$P = \omega^4 (dq\epsilon_0)^2/16\pi^2\epsilon_0 c^3 \int \sin^3 \theta\, d\theta$$

where:

$$0 \leq \theta \leq \pi.$$

The integral when evaluated results in:

$$\int \sin^3 \theta\, d\theta = \frac{4}{3}.$$

Therefore, the average total power is:

$$\omega^4 (dq\, \epsilon_0)^2/12\pi\epsilon_0 c^3.$$

58. (A)

A turbine meter consists of a bladed rotor installed in a flow tube. The rotor is suspended axially in the direction of flow. As fluid passes through the tube, the rotor spins on its axis at a rate proportional to the fluid velocity. Turbine meters provide high accuracy and repeatability over a wide flow range. Typical accuracy varies between ±0.15% to ±0.50% over flow ranges of 10–35:1.

The Venturi tube has a tapered inlet and diverging outlet. The Venturi can measure moderately dirty fluids since there are no places for dirt to build up in the tube. The discharge coefficient of a Venturi is constant and predictable to ±1%.

A magnetic flowmeter consists of a section of pipe, a nonconductive liner material, and flush-mounted electrodes. Electromagnetic coils surrounding the section of pipe induce a magnetic field. The fluid moving through the pipe acts as a conductor. This results in an induced voltage at the electrodes, which is only a function of the fluid velocity. The magnetic flowmeter has accuracies of ±0.5% to ±1% over a flow range of 10:1.

Vortex shedding is the formation of whirlpools or eddies by turbulent flow about a blunt-faced object. The rate of vortex formation is directly proportional to volumetric flow above a minimum threshold flow rate. A sensor placed in close proximity to the initiating object measures the frequency of the pressure fluctuation associated with the vortex formation.

Accuracy varies from a value of ±0.75% to ±1.25% over a 10–15:1 flow range for liquids.

59. **(B)**

Planck's black body radiation equation is given by:

$$W_\lambda = C_1 \lambda^{-5} (e^{c/\lambda T} - 1)^{-1}.$$

Planck's equation is reduced to Wien's equation at high temperatures and short wavelengths. Thus, we obtain:

$$W_\lambda = C_1 \lambda^{-5} (e^{c/\lambda T})^{-1},$$

where C_1 and C are constants, λ is the radiation wavelength, and T is the temperature. Actual "real-world" objects are approximated by $W_\lambda = \varepsilon C_1 \lambda^{-5} (e^{c/\lambda T})^{-1}$, where ε is the emissivity of the metal surface. Measuring the radiation at two different fixed wavelengths and taking the ratio of the energies, we obtain:

$$\frac{W_{\lambda 1}}{W_{\lambda 2}} = \left(\frac{\lambda_1}{\lambda_2}\right)^{-5} e^{-c[(\lambda_2 - \lambda_1)/\lambda_2 \lambda_1]T}.$$

Expanding the exponential in a power series and eliminating the constants via calibration, we obtain the following:

$$\frac{W_{\lambda 1}}{W_{\lambda 2}} \propto T.$$

Thus:

$$\frac{W_{\lambda 1}}{W_{\lambda 2}} \cong -\frac{K}{T}.$$

60. **(C)**

The optical probe is not affected by most external parameters. Ambient light conditions are eliminated by pulsed light sources and narrowband wavelength filters. Using a capacitance or magnetic proximity probe for displacement measurements of the machine's surface during vibration requires the design analysis of stray electromagnetic fields. Massive amounts of conductive, or nonconductive, magnetic, or nonmagnetic, properties of machine material produce extraneous or fringe fields. These fields in turn will effect the accuracy of the measured displacement information. Acoustic sensors have a limited frequency range.

FE/EIT

FE: PM Electrical Engineering Exam

Answer Sheets

FE: PM ELECTRICAL ENGINEERING
Test 1
ANSWER SHEET

1. Ⓐ Ⓑ Ⓒ Ⓓ
2. Ⓐ Ⓑ Ⓒ Ⓓ
3. Ⓐ Ⓑ Ⓒ Ⓓ
4. Ⓐ Ⓑ Ⓒ Ⓓ
5. Ⓐ Ⓑ Ⓒ Ⓓ
6. Ⓐ Ⓑ Ⓒ Ⓓ
7. Ⓐ Ⓑ Ⓒ Ⓓ
8. Ⓐ Ⓑ Ⓒ Ⓓ
9. Ⓐ Ⓑ Ⓒ Ⓓ
10. Ⓐ Ⓑ Ⓒ Ⓓ
11. Ⓐ Ⓑ Ⓒ Ⓓ
12. Ⓐ Ⓑ Ⓒ Ⓓ
13. Ⓐ Ⓑ Ⓒ Ⓓ
14. Ⓐ Ⓑ Ⓒ Ⓓ
15. Ⓐ Ⓑ Ⓒ Ⓓ
16. Ⓐ Ⓑ Ⓒ Ⓓ
17. Ⓐ Ⓑ Ⓒ Ⓓ
18. Ⓐ Ⓑ Ⓒ Ⓓ
19. Ⓐ Ⓑ Ⓒ Ⓓ
20. Ⓐ Ⓑ Ⓒ Ⓓ
21. Ⓐ Ⓑ Ⓒ Ⓓ
22. Ⓐ Ⓑ Ⓒ Ⓓ
23. Ⓐ Ⓑ Ⓒ Ⓓ
24. Ⓐ Ⓑ Ⓒ Ⓓ
25. Ⓐ Ⓑ Ⓒ Ⓓ
26. Ⓐ Ⓑ Ⓒ Ⓓ
27. Ⓐ Ⓑ Ⓒ Ⓓ
28. Ⓐ Ⓑ Ⓒ Ⓓ
29. Ⓐ Ⓑ Ⓒ Ⓓ
30. Ⓐ Ⓑ Ⓒ Ⓓ

31. Ⓐ Ⓑ Ⓒ Ⓓ
32. Ⓐ Ⓑ Ⓒ Ⓓ
33. Ⓐ Ⓑ Ⓒ Ⓓ
34. Ⓐ Ⓑ Ⓒ Ⓓ
35. Ⓐ Ⓑ Ⓒ Ⓓ
36. Ⓐ Ⓑ Ⓒ Ⓓ
37. Ⓐ Ⓑ Ⓒ Ⓓ
38. Ⓐ Ⓑ Ⓒ Ⓓ
39. Ⓐ Ⓑ Ⓒ Ⓓ
40. Ⓐ Ⓑ Ⓒ Ⓓ
41. Ⓐ Ⓑ Ⓒ Ⓓ
42. Ⓐ Ⓑ Ⓒ Ⓓ
43. Ⓐ Ⓑ Ⓒ Ⓓ
44. Ⓐ Ⓑ Ⓒ Ⓓ
45. Ⓐ Ⓑ Ⓒ Ⓓ
46. Ⓐ Ⓑ Ⓒ Ⓓ
47. Ⓐ Ⓑ Ⓒ Ⓓ
48. Ⓐ Ⓑ Ⓒ Ⓓ
49. Ⓐ Ⓑ Ⓒ Ⓓ
50. Ⓐ Ⓑ Ⓒ Ⓓ
51. Ⓐ Ⓑ Ⓒ Ⓓ
52. Ⓐ Ⓑ Ⓒ Ⓓ
53. Ⓐ Ⓑ Ⓒ Ⓓ
54. Ⓐ Ⓑ Ⓒ Ⓓ
55. Ⓐ Ⓑ Ⓒ Ⓓ
56. Ⓐ Ⓑ Ⓒ Ⓓ
57. Ⓐ Ⓑ Ⓒ Ⓓ
58. Ⓐ Ⓑ Ⓒ Ⓓ
59. Ⓐ Ⓑ Ⓒ Ⓓ
60. Ⓐ Ⓑ Ⓒ Ⓓ

FE: PM ELECTRICAL ENGINEERING
Test 2
ANSWER SHEET

1. Ⓐ Ⓑ Ⓒ Ⓓ
2. Ⓐ Ⓑ Ⓒ Ⓓ
3. Ⓐ Ⓑ Ⓒ Ⓓ
4. Ⓐ Ⓑ Ⓒ Ⓓ
5. Ⓐ Ⓑ Ⓒ Ⓓ
6. Ⓐ Ⓑ Ⓒ Ⓓ
7. Ⓐ Ⓑ Ⓒ Ⓓ
8. Ⓐ Ⓑ Ⓒ Ⓓ
9. Ⓐ Ⓑ Ⓒ Ⓓ
10. Ⓐ Ⓑ Ⓒ Ⓓ
11. Ⓐ Ⓑ Ⓒ Ⓓ
12. Ⓐ Ⓑ Ⓒ Ⓓ
13. Ⓐ Ⓑ Ⓒ Ⓓ
14. Ⓐ Ⓑ Ⓒ Ⓓ
15. Ⓐ Ⓑ Ⓒ Ⓓ
16. Ⓐ Ⓑ Ⓒ Ⓓ
17. Ⓐ Ⓑ Ⓒ Ⓓ
18. Ⓐ Ⓑ Ⓒ Ⓓ
19. Ⓐ Ⓑ Ⓒ Ⓓ
20. Ⓐ Ⓑ Ⓒ Ⓓ
21. Ⓐ Ⓑ Ⓒ Ⓓ
22. Ⓐ Ⓑ Ⓒ Ⓓ
23. Ⓐ Ⓑ Ⓒ Ⓓ
24. Ⓐ Ⓑ Ⓒ Ⓓ
25. Ⓐ Ⓑ Ⓒ Ⓓ
26. Ⓐ Ⓑ Ⓒ Ⓓ
27. Ⓐ Ⓑ Ⓒ Ⓓ
28. Ⓐ Ⓑ Ⓒ Ⓓ
29. Ⓐ Ⓑ Ⓒ Ⓓ
30. Ⓐ Ⓑ Ⓒ Ⓓ

31. Ⓐ Ⓑ Ⓒ Ⓓ
32. Ⓐ Ⓑ Ⓒ Ⓓ
33. Ⓐ Ⓑ Ⓒ Ⓓ
34. Ⓐ Ⓑ Ⓒ Ⓓ
35. Ⓐ Ⓑ Ⓒ Ⓓ
36. Ⓐ Ⓑ Ⓒ Ⓓ
37. Ⓐ Ⓑ Ⓒ Ⓓ
38. Ⓐ Ⓑ Ⓒ Ⓓ
39. Ⓐ Ⓑ Ⓒ Ⓓ
40. Ⓐ Ⓑ Ⓒ Ⓓ
41. Ⓐ Ⓑ Ⓒ Ⓓ
42. Ⓐ Ⓑ Ⓒ Ⓓ
43. Ⓐ Ⓑ Ⓒ Ⓓ
44. Ⓐ Ⓑ Ⓒ Ⓓ
45. Ⓐ Ⓑ Ⓒ Ⓓ
46. Ⓐ Ⓑ Ⓒ Ⓓ
47. Ⓐ Ⓑ Ⓒ Ⓓ
48. Ⓐ Ⓑ Ⓒ Ⓓ
49. Ⓐ Ⓑ Ⓒ Ⓓ
50. Ⓐ Ⓑ Ⓒ Ⓓ
51. Ⓐ Ⓑ Ⓒ Ⓓ
52. Ⓐ Ⓑ Ⓒ Ⓓ
53. Ⓐ Ⓑ Ⓒ Ⓓ
54. Ⓐ Ⓑ Ⓒ Ⓓ
55. Ⓐ Ⓑ Ⓒ Ⓓ
56. Ⓐ Ⓑ Ⓒ Ⓓ
57. Ⓐ Ⓑ Ⓒ Ⓓ
58. Ⓐ Ⓑ Ⓒ Ⓓ
59. Ⓐ Ⓑ Ⓒ Ⓓ
60. Ⓐ Ⓑ Ⓒ Ⓓ

FE/EIT

FE: PM Electrical Engineering Exam

Appendix

VARIABLES

a	=	acceleration
a_t	=	tangential acceleration
a_r	=	radial acceleration
d	=	distance
e	=	coefficient of restitution
f	=	frequency
F	=	force
g	=	gravity = 32.2 ft/sec^2 or 9.81 m/sec^2
h	=	height
I	=	mass inertia
k	=	spring constant, radius of gyration
KE	=	kinetic energy
m	=	mass
M	=	moment
PE	=	potential energy
r	=	radius
s	=	position
t	=	time
T	=	tension, torsion, period
v	=	velocity
w	=	weight
x	=	horizontal position
y	=	vertical position
α	=	angular acceleration
ω	=	angular velocity
θ	=	angle
μ	=	coefficient of friction

EQUATIONS

Kinematics

Linear Particle Motion

Constant velocity

$$s = s_o + vt$$

Constant acceleration

$$v = v_o + at$$

$$s = s_o + v_o t + \left(\frac{1}{2}\right) at^2$$

$$v^2 = v_o^2 + 2a(s - s_o)$$

Projectile Motion

$$x = x_o + v_x t$$

$$v_y = v_{yo} - gt$$

$$y = y_o + v_{yo}t - \left(\frac{1}{2}\right)gt^2$$

$$v_y^2 = v_{yo}^2 - 2g\,(y - y_o)$$

Rotational Motion

Constant rotational velocity

$$\theta = \theta_o + \omega t$$

Constant angular acceleration

$$\omega = \omega_o + \alpha t$$

$$\theta = \theta_o + \omega_o t + \left(\frac{1}{2}\right)\alpha t^2$$

$$\omega^2 = \omega_o^2 + 2\alpha\,(\theta - \theta_o)$$

Tangential velocity

$$v_t = r\omega$$

Tangential acceleration

$$a_t = r\alpha$$

Radial acceleration

$$a_r = r\omega^2 = \frac{v_t^2}{r}$$

Polar coordinates

$$a_r = \frac{d^2r}{dt^2} - r\left(\frac{d\theta}{dt}\right)^2 = \frac{d^2r}{dt^2} - r\omega^2$$

$$a_\theta = r\left(\frac{d^2\theta}{dt^2}\right) + 2\left(\frac{dr}{dt}\right)\left(\frac{d\theta}{dt}\right) = r\alpha + 2\left(\frac{dr}{dt}\right)\omega$$

$$v_r = \frac{dr}{dt}$$

$$v_\theta = r\left(\frac{d\theta}{dt}\right) = r\omega$$

Relative and Related Motion

Acceleration

$$a_A = a_B + a_{A/B}$$

Velocity

$$v_A = v_B + v_{A/B}$$

Position

$$x_A = x_B + x_{A/B}$$

Kinetics

$$w = mg$$

$$F = ma$$

$$F_c = ma_n = \frac{mv_t^2}{r}$$

$$F_f = \mu N$$

Kinetic Energy

$$KE = \left(\frac{1}{2}\right)mv^2$$

Work of a force $= \int F ds$

$$KE_1 + \text{Work}_{1-2} = KE_2$$

Potential Energy

Spring $PE = \left(\frac{1}{2}\right)kx^2$

Weight $PE = wy$

$$KE_1 + PE_1 = KE_2 + PE_2$$

Power

Linear power $P = Fv$

Torsional or rotational power $P = T\omega$

Impulse-Momentum

$$mv_1 + \int F dt = mv_2$$

Impact

$$m_A v_{A1} + m_B v_{B1} = m_A v_{A2} + m_B v_{B2}$$

$$e = \frac{v_{B2} - v_{A2}}{v_{A1} - v_{B1}}$$

Perfectly plastic impact ($e = 0$)

$$m_A v_{A1} + m_B v_{B1} = (m_A + m_B)v'$$

One mass is infinite

$$v_2 = e v_1$$

Inertia

Beam $\quad I_A = \left(\frac{1}{12}\right)ml^2 + m\left(\frac{1}{2}\right)^2 = \left(\frac{1}{3}\right)ml^2$

Plate

$$I_A = \left(\frac{1}{12}\right)m(a^2 + b^2) + m\left[\left(\frac{a}{b}\right)^2 + \left(\frac{b}{2}\right)^2\right] = \left(\frac{1}{3}\right)m(a^2 + b^2)$$

Wheel $\quad I_A = mk^2 + mr^2$

Two-Dimensional Rigid Body Motion

$$F_x = ma_x$$
$$F_y = ma_y$$
$$M_A = I_A \alpha = I_{cg}\,\alpha + m(a)d$$

Rolling Resistance

$$F_r = \frac{mga}{r}$$

Energy Methods for Rigid Body Motion

$$KE_1 + \text{Work}_{1-2} = KE_2$$

$$\text{Work} = \int F ds + \int M d\theta$$

Mechanical Vibration

Differential equation

$$\frac{md^2 x}{dt^2} + kx = 0$$

Position

$$x = x_m \sin\left[\sqrt{\frac{k}{m}}\,t + \theta\right]$$

Velocity

$$v = \frac{dx}{dt} = x_m\sqrt{\frac{k}{m}}\cos\left[\sqrt{\frac{k}{m}}\,t + \theta\right]$$

Acceleration

$$a = \frac{d^2x}{dt^2} = -x_m\left(\frac{k}{m}\right)\sin\left[\sqrt{\frac{k}{m}}\,t + \theta\right]$$

Maximum values

$$x = x_m, v = x_m\sqrt{\frac{k}{m}},\, a = -x_m\left(\frac{k}{m}\right)$$

Period

$$T = \frac{2\pi}{\left(\sqrt{\dfrac{k}{m}}\right)}$$

Frequency

$$f = \frac{1}{T} = \frac{\sqrt{\dfrac{k}{m}}}{2\pi}$$

Springs in parallel

$$k = k_1 + k_2$$

Springs in series

$$\frac{1}{k} = \frac{1}{k_1} + \frac{1}{k_2}$$

AREA UNDER NORMAL CURVE

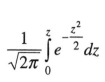

$$\frac{1}{\sqrt{2\pi}}\int_{0}^{z}e^{-\frac{z^2}{2}}dz$$

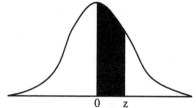

Z	0	1	2	3	4	5	6	7	8	9
0.0	.0000	.0040	.0080	.0120	.0160	.0199	0239	.0279	.0319	.0359
0.1	.0398	.0438	.0478	.0517	.0557	.0596	.0636	.0675	.0714	.0754
0.2	.0793	.0832	.0871	.0910	.0948	.0987	.1026	.1064	.1103	.1141
0.3	.1179	.1217	.1255	.1293	.1331	.1368	.1406	.1443	.1480	.1517
0.4	.1554	.1591	.1628	.1664	.1700	.1736	.1772	.1808	.1844	.1879
0.5	.1915	.1950	.1985	.2019	.2054	.2088	.2123	.2157	.2190	.2224
0.6	.2258	.2291	.2324	.2357	.2389	.2422	.2454	.2486	.2518	.2549
0.7	.2580	.2612	.2642	.2673	.2704	.2734	.2764	.2794	.2823	.2852
0.8	.2881	.2910	.2939	.2967	.2996	.3023	.3051	.3078	.3106	.3133
0.9	.3159	.3186	.3212	.3238	.3264	.3289	.3315	.3340	.3365	.3389
1.0	.3413	.3438	.3461	.3485	.3508	.3531	.3554	.3577	.3599	.3621
1.1	.3643	.3665	.3686	.3708	.3729	.3749	.3770	.3790	.3810	.3830
1.2	.3849	.3869	.3888	.3907	.3925	.3944	.3962	.3980	.3997	.4015
1.3	.4032	.4049	.4066	.4082	.4099	.4115	.4131	.4147	.4162	.4177
1.4	.4192	.4207	.4222	.4236	.4251	.4265	.4279	.4292	.4306	.4319
1.5	.4332	.4345	.4357	.4370	.4382	.4394	.4406	.4418	.4429	.4441
1.6	.4452	.4463	.4474	.4484	.4495	.4505	.4515	.4525	.4535	.4545
1.7	.4554	.4564	.4573	.4582	.4591	.4599	.4608	.4616	.4625	.4633
1.8	.4641	.4649	.4656	.4664	.4671	.4678	.4686	.4693	.4699	.4706
1.9	.4713	.4719	.4726	.4732	.4738	.4744	.4750	.4756	.4761	.4767
2.0	.4772	.4778	.4783	.4788	.4793	.4798	.4803	.4808	.4812	.4817
2.1	.4821	.4826	.4830	.4834	.4838	.4842	.4846	.4850	.4854	.4857
2.2	.4861	.4864	.4868	.4871	.4875	.4878	.4881	.4884	.4887	.4890
2.3	.4893	.4896	.4898	.4901	.4904	.4906	.4909	.4911	.4913	.4916
2.4	.4918	.4920	.4922	.4925	.4927	.4929	.4931	.4932	.4934	.4936
2.5	.4938	.4940	.4941	.4943	.4945	.4946	.4948	.4949	.4951	.4952
2.6	.4953	.4955	.4956	.4957	.4959	.4960	.4961	.4962	.4963	.4964
2.7	.4965	.4966	.4967	.4968	.4969	.4970	.4971	.4972	.4973	.4974
2.8	.4974	.4975	.4976	.4977	.4977	.4978	.4979	.4979	.4980	.4981
2.9	.4981	.4982	.4982	.4983	.4984	.4984	.4985	.4985	.4986	.4986
3.0	.4987	.4987	.4987	.4988	.4988	.4989	.4989	.4989	.4990	.4990
3.1	.4990	.4991	.4991	.4991	.4992	.4992	.4992	.4992	.4993	.4993
3.2	.4993	.4993	.4994	.4994	.4994	.4994	.4994	.4995	.4995	.4995
3.3	.4995	.4995	.4995	.4996	.4996	.4996	.4996	.4996	.4996	.4997
3.4	.4997	.4997	.4997	.4997	.4997	.4997	.4997	.4997	.4997	.4998
3.5	.4998	.4998	.4998	.4998	.4998	.4998	.4998	.4998	.4998	.4998
3.6	.4998	.4998	.4999	.4999	.4999	.4999	.4999	.4999	.4999	.4999
3.7	.4999	.4999	.4999	.4999	.4999	.4999	.4999	.4999	.4999	.4999
3.8	.4999	.4999	.4999	.4999	.4999	.4999	.4999	.4999	.4999	.4999
3.9	.5000	.5000	.5000	.5000	.5000	.5000	.5000	.5000	.5000	.5000

POWER SERIES FOR ELEMENTARY FUNCTIONS

$$\frac{1}{x} = 1 - (x-1) + (x-1)^2 - (x-1)^3 + (x-1)^4 - \ldots + (-1)^n (x-1)^n + \ldots,$$
$$0 < x < 2$$

$$\frac{1}{1+x} = 1 - x + x^2 - x^3 + x^4 - x^5 + \ldots + (-1)^n x^n + \ldots, \qquad -1 < x < 1$$

$$\ln x = (x-1) - \frac{(x-1)^2}{2} + \frac{(x-1)^3}{3} - \frac{(x-1)^4}{4} + \ldots + \frac{(-1)^{n-1}(x-1)^n}{n} + \ldots,$$
$$0 < x \le 2$$

$$e^x = 1 + x + \frac{x^2}{2!} + \frac{x^3}{3!} + \frac{x^4}{4!} + \frac{x^5}{5!} + \ldots + \frac{x^n}{n!} + \ldots, \qquad -\infty < x < \infty$$

$$\sin x = x - \frac{x^3}{3!} + \frac{x^5}{5!} - \frac{x^7}{7!} + \frac{x^9}{9!} - \ldots + \frac{(-1)^n x^{2n+1}}{(2n+1)!} + \ldots, \qquad -\infty < x < \infty$$

$$\cos x = x - \frac{x^2}{2!} + \frac{x^4}{4!} - \frac{x^6}{6!} + \frac{x^8}{8!} - \ldots + \frac{(-1)^n x^{2n}}{(2n)!} + \ldots, \qquad -\infty < x < \infty$$

$$\arctan x = x - \frac{x^3}{3} + \frac{x^5}{5} - \frac{x^7}{7} + \frac{x^9}{9} - \ldots + \frac{(-1)^n x^{2n+1}}{2n+1} + \ldots, \qquad -1 \le x \le 1$$

$$\arctan x = x - \frac{x^3}{3} + \frac{x^5}{5} - \frac{x^7}{7} + \frac{x^9}{9} - \ldots + \frac{(-1)^n x^{2n+1}}{2n+1} + \ldots, \qquad -1 \le x \le 1$$

$$(1+x)^k = 1 + kx + \frac{k(k-1)x^2}{2!} + \frac{k(k-1)(k-2)x^3}{3!}$$
$$+ \frac{k(k-1)(k-2)(k-3)x^4}{4!} + \ldots, \qquad\qquad -1 < x < 1$$

$$(1+x)^{-k} = 1 - kx + \frac{k(k+1)x^2}{2!} - \frac{k(k+1)(k+2)x^3}{3!}$$
$$+ \frac{k(k+1)(k+2)(k+3)x^4}{4!} - \ldots, \qquad\qquad -1 < x < 1$$

TABLE OF MORE COMMON LAPLACE TRANSFORMS

$f(t) = L^{-1}\{F(s)\}$	$F(s) = L\{f(t)\}$
1	$\dfrac{1}{s}$
t	$\dfrac{1}{s^2}$
$\dfrac{t^{n-1}}{(n-1)!}; n = 1, 2, \dots$	$\dfrac{1}{s^n}$
e^{at}	$\dfrac{1}{s-a}$
$t\,e^{at}$	$\dfrac{1}{(s-a)^2}$
$\dfrac{t^{n-1}e^{-at}}{(n-1)!}$	$\dfrac{1}{(s+a)^n}; n = 1, 2, \dots$
$\dfrac{e^{-at} - e^{-bt}}{b-a}; a \neq b$	$\dfrac{1}{(s+a)(s+b)}$
$\dfrac{a\,e^{-at} - b\,e^{-bt}}{a-b}; a \neq b$	$\dfrac{s}{(s+a)(s+b)}$
$\sin st$	$\dfrac{a}{s^2 + a^2}$
$\cos at$	$\dfrac{s}{s^2 + a^2}$
$\sinh at$	$\dfrac{a}{s^2 - a^2}$

$f(t) = L^{-1}\{F(s)\}$	$F(s) = L\{f(t)\}$
$\cosh at$	$\dfrac{s}{s^2 - a^2}$
$\dfrac{1}{a^2}(1 - \cos at)$	$\dfrac{1}{s(s^2 + a^2)}$
$\dfrac{1}{a^3}(at - \sin at)$	$\dfrac{1}{s(s^2 + a^2)}$
$\dfrac{t}{2a}\sin at$	$\dfrac{s}{(s^2 + a^2)^2}$
$\dfrac{1}{b}e^{-at}\sin bt$	$\dfrac{1}{(s + a)^2 + b^2}$
$e^{-at}\cos bt$	$\dfrac{s + a}{(s + a)^2 + b^2}$
$h_1(t - a)$ 	$\dfrac{1}{s}e^{-as}$
$h_1(t) - h_1(t - a)$ 	$\dfrac{1 - e^{-as}}{s}$
$\dfrac{1}{t}\sin kt$	$\arctan\dfrac{k}{s}$

The
HANDBOOK of
ELECTRICAL
ENGINEERING

Staff of Research and Education Association

Available at your local bookstore or order directly from us by sending in coupon below.

HANDBOOK of MATHEMATICAL, SCIENTIFIC, & ENGINEERING FORMULAS, FUNCTIONS, GRAPHS, TABLES, & TRANSFORMS

RESEARCH & EDUCATION ASSOCIATION

A particularly useful reference for those in math, science, engineering and other technical fields. Includes the most-often used formulas, tables, transforms, functions, and graphs which are needed as tools in solving problems. The entire field of special functions is also covered. A large amount of scientific data which is often of interest to scientists and engineers has been included.

REA's Problem Solvers

The "PROBLEM SOLVERS" are comprehensive supplemental text-books designed to save time in finding solutions to problems. Each "PROBLEM SOLVER" is the first of its kind ever produced in its field. It is the product of a massive effort to illustrate almost any imaginable problem in exceptional depth, detail, and clarity. Each problem is worked out in detail with a step-by-step solution, and the problems are arranged in order of complexity from elementary to advanced. Each book is fully indexed for locating problems rapidly.

ACCOUNTING
ADVANCED CALCULUS
ALGEBRA & TRIGONOMETRY
AUTOMATIC CONTROL
   SYSTEMS/ROBOTICS
BIOLOGY
BUSINESS, ACCOUNTING, & FINANCE
CALCULUS
CHEMISTRY
COMPLEX VARIABLES
DIFFERENTIAL EQUATIONS
ECONOMICS
ELECTRICAL MACHINES
ELECTRIC CIRCUITS
ELECTROMAGNETICS
ELECTRONIC COMMUNICATIONS
ELECTRONICS
FINITE & DISCRETE MATH
FLUID MECHANICS/DYNAMICS
GENETICS
GEOMETRY
HEAT TRANSFER

LINEAR ALGEBRA
MACHINE DESIGN
MATHEMATICS for ENGINEERS
MECHANICS
NUMERICAL ANALYSIS
OPERATIONS RESEARCH
OPTICS
ORGANIC CHEMISTRY
PHYSICAL CHEMISTRY
PHYSICS
PRE-CALCULUS
PROBABILITY
PSYCHOLOGY
STATISTICS
STRENGTH OF MATERIALS &
   MECHANICS OF SOLIDS
TECHNICAL DESIGN GRAPHICS
THERMODYNAMICS
TOPOLOGY
TRANSPORT PHENOMENA
VECTOR ANALYSIS

If you would like more information about any of these books,
complete the coupon below and return it to us or visit your local bookstore.

REA's Test Preps
The Best in Test Preparation

- REA "Test Preps" are **far more** comprehensive than any other test preparation series
- Each book contains up to **eight** full-length practice tests based on the most recent exams
- **Every** type of question likely to be given on the exams is included
- Answers are accompanied by **full** and **detailed** explanations

REA has published over 60 Test Preparation volumes in several series. They include:

Advanced Placement Exams (APs)
Biology
Calculus AB & Calculus BC
Chemistry
Computer Science
English Language & Composition
English Literature & Composition
European History
Government & Politics
Physics
Psychology
Statistics
Spanish Language
United States History

College-Level Examination Program (CLEP)
Analyzing and Interpreting Literature
College Algebra
Freshman College Composition
General Examinations
General Examinations Review
History of the United States I
Human Growth and Development
Introductory Sociology
Principles of Marketing
Spanish

SAT II: Subject Tests
American History
Biology E/M
Chemistry
English Language Proficiency Test
French
German

SAT II: Subject Tests (cont'd)
Literature
Mathematics Level IC, IIC
Physics
Spanish
Writing

Graduate Record Exams (GREs)
Biology
Chemistry
Computer Science
Economics
Engineering
General
History
Literature in English
Mathematics
Physics
Psychology
Sociology

ACT - ACT Assessment

ASVAB - Armed Services Vocational Aptitude Battery

CBEST - California Basic Educational Skills Test

CDL - Commercial Driver License Exam

CLAST - College Level Academic Skills Test

ELM - Entry Level Mathematics

ExCET - Exam for the Certification of Educators in Texas

FE (EIT) - Fundamentals of Engineering Exam

FE Review - Fundamentals of Engineering Review

GED - High School Equivalency Diploma Exam (U.S. & Canadian editions)

GMAT - Graduate Management Admission Test

LSAT - Law School Admission Test

MAT - Miller Analogies Test

MCAT - Medical College Admission Test

MSAT - Multiple Subjects Assessment for Teachers

NJ HSPT- New Jersey High School Proficiency Test

PPST - Pre-Professional Skills Tests

PRAXIS II/NTE - Core Battery

PSAT - Preliminary Scholastic Assessment Test

SAT I - Reasoning Test

SAT I - Quick Study & Review

TASP - Texas Academic Skills Program

TOEFL - Test of English as a Foreign Language

TOEIC - Test of English for International Communication

RESEARCH & EDUCATION ASSOCIATION
61 Ethel Road W. • Piscataway, New Jersey 08854
Phone: (732) 819-8880   **website: www.rea.com**

Please send me more information about your Test Prep books

Name _____

Address _____

City _____ State _____ Zip _____

REA's Test Prep Books Are The Best!

(a sample of the <u>hundreds of letters</u> REA receives each year)

" I am writing to congratulate you on preparing an exceptional study guide. In five years of teaching this course I have never encountered a more thorough, comprehensive, concise and realistic preparation for this examination. "
Teacher, Davie, FL

" I have found your publications, *The Best Test Preparation...*, to be exactly that. "
Teacher, Aptos, CA

" I used your *CLEP Introductory Sociology* book and rank it 99% – thank you! "
Student, Jerusalem, Israel

" Your GMAT book greatly helped me on the test. Thank you. "
Student, Oxford, OH

" I recently got the French SAT II Exam book from REA. I congratulate you on first-rate French practice tests."
Instructor, Los Angeles, CA

" Your AP English Literature and Composition book is most impressive."
Student, Montgomery, AL

" The REA LSAT Test Preparation guide is a winner! "
Instructor, Spartanburg, SC

(more on front page)